Technocrime

Technocrime

Technology, crime and social control

**Edited by
Stéphane Leman-Langlois**

WILLAN
PUBLISHING

Published by

Willan Publishing
Culmcott House
Mill Street, Uffculme
Cullompton, Devon
EX15 3AT, UK
Tel: +44(0)1884 840337
Fax: +44(0)1884 840251
e-mail: info@willanpublishing.co.uk
website: www.willanpublishing.co.uk

Published simultaneously in the USA and Canada by

Willan Publishing
c/o ISBS, 920 NE 58th Ave, Suite 300,
Portland, Oregon 97213-3786, USA
Tel: +001(0)503 287 3093
Fax: +001(0)503 280 8832
e-mail: info@isbs.com
website: www.isbs.com

First published 2008

ISBN   978-1-84392-385-5 paperback
       978-1-84392-386-2 hardback

British Library Cataloguing-in-Publication Data

A catalogue record for this book is available from the British Library

Project managed by Deer Park Productions, Tavistock, Devon
Typeset by GCS, Leighton Buzzard, Bedfordshire
Printed and bound by T.J. International, Padstow, Cornwall

Contents

Foreword by Gary T. Marx   *vii*
Notes on contributors   *xxi*
Acknowledgement   *xxv*

1   **Introduction: technocrime**   **1**
    Stéphane Leman-Langlois

2   **Crime and lawfulness in the age of all-seeing**
    techno-humanity   **14**
    David Brin

3   **The local impact of police videosurveillance on**
    the social construction of security   **27**
    Stéphane Leman-Langlois

4   **Cyberwars and cybercrimes**   **46**
    Benoît Gagnon

5   **Policing through nodes, clusters and bandwidth**   **66**
    Johnny Nhan and Laura Huey

6   **Second Life and governing deviance in virtual worlds**   **88**
    Jennifer Whitson and Aaron Doyle

7   **Privacy as currency: crime, information and**
    control in cyberspace   **112**
    Stéphane Leman-Langlois

  8 Information technology and criminal intelligence   139
     a comparative perspective
     Frédéric Lemieux

  9 Scientific policing and criminal investigation   169
     Jean-Paul Brodeur

 10 Sorting systems: identification by database   194
     David Lyon

 11 A view of surveillance   209
     Peter K. Manning

 12 Afterword: technopolice   243
     Stéphane Leman-Langlois

 Index   247

Foreword

Something's happening here and we are there[1]

Gary T. Marx

He that will not apply new remedies must expect new evils.
Sir Francis Bacon

As long as the genuine security problem exists, there will be persons whose imagination will be set boiling with excited apprehension.
E. Shils

Of course I'll not deceive her I'm not there, I'm gone It's all about confusion and I cry for her
Bob Dylan, I'm Not There

As a good multi-tasking modern, I finished reading this cornucopian volume while watching the Bob Dylan film *I'm Not There*. I was struck by their parallels and the clarity of the haze surrounding both. The topics are enigmatic and rich in contradiction and paradox, resisting efforts at didactic, fixed and linear interpretation. At the same time there are abundant reoccurring social patterns and processes. Therein lays (and at time lies as well) their appeal and challenge.

The ever optimistic scholar, whether studying the work of the artist or the social impact of computer technology, seeks the light beyond the fog and the truth(s) behind the masks. The contributors to this timely volume find both.

In the case of computers and society, we know a lot is happening here, but what is it? One is even led to suspect, with Gertrude Stein, that maybe there is no there there because there is here, or that there is no past or future because they are ever present – as a result of improved record keeping, simulation and prediction.

Yet, however varied, the realities of a multi-perspectival world do not prevent the authors from finding bedrocks of meaning, structure and process striated throughout the heterogeneity of *techno-police* and *technocrime*.

In the beginning there are the questions. These authors identify the fundamental issues and carefully strain them through an informing mesh of social theory and empirical research. This pioneering tapestry in progress is necessary reading for students interested in the myriad and shifting ties between technology and law and society, social control, criminology and deviance.

Consistent with the social constructionist tenor of the volume, much of what readers will find here is conditioned by what they bring to the book. With that disclaimer, let me briefly note some approaches and themes that I found particularly resonate and worthy of continuing attention for researchers and practitioners. Among topics I will briefly consider: ways of conceptualizing the changes and alterations in border conditions, aggregation and disaggregation, system complexity and dynamics, rhetorical excesses, ironies and value conflicts and symbolic communication.

With respect to technology and social control it is clear that a great deal is happening here. This volume emphasizes techno-police and technocrime. These are found within and contribute to contexts involving globalization, deterritorialization and the breaking, blurring, merging, morphing of traditional borders and the appearance of new barriers (whether spatial, geographical, juridical, organizational, functional or of the senses).[2]

Boundaries

In response to threats, risks, disasters, pandemics, fear and critical incidents, means based on profiling, pattern recognition, transactional data, data-mining, embedded sensors/ambient intelligence, intercepts, satellites, passwords, spyware, biometrics, authentication, audit trails and target hardening are applied. There is an emphasis on prevention, pro-activity and preparedness.

Cyberspace technologies and behaviours, by definition, alter our understanding of the borders of space, time, property, hierarchy, the person and national boundaries. They can also weaken, blur and reconfigure traditional borders between, as well as within, countries and across forms and subjects/targets of control.

Terms such as centralization–decentralization and centre–periphery, the public and the private, privacy and openness can no longer be as easily applied. We see a new kind of mobile total institution portaged by individuals in their bodies, minds and everyday activities as they radiate, communicate and behave, still in the shadow, but not in the physical presence of overseers.

New organizational forms related to the spread of a techno-control ethos stimulated by entrepreneurs, perceptions of shared threats and the use of the same tools (including the sharing of information) have profound implications for the traditional distinctions between public and private police, law enforcement and national security, the police and the military, operational and intelligence agencies, national and international law enforcement and local and international criminal activities and organizations.

Even when organizational borders remain intact, the behaviour of control agents appears to be increasingly similar, there appears to be an increase in joint operations and there is increased circulation of control agents across organizations.

Johnny Nhan and Laura Huey note this blurring of borders in describing the emergent network of private and public agencies concerned with cybercrime. Benoît Gagnon notes that in spite of (or perhaps because of) the transnational, non-spatial borders of cyberspace, governments seek to define it as national space analogous to geographical space.

The topic requires both disaggregation and aggregation. We need to disentangle the multiple dimensions frequently found with ideal types and to find ways of measuring these so their distribution and interrelations can be empirically documented and subject to hypothesizing.

Systems

Many of the articles admirably break the shifting worlds of technology, rules, control and violation into manageable analytic and empirically measurable bites. This is not matched by equivalent efforts at aggregation or the offering of middle-range testable theories. However, given the newness of the topics, the richness and variety of the empirical, the relative weaknesses of our methods and the organization and values of social science, this is not surprising. Studying implementation, neutralization, counter-neutralization, displacement, escalation, evolution, devolution, atrophy, entropy, contraction and border changes must be central to inquiry.

In early 1960 Professor Erving Goffman observed that 'for a nickel and a theory all you can get is a cup of coffee.' A bit strong, but it is only after empirical inquiries and unpacking the pieces that we know what to put back together and what needs to be explained. Most of the chapters in this volume adopt a systems approach that acknowledges the contextual interdependence of rule enforcers and rule violators. A systems approach can acknowledge the interaction of the technical and the social while helping avoid technological and social determinism.

Technology offers new resources to agents and subjects of social control who apply, and respond, in imaginative and unexpected ways. In conflict settings, new technologies almost invariably bring reciprocal responses. As Simmel observed, adversaries may come in many ways to resemble each other (Coser 1956). This point can be easily missed when the topic is only approached in absolute moralistic terms of the good guys and the bad guys.

Rules and rule violations must be studied as an interaction process. The dynamic, 'no final victory' quality of many control settings calls attention to game like qualities (note the parallel of cyberspace games to actual life and their intermingling noted in the article by Jennifer Whitson and Aaron Doyle).

A systems approach encourages us to be cautious about claims for 'independent' variables unsullied by their environments and to identify feedback processes and reciprocal influences.

Not so old, not so new

Yet loose systems of social orders (even as they have borders, histories, culture and social organization) are hardly hermetically sealed, nor do all variables (or inputs) count equally. As these articles make very clear, some things change even amidst stability and there are endless combinations of the age of both the bottles and the wine, depending on where one looks and where one chooses to draw the line between changes in degree and in kind.

There is need to locate the broad constants found in control settings, and within these, the major areas where variation and reoccurring forms and processes can be identified. But there is equivalent need to be alert for changes as suggested by the concepts mentioned above and to subject claims about radical change to empirical analysis.

Given the multiple goals of any complex organization or individual and their embedding in political, legal and social cultures, the conclusions from the articles by Frederic Lemieux, Jean-Paul Brodeur and Peter K. Manning that little has changed re the broad goals of national security, crime prevention or crime solving and local police routines is not surprising. But that does not mean impacts do not occur elsewhere (e.g. as with styles of work, efficiency, priorities among goals or in popular culture), nor that at some point small changes do not cumulate into something more (even as this can be hard to see because change is gradual and we are a part of what we study).

The continuing development and application of technologies that extend the senses and are of low visibility, involuntarily, remotely and often softly applied, cheaper, integrated and automated, abstract the rich variability of local contexts into general categories involve real time data flows, the folding of surveillance into routine activities, immediate links between data collection and action and categorical suspicion are hardly insignificant.

A dynamic view of technology and social control can encourage a historical perspective, attention to the careers of techniques, rules and violations and awareness of the possibility of cycles. If I had a dime for every supposed empirical trend that turned out to be merely a blip or to represent a lag factor or a cyclical process, I would not travel coach class to academic meetings. Our research must be continually in process, responding to changes in the game and moves of the players.

Attention to the complexity these authors document can counter the rhetorical excesses of control entrepreneurs and doomsday prophets. The commercialization and privatization of crime control too easily leads to exaggerating a technology's power, overstating risks and marketing fear. The verbiage collapsing a technology's potential (as perhaps demonstrated in pristine laboratory settings, even if the data are made available to outside researchers) with the smudgier world of real applications pollutes public discourse.

This book offers a needed reality check in finding that claims – whether about the revolutionary implications of the technologies for policing and national security or for converting dystopian visions to reality, or the takeover of the world by international criminals are greatly exaggerated.

Rhetorical excess and the failure of the best made plans have many sources including those Stéphane Leman-Langlois suggests in the introduction such as dysfunctional technologies, incompetent users, lower priority and a high number of targets. The gaps (and even chasms) between stated intentions and the fullness of outcomes may also reflect self-serving entrepreneurial spin (or bullshit), outright prevarication, selective and misperception, wish-fulfillment, paranoia, stupidity and tunnel vision, lack of motivation, system incompatibilities and the inability to anticipate system complexities, contingencies and confounding factors.

Value conflicts (even assuming we can agree on what abstract values mean in practice) are an additional limiting factor. We can rarely have it all and obtaining more of one value often implies less of another. Consider for example the tensions between:

- liberty and order;
- communalism and individualism;
- the security offered by hard, presumably fail-safe, no choice engineering solutions vs. the need and advantages of freely chosen self-control in consensual settings;
- aggregate (often statistical) rationality and efficiency against due process, justice, and fairness for each individual;
- security and safety vs. cost, convenience and timeliness universalism (equality), standardization, elimination of discretion vs. particularism (differentiation) and the flexibility to respond to unique situations;
- automatic machine processing for reliability, consistency and fairness ('get the human out of the loop') vs. reliance on human judgement and review and the ability to better interpret contexts;
- control as repression/domination/colonization/homogenization or as responsible management/oversight/care/guidance;
- protection through isolation and exclusion vs. rehabilitation through inclusion;
- anti-theft barriers designed to keep others out (or inmates within) may prevent the contained from leaving when there is an emergency such as a fire;
- the desire to be noticed and the desire to be left alone;
- prevention (with uncertainty about whether an event would have occurred) vs. response after the fact;
- deterrence vs. apprehension;
- the control of, or access to, information as property or as a right;

- publicity/visibility as accountability but also as deterrents to creativity, experimentation, civility and diplomacy;
- freedom of expression and the avoidance of defamation/harassment/slander/irresponsible and mendacious speech, unwanted encroachments;
- information control as central to selfhood, intimacy and group borders but also to hiding dishonesty, violations, conspiracies and the communication of distrust.

Goals and results

Even when a tactic clearly 'works' and the meaning of work is not at issue (e.g. who says it works and by what measurements and standards?), we must ask a series of questions such as, has the decision to apply it involved democratic and self-critical procedures? Are the means and goals ethical, as well as legal? Are there alternative means that would work as well, or better? What collateral costs and benefits may accompany a tactic (in the long, as well as the short run and for a variety of groups)? Without denying the seriousness of the problem a tactic is intended to address, are there times when it is better to do nothing?

Even when it clearly doesn't work in an instrumental way, it may still serve other goals involving symbolic communication and be a statement about what an organization represents and what it wishes to say to an audience.[3]

Both the means for, and the content of, communication can reflect political struggle. The meaning of a technology and any mandates about, or restrictions upon, its use must be sought beyond its objective specifications. We need to understand the political processes involved in its labelling and how control and violations (whether of self-serving malefactors who harm others or those with communal goals) are defined. Understanding linguistic conflicts over the appropriate analogy for a new form is central to this.

Consider the well known example of email. Is this most like a conversation in public, a post card or a first class letter or is it something else all together? How should we *conceive* offerings and emanations that are in a sense delivered (voluntarily?) by the person but collected by others (often without the subject's knowledge – either because data collection has low visibility, being built into the process, or because of deception)? These may come through traditional borders such as the body, buildings, packages and clothes. Examples include brain (and other) electrical waves, heat and scent, biological waste, garbage and appearance including gait. What of the mosaic dossiers created from publicly available (as in accessible) sources? Are these public or private in a normative sense? Are they a form of property belonging to their originator or whomever gets in the data stream? Do they constitute a search? When should taking (or creating) them require informed consent or at least a warrant? The answer depends on how the context is socially defined beyond any objective aspects per se.

The book offers a useful case study of a major area where new technologies are being applied. Criminal justice differs from other institutional areas such as commerce, work, health care and education, because the human rights and non-consensual aspects are more pronounced as a result of government's greater power (although this ironically, and of necessity, often comes with greater restrictions and citizen rights). Yet there are also parallels.

Issues of technology, rules and violations cut across institutional areas. This reflects structural universals involving the centrality of rules to social organization and behaviour (whether as conformity or deviance). It can also reflect fads and fashions.

Across social fields we increasingly see common technical control practices reflecting a society with attenuated tolerance for risk and with an emphasis on prevention. The methods often involve data presumed to be converted to information and knowledge.

As popularly seen the most media visible forms of new control have a 'technologically' based 'hard' material or engineering quality relying on recent developments in computerization, electronics, biochemistry, materials science and architecture under a legitimating halo of science. But contemporary control goes far beyond these to research tinged efforts at persuasion, seduction, manipulation and deception, whether involving interpersonal relations, advertising, political messages or education.[4] In his chapter on the changing meanings of privacy Stéphane Leman-Langlois suggests that given the benefits, offering personal information as a necessary condition for some advantage seems to many people to be a modest price to pay.

There are efforts to engineer behaviour in both a hard and soft sense through increased transparency, documentation and identification associated with suspicion, the use of predictive statistical models, the offering of rewards, and the encouragement of self-monitoring.[5] This occurs within a networked society of ambient and ubiquitous sensors in constant communication. Such a society continually asks, 'who are you?' and protean identities are both asserted by, and imposed upon, individuals. It is also a society of mobility and location, asking, 'where are you, where have you been and who else is there?'

Consider the continuing trend toward rationalization of control and violation to ever more areas. As David Lyon observes with the modern state and economy there has been a vast proliferation of rules and standards for inclusion and exclusion. With this comes the need for greatly expanded inspections and the need to prove innocence (or at least eligibility) and new technologies and rules involving transparency and documentation. The reverse side of the fair allocation of benefits is the equivalent fair distribution of penalties which also requires enhanced penetration of civil society and crossing personal borders.

The new information technologies related to expanded and enhanced regulation, management and manipulation create new forms of violation and predation – whether on the part of authorities or citizens. David Brin, in arguing for greater equality in the application of technologies of visibility notes that the technologies can be applied bi-directionally, even as there is a pronounced formal tilt away from this favouring the more powerful (whether state agents, employers, merchants, or adults) and an informal tilt favouring males and dominant group members.

Yet the potential of turning control technologies against the controllers and élites more broadly (whether in search of accountability or in pursuit of more efficient means of predation) is one of the ironies that make this field so fascinating. A scene at the end of the film *Chinatown* nicely illustrates this. Jack Nicholson tries to determine how Faye Dunaway is related to a young woman in her family. At first Dunaway responds, 'She's my sister,' then 'She's my daughter,' and under Nicholson's grilling she continues to say, 'She's my sister,' then 'She's my daughter.' Finally, in response to Nicholson's demanding which it is, she replies, 'Both,' indicating an atypical relationship with her father. The non binary nature of that encounter illustrates a central contemporary social control theme involving the presence of the opposing trends this volume illustrates.

As several articles suggest, the tools that deny liberty and facilitate predation can also be used to enhance liberty and security. We see many new ways to cross the borders of the person and the organization, but we also see a profusion of new technologies to guard against this and laws and policies limiting the use of technology. A decision to use any technology involves an implicit trade-off between its advantages and disadvantages and forgoing those of other means. All tools have an (or many) Achilles heel(s) and can be neutralized. For example, high tech means of intercepting communication are of little help when couriers are used. A perfect DNA match under ideal collection and analysis conditions can only reveal an empirical correlation not legal guilt, intentions or how the sample got there.

Consider also current trends involving both the hardening and the softening of social control. The case for the latter is seen in a letter Huxley wrote to Orwell after the publication of *1984* (quoted in Grover 1969):

Dear Mr Orwell
Within the next generation I believe that the world's rulers will discover that infant conditioning and narco-hypnosis are more efficient as instruments of government, than clubs and prisons, and that the lust for power can be just as completely satisfied by suggesting people into loving their servitude as by flogging and kicking them into obedience. In other words, I feel that the nightmare of *Nineteen Eighty-Four* is destined to modulate into the nightmare of a world having more resemblance to that which I imagined in *Brave New World*. The change will be brought about as a result of a felt need for efficiency [*and we can note seduction and fear – as viewed 60 years later*].

The softening of control, particularly as applied domestically, fits well with contemporary democratic sensibilities. But rather than displacing, it exists alongside of, enhanced hard forms. While these may not be coercive in the traditional sense, they are in denying the actor any choice. The world is engineered in such a fashion that the resources and/or opportunity to do the wrong thing (or at least to not do what the more powerful do not want done – whether this involves the law, commerce or work) is absent.[6]

Physically engineered environments such as improved locks, graffiti-resistant building materials, biometric access means and the replacement of credit for cash are increasingly found along side of seductive efforts that can hardly be refused such as frequent shopper rewards, faster and more efficient processing (e.g. at airports or on toll roads) and sexy advertising role models and media product placement. For those in the control business this may appear as a win/ win situation – either the ability to violate rules is made impossible or individuals are socialized and manipulated such that they make the choices desired by those with the technology and authority. This of course leaves the question of when is a choice 'really' a choice begging.[7]

Both Orwell and Huxley continue to apply, if in qualified form, since reality is usually more complicated than the simplifications which words offer – whether in fiction or the ideal types of the social inquirer.[8] But in addition, in noting the complexities and the screw-ups and absurdities that may accompany technical, usually acontextual, control efforts into complex and dynamic systems, Franz Kafka can't be ignored.[9] Nor can William Gibson or Philip K. Dick, who anticipated so many contemporary themes in their writing (e.g. the latter's use of prevention as expressed in the film *Minority Report* based on his short story).

The search for technical solutions to social problems (even given the variability in how these are defined) is fundamental to our ambivalent age. We both welcome technology and fear it. The basic issue is not with the implied effort to improve – something reflecting the highest aspirations of our reaching civilization. Rather the concern is with the narrowing of focus that may accompany this and inequality with respect to how problems are defined and resources for solutions are allocated. We must avoid mechanical solutions that are not accompanied by asking why some individuals break the rules and how social organization may encourage social problems.

Stand-alone technical solutions (increasingly privatized and focusing on the individual) seek to by-pass the need to create a society in which there is communal responsibility and in which individuals act responsibly as a result of voluntary commitment to the rules, not because they have no choice, or only out of fear of reprisals. Emphasis on the latter can encourage social neglect and more problems, leading to calls for more intensive and extensive reliance on technology and more rules, in a seemingly endless self-reinforcing and self-defeating spiral.

There is little room left for political debate or negotiation or time for reflection on broad consequences when technical weapons are drawn too quickly and accompanied by the belief that the means are neutral, the goals universal and the opposition personifies unadulterated evil.

Technological controls, presumably being science based, are justified as valid, objective, neutral, universal, consensual and fair. In the best of all possible worlds they can be. Yet we need to be mindful of the fact that tools and results are socially created and interpreted (and thus potentially disputable)[10] and exist in dynamic interdependent systems where interests may conflict, inequality is often present and where full impacts are difficult to anticipate. The critical inquiry and humility expressed by the authors in this volume are as needed as are innovation and experimentation.

References

Coser, L. (1956) *The Functions of Group Conflict*. New York: The Free Press.

Dupont, B. (2004) 'La Technicisation du Travail Policier: Ambivalences et Contradicitons Internes', *Criminologie*, 37(1): 107–126.

Grover, S. (1969) *Letters of Aldous Huxley*. London: Chatto & Windus.

Marx, G. (2006) 'Soft Surveillance: The Growth of Mandatory Voluntarism in Collecting Personal Information', in T. Monahan (ed.) *Surveillance and Security*. New York: Routledge.

Nogala, D. (1995) 'The Future Role of Technology in Policing' in J.P. Brodeur (ed.) *Comparison in Policing: An International Perspective*. Aldershot: Avebury (pp.191–210).

Shils, E. (1956) *The Torment of Secrecy*. Chicago: University of Chicago Press.

Notes

1 These remarks draw from *Windows into the Soul: Surveillance and Society in an Age of High Technology*, (G.T. Marx) University of Chicago, forthcoming, and 'The Engineering of Social Control: Intended and Unintended Consequences' in J. Byrne and D. Rebovich, *The New Technology of Crime, Law and Social Control*, Monsey, NY: Criminal Justice Press.

2 Among some related broad terms for characterizing various aspects of contemporary controls in the vast literature on the topic: the panopticon, the gaze, superpanopticon, post-panopticon, synopticon, banopticon, surveillance society, the new surveillance, maximum security society, high policing, securitization, viewer society, surveillance creep, soft cage and glass cage. Or consider computer-related concepts such as cyberspace, digitalization, dataveillance, miniaturization, encryption and decryption, virtual, simulation, codes, networks, integrated information systems and surveillant assemblage.

3 Consider the interesting topic of tactics that 'work' but only because of deception on the part of the agent. One of the justifications for the polygraph is that if people are conned into thinking it works then they will be truthful. The same is claimed for the deterrent effect of video cameras without film or that are never reviewed. But, aside from the ethical issues around control via deception, if the deception is discovered it may serve to delegitimate other truthful claims.

4 This of course raises the issue of what is a modern technology. Here it refers to a strategic application of means to ends involving some pragmatic

theory of why this should work (whether it has a tangible material base is thus irrelevant). The controls of interest are 'technologically' based, but what is a technology? Are magic and prayer technologies? The pragmatic empirical justification for most current control techniques contrasts with other sources of legitimation such as role relationships, tradition, the supernatural and unabashed power. Given the issues around definition, measurement and interpretation there is much room for self and other deception in concluding that a modern tactic does work. In 1995, Detlef Nogala chronicled emerging 'techno-police' trends in the US and Germany and suggested a way to systematize these based largely on their intended function. He used the term broadly to refer to all police 'policies, strategies, tactics' based on the capacities of advanced technologies. That leaves undefined just what an advanced technology is. His examples primarily involve what Byrne and Rebovich (2007) refer to as 'hard' technologies in contrast to 'soft' information based means. But one can also apply those terms to direct coercion vs. tactics that are deceptive, manipulative and relatively passive, non-invasive and of low visibility, not requiring the subject's cooperation or those in which subjects voluntarily cooperate (see Note 6).

5 For the latter engineered cases consider efforts to educate and help citizens as seen in anti-drunk driving advertizing campaigns, the creation of designated driver systems, signs indicating one's auto speed, and devices for monitoring alcohol level. The effort to create a sense of social responsibility through neighborhood community policing activities can also be seen as soft engineering.

6 Some basic forms here are target removal, target devaluation, target insulation, offender weakening or incapacitation, exclusion and offense/offender/target identification.

7 The issues and trade offs from order sought by hard and soft control, coercion and deception, force and manipulation or seduction, threat and socialization are profound indeed. One approach is in Marx (2006). Coercion is at least honest. But in a mannered society valuing the dignity and liberty of the individual, voluntarism and consensus, it is seen as less desirable and even primitive.

8 Benoit Dupont (2004) notes the limitations on both the Orwellian and a techno-optimism perspective to capture the ambiguities and contradictions in applying technology to police work.

9 Consider the bizarre encounters of travelers deemed as suspicious by the Homeland Security Agency who are on 'no fly lists' and who have trouble finding out why they are on the list and in having their names removed.

10 That meanings are socially created does not of course mean that all meanings are equal with respect to logic, empirical support or morality.

Notes on contributors

David Brin published his non-fiction book, *The Transparent Society: Will Technology Force us to Choose between Freedom and Privacy?*, in 1998. This deals with a wide range of threats and opportunities facing our wired society during the information age. His chief argument, that openness is more effective than secrecy at fostering freedom, sparked controversy and garnered the Freedom of Speech Prize from the American Library Association. His papers in scientific journals cover an eclectic range of topics, from astronautics, astronomy and optics to alternative dispute resolution and the role of neoteny in human evolution. His PhD in space physics from the University of California at San Diego followed a masters in optics and an undergraduate degree in astrophysics from Caltech. He was a postdoctoral fellow at the California Space Institute and the Jet Propulsion Laboratory.

Jean-Paul Brodeur is currently a professor at the École de criminologie of the University of Montréal, where he is also the Director of the International Centre for Comparative Criminology. He is the author of some 102 refereed articles, 70 book chapters, and 19 books and Canadian government reports. He publishes in French, his native tongue, and also in English and German. Some of his books and articles have been translated into Spanish and Portuguese. He was the director of research of several Canadian government commissions of inquiry on policing, sentencing, national security and the Canadian armed forces. He was awarded a Killam scholarship for the years 2002–4. He spent these years alternately in France, at the Centre national de la recherche scientifique, and in the UK, where he was an invited fellow at the University of Cambridge. He is also a fellow of the Royal Society of Canada.

Aaron Doyle is Associate Professor of Sociology at Carleton University. His books include *Arresting Images: Crime and Policing in Front of the Television Camera* (2003), *Insurance as Governance* (2003, with Richard Ericson and Dean Barry), *Uncertain Business: Risk, Insurance and the Limits of Knowledge* (2004, with Richard Ericson) and *Risk and Morality* (2003, co-edited with Richard Ericson). Current research also includes work on risky occupations, gender and the body, and on the distinctive punitive properties of jails and detention and remand centres as opposed to prisons.

Benoît Gagnon is a PhD candidate in crimnology at the University of Montréal. As Associated Researcher at the Chaire du Canada en sécurité, identité et technologie, he works on such areas as cybercriminality, terrorism, security studies and the role of technologies in securitization processes. He is also a member of the Commission de l'éthique de la science et de la technologie of the government of Quebec.

Laura Huey is an Assistant Professor of Sociology at the University of Western Ontario. She is the author of several publications in the fields of policing, surveillance and cybercrime. Her most recent project, *Negotiating Demands: The Politics of Policing of Skid Row in Edinburgh, San Francisco and Vancouver*, was published in 2007.

Stéphane Leman-Langlois received his PhD in criminology from the University of Toronto in 2000, and he is Associate Professor of Criminology at the University of Montréal's School of Criminology. He is a member of the International Centre for Comparative Criminology and has worked on crimes against humanity, policing, technologies, terrorism and cybercrime. His concerns include the social construction of (in)security and the symbolic aspects of technology in the production of security and insecurity. His most recent publications include *Sociocriminologie* (2007), 'The myopic panopticon: the social consequences of policing through the lens' (*Policing and Society*, 2003, also published in V. Kappeler (ed.) *The Police and Society*, 2006), 'La surveillance totale' (*Cahiers de l'IHESI*, 2005, with Jean-Paul Brodeur), 'Theft in the information age: music, technology, crime and claims-making' (*Knowledge, Technology and Policy*, 2005), 'Surveillance-fiction: high and low policing revisited' (with Jean-Paul Brodeur, in R.V. Ericson and K. Haggerty (eds) *The New Politics of Surveillance* *and Visibility*, 2006), 'Le cybercrime comme moyen de contrôle du cyberespace', (*Criminologie*, 2006), 'Les technologies de l'identification, une note de recherche', (*Revue internationale de criminologie et de police technique et scientifique*, 2005, with Jean-Paul Brodeur) and 'Les technologies de protection des espaces' (with Lucie Dupuis, in M. Cusson *et al.* (eds), *Traité de la sécurité intérieure*, 2007).

Frédéric Lemieux is Assistant Professor at the School of Criminology of the University of Montréal and a researcher at the International Centre for Comparative Criminology. Much of his research has focused on social control. He is currently conducting studies on the function of criminal intelligence as a formal social control tool. He has published various journal articles examining social control and crime, as well as two books, the first one on the militarization of the police, in 2005, and the second on an international comparison of rules and practices in criminal intelligence, in 2006.

David Lyon is Queen's Research Chair in Sociology and Director of the Surveillance Project at Queen's University, Kingston, Ontario. He obtained a Killam research fellowship (2008–10) to examine national ID card systems and has authored and/or edited a number of books on surveillance, the most recent of which are *Surveillance after September 11* (2003), *Theorizing Surveillance: The Panopticon and Beyond* (ed. 2006) and *Surveillance Studies: An Overview* (2007).

Peter K. Manning holds the Elmer V.H. and Eileen M. Brooks trustees' Chair in the College of Criminal Justice at Northeastern University, Boston, MA. He has taught at Michigan State, MIT, Oxford, the University of Michigan and elsewhere, and was a Fellow of the National Institute of Justice, Balliol and Wolfson Colleges, Oxford, the American Bar Foundation, the Rockefeller Villa (Bellagio) and the Centre for Socio-legal Studies, Wolfson College, Oxford. Listed in *Who's Who in America* and *Who's Who in the World*, he has been awarded many contracts and grants, the Bruce W. Smith and the O.W. Wilson Awards from the Academy of Criminal Justice Sciences and the Charles Horton Cooley Award from the Michigan Sociological Association. The author and editor of some 13 books, including *Privatization of Policing: Two Views* (2000, with Brian Forst), his research interests include the rationalizing and interplay of private and public policing, democratic policing as a social form, homeland security, crime mapping and crime analysis, the uses of information technology and qualitative methods. The 2nd edition of *Narcs'*

Game appeared in 2004. His monograph, *Policing Contingencies*, was published in 2003, and his book, *Technology's Ways*, is forthcoming.

Gary T. Marx is Professor Emeritus at the Massachusetts Institute of Technology (MIT). He has also taught at the University of California at Berkeley (from where he received his PhD), Harvard University, the University of Colorado and for shorter periods at 20 other schools. He has written several books including *Protest and Prejudice: A Study of Belief in the Black Community* (1969); *Undercover: Police Surveillance in America* (1988); and the forthcoming *Windows Into the Soul: Surveillance and Society in an Age of High Technology.*

Johnny Nhan is a doctoral student at the University of California, Irvine. His current research is in the area of cyber-based crimes, particularly in relation to the intersection of public and private policing forms. He has also written in the field of Internet piracy.

Jennifer Whitson is a PhD student in sociology at Carleton University. She is researching and publishing in the areas of communications technologies and identity theft, software and social control, and law and morality in online domains. In 2005 she co-edited a special double volume of the *Journal Surveillance and Society* on 'Doing surveillance studies'. A recent article on identity theft and the care of the virtual self, co-authored with Kevin Haggerty, is forthcoming in the journal *Economy and Society.*

Acknowledgement

We would like to thank the *Fonds Québécois de recherche sur la société et la culture* (FQRSC, Grant 2008-SE-118600) for its financial support in the preparation of this book. The research of several of the contributors was also supported by the FQRSC.

Chapter 1

Introduction: technocrime

Stéphane Leman-Langlois

Technocrime does not exist. It is a figment of our imaginations. It is simply a convenient way to refer to a set of concepts, practices, frames and knowledges shaping the ways in which we understand matters having to do with the impact of technology on crime, criminals and our reactions to crime – and vice versa: since crime, criminals and reactions also transform technology. Technocrime includes crimes against computers; crimes committed with computers; cybercrimes; and crimes involving credit cards, automated telling machines, communications apparatuses (such as satellite signal theft) or the violation of protection strategies (including alarm systems and CD/DVD copy protection schemes). Technocrime gives rise to technosecurity and technopolice, as sets of various activities explicitly designed to prevent or repress it (for a complete inventory, see Byrne and Rebovich 2007). These responses are openly justified by descriptions of 'new' technocrimes, with more lurid or horrifying behaviours calling for stricter laws, restrictions of due process rules and higher enforcement budgets. But it should not be assumed that technopolicing follows technocrimes. It may also simply be the logical extension of security and policing into the high-tech world.

Though private forms of technosecurity are clearly at the vanguard of high-tech crime protection, the state remains the leader in more exotic, generalized forms of applied, high-tech security (national security, military security) – though it relies on private industries for most of the tech provision, of course.

Much has already been written on new technologies, crime and security. Most of it leaves the sociologically inclined mind unsatisfied:

crime, like technology, comprises objects not easily observed or measured and it involves various practices. These are sociological objects: they are modified by culture and they modify culture. This book attempts to explore new avenues and to re-examine a number of trends in the literature about crime and technology:

- *Technology is a new way of doing crime*: the emerging high-tech toolset that criminals have at their disposal makes them more dangerous, to more people – crooks can con better with technology; paedophiles can lure their victims better; and anyone can harass, defame, threaten or blackmail better with technology. In other cases, technology makes criminals dangerous to new people in entirely new ways: previously unthinkable crimes have appeared, such as website defacing, circumventing copy protection schemes, the denial of service attacks and digital rape. Cybercrime and computer crime are the bane of the information society.

- *Technology is a new way of doing policing*: the policing tech toolbox has drawn much attention in professional publications, in official government reports, in the media and, to a lesser extent, in the scientific literature. New cybercops and netdetectives have been at the centre of news reports. Their cyberwatch and netvigilance outfits have not been thoroughly studied but certainly have grabbed media attention as the new professional, expert police elite, or at least one form of an advanced, future-oriented way of doing policing. New tools in the fight against crime have created controversy, such as the Taser and other so-called 'less than lethal' weapons. Others seem drawn from science-fiction movies: pulsed energy projectiles, infra sound, lasers, microwave and chemical riot-disruption weapons, as well as many others.

- *Technology is a new way of threatening national security*: cyberterrorists have been using advanced steganography and other advanced encryption tools to disseminate crucial information to their accomplices. They have plotted online in chatrooms and on Arabic language bulletin boards. Canadian Momin Khawadja sent UK bomb plotters emails telling them how he could build efficient detonators for them – fortunately, he was caught in the National Security Agency's top-secret SIGINT communication interception net. A 'cyber Pearl Harbour' is looming, with attackers targeting essential infrastructures in attempts to cripple economies. They will co-ordinate attacks on supervisory control and data acquisition (SCADA) computer systems and on other targets selected to produce cascading failures along our highly interconnected infrastructures.

- *Technology is a new way to protect national security*: massive database analysis, information sharing across state and private entities, real-time crime mapping, transaction surveillance, and more efficient communication between security and police entities, as well as *within* those agencies, will enhance our ability to fight crime, terrorism, subversion, industrial spying and other international threats. It will also help manage emergencies when prevention was insufficient or when natural, unpredictable events occur. Later, technology will help us prosecute, punish and watch those responsible.

- *Technology is a new way to encroach on civil liberties*: physical surveillance technologies include CCTV and an increasing number of innovations, such as night vision, face recognition, gait recognition, computerized emotional state visual recognition, behavioural analysis and cross-system, camera-to-camera tracking. Physical surveillance also includes satellite imaging, city-wide sound analysis and location, mobile-phone radars, backscatter X-ray and many other technologies in development or already in use. To this must be added information surveillance or 'dataveillance' technologies, through biometrics, datamining and database interoperability. Linking those various forms of information and structuring them with social and psychological behavioural models will allow the creation of individual profiles more complete than the image individuals have of themselves.

- *Technology is a new way to protect civil liberties*: automated systems may see, hear and read everything, but they are devoid of ill-intentions, have no interest in publishing personal information, cannot benefit from blackmail, are free from political bias and do not care about our sexual preferences, personal quirks or the stupid mistakes we make. Automated systems are programmed to recognize threats to national and personal security only (of course, they are still programmed by humans).

The above contradictions should cause no surprise. Behind the new jargon of technology, mostly influenced by science fiction (for instance, the omnipresent 'cyber-' prefix inspired by Willam Gibson's 1984 *Neuromancer*), hide the same hesitation, controversy, conflicting politics and cultural constructs that have always been integral to all attempts at defining crime and criminals and to devising our responses to them. In fact, much of technocrime shows that constructivist approaches are much more powerful ways to account for reality than conventional, more essentialist or naturalistic approaches. More than ever, crime is what 'we' make of it and is 'real in its consequences', to paraphrase W.I. Thomas. Furthermore, as the chapters below show, this 'we' is more problematic than ever – most obviously when new laws criminalize mass behaviours. It is not surprising, therefore, that much of the analysis and nearly all the political discourse about technocrimes, consists of analogies with conventional crimes (filesharing is high-tech shoplifting).

Though much of the activity of the social sciences has also contributed to establish crime as a natural, objective, essential behaviour, the tech language offers an even stronger gloss of objective certainty. Contrary to the social disciplines, technology from the 'hard' or natural sciences takes human beings to space, allows remote-controlled surgery, helps us travel around the world, cures diseases, etc. Its less spectacular achievements are closely enmeshed in our daily activities: our work, entertainment, communications, learning, our very awareness of our world. When we are told there is such a thing as 'computer crime,' the concept seems closer to the natural laws that gave us computers than to the artificial laws that gave us crimes.

In many ways, technocrime also points to the critical flaws of late-modern society, the fragility of its technological structure, the unknown consequences of the deep demographic and social changes it has triggered and the general insecurity it has failed to alleviate. For others, technocrime encompasses an ordinary voyeuristic fascination with criminal behaviour, intriguing police drama and exciting technological gadgets. Either way, it makes good copy.

In reality, technocrime is a Gordian knot of political interests, economic interests, legal rules, technological developments, police, private security and forensics expertise, mass individual desires, geopolitical strategies and other forms of power we have yet to map. Some of the chapters in this volume, through their investigations of certain forms of 'crime' in the cyberworld, show how some of the most fundamental theoretical questions pop up in the most common activities of netizens. Is it possible to 'rape' an avatar? Can a virtual object actually be 'stolen'? (see Chapter 6)? Or are we just pasting our common understandings of damage and tort on new, uncharted regions of human behaviour and stretching language in order to describe things that it is clearly inadequate to describe?

Governing through technocrime

In a recent book, Simon (2007) described the increasing tendency of western societies to organize life with the help of systematic criminalization and police control. Wasteful, dangerous, risky, unhealthy, economically threatening and merely irritating behaviours are constituted into crimes or other forms of penal offences and watched, prevented, repressed and punished with the classical tools of the penal state. The mentally ill, the working poor, children, social assistance beneficiaries, immigrants, drivers and many others are being watched for potential criminal activity. Phenomena previously taken as social problems are now crime problems.

State response to such problems takes two broad forms: first, the penal system is used to individualize responsibility for crimes. 'Justice' will make those responsible pay for their actions. The previous failure of mega-social programmes to eradicate a variety of target problems (poverty, addictions, etc.) also helps funnel resources towards individualized conceptions of the problems. While crime was previously taken to be a symptom of social problems, it is not rare today to hear the exact opposite discourse, where poverty, social disorganization and citizens' retreat from public spaces in their neighbourhoods are the symptoms of a deeper crime problem (especially since Wilson and Kelling's famous 1982 paper). Secondly, since crime problems are conceived of as constant, background risks for all citizens, which must be *managed* through behaviour modification, situational prevention and target-hardening, much of the actual work needed can be left to individual citizens (and their private agents, should they choose – and if they can afford it – to entrust professionals with their security).

Much of technocrime operates in the same way. For instance, cybercrime is being used to justify and to encourage the monitoring of online activities and to create new responsibilities for various actors: parents watching (over) their children, employees watching other employees, employees watching their employers, employers watching their employees, spouses watching (out for) each other, Internet service providers (ISPs) watching their customers and retaining data about their activities online, etc. The cyberworld, much like the real world, is fraught with ill-intentioned individuals who are adept at disappearing into the massive quantity of activities and people online. Therefore, all must be watched.

More than in any other type of late-modern policing, technopolicing involves multiple entities, and conventional, state-centred police organizations are but one actor in the overall production of technosecurity. The actual breadth, depth or intensity of corporate policing online will never be known, but indications are that it is quite extensive. Traditional police organizations routinely ask corporations to produce near-complete investigations and evidence packages before they take over and proceed to submit the case to prosecuting attorneys. This is in part because the police have little resources, both in terms of tech-savvy investigators and analysts and in terms of the technology itself. Corporations and especially those most at risk of cyber-victimization, have, on the contrary, the required know-how, technology and, of course, a much more immediate, pressing motivation. However, it would be a mistake to conclude that actual, concrete surveillance and control of our activities are rampant. Because of dysfunctional technologies, incompetent users, low priority or simply the extremely high number of targets, technosecurity remains (for now) more talk than consequence.

In fact, one interesting aspect of technopolicing is how it is functionally split from traditional, conservative and far more common policing. In the case of conventional crime analysis, civilian expert analysts are typically at the bottom of the police respect/influence ladder. They do not have on-the-street crime experience and are not trained crime investigators; they have not proven themselves in the field; and they are thought of as 'outsiders' which, in police culture, means untrustworthy. This attitude is only worsened for analysts who focus on weird, complex or non-physical crimes.

However, a 'technopolice brigade' also exists: officers and administrators whose actions and influence pull the other way – the more the tech, the better the policing. The most spectacular success story for technopolice enthusiasts is the adoption of the 'Compstat' ethos and technologies, introduced by Bill Bratton in New York in the 1990s, but slowly making its presence felt throughout the world (with various degrees of success; I witnessed a 'Compstat' session in Philadelphia in 2005 where crime mapping was at best a form of visual support for an otherwise rather ordinary police briefing). British 'intelligence-led policing' (ILP) is also tech-heavy. Compstat relies in part on crime mapping software (MapInfo) and on the experts needed to make it work. However, crime mapping was introduced primarily as a management tool and is only beginning to be used to devise responses to crime. For now, such responses are limited to the conventional forms of increased (visible and invisible) presence and crackdowns. The *reasons* why crimes occur are deemed immaterial to police work. Paradoxically, then, the new technology has allowed the police to revert to ancient tactics.

Technology certainly permeates policing in one area: in North America and elsewhere, *weapons* technologies and often military technologies, are increasingly adopted by civilian police forces and by private security services. Many authors (but especially Kraska 1999) have already described how the militarization of policing is mainly driven by the increasing adoption of military weapons and the tactics and strategies they impose. Current controversy about the misuse of electrical pulse weapons, commercialized mostly by Taser International, shows how police safety is currently perceived as depending on the correct technological tools (which would include powerful firearms, bulletproof vests, CS/mace/pepper spray-cans, etc.) – in other words, despite declining crime rates, public policing is increasingly seen as an antagonistic, violent, high-danger occupation.

Robots are mission-oriented, autonomous systems and, as such, police robots remain in the realm of science fiction. However, current remote-operated observation and intervention platforms, though always mistakenly referred to as 'robots,' do open the way to even more spectacular technologies, like the eventual operation of 'real' robots. These are already available on the private market: small devices making random surveillance rounds in empty buildings, swapping their own battery when needed, notifying human watchers when suspicious occurrences are detected; and some can be equipped with weapons. It is difficult, at this time, to imagine how policing, security and crime will be modified by the probably inevitable adoption of such technology – but it is certainly a fascinating exercise.

Strangely, as is apparent in Peter Manning's chapter (Chapter 11), technopolicing, by and large, *does not work*: 1) it does not reduce crime, it does not make citizens less afraid of crime, it does not make cops happier with their work; 2) it also does not work for purely technical reasons; 3) and, finally, it does not work because it does not match the conception police have of their mission. Of course, one might argue that the situation is not unlike that of conventional policing: though crime will never be eradicated by policing and actual policing effects on crime are not often measurable, the complete *absence* of policing could conceivably result in an explosion of criminality. In other words, without technopolicing, the technocrime problem might be *worse*. Whether or not one is sceptical about such pronouncements, they are certainly far too vague to provide any form of interesting conclusion about the nature, effects and interactions of technopolicing with technocrime. Be that as it may, regardless of the actual impact of technopolice on our reality, its vertiginous amplification and spiralling costs certainly make it an interesting social and political phenomenon.

Structure of the book

This book covers many aspects of the technocrime question, though many, many more remain untouched. Chapters vary not only in their subject matter but also in their theoretical and empirical density. Chapter 2, by David Brin, accomplished science-fiction author, is an extension of his controversial opus, *The Transparent Society* (1998). Brin offers a thought experiment: what if the technology of surveillance could become sufficiently democratized to offer viable counter-surveillance? There is an abundance of evidence showing that watching those in authority renders them more accountable. The news is full of politicians captured by mobile-phone cameras after hit-and-run incidents, of videos of police officers beating suspects (the most famous case remains that of Rodney King in Los Angeles) or tazering them to death, of military public-relations personnel adjusting Wikipedia entries to reflect a better image of operations abroad, etc. Brin concludes that counter-watching, or what Mann (Mann *et al.* 2003) calls 'sousveillance', is not a techno-fantasy or a gadget obsession – one might add that it may never work very well – but is the only means by which we will maintain a modicum of ruling-class and institutional accountability in the future.

In Chapter 3, Stéphane Leman-Langlois reports on an ongoing study of ordinary people's perception of police CCTV. The author ran some group interviews in an area of downtown Montreal (Canada) and asked residents, shop owners and employees whether cameras had an effect on them: did they feel safer; did they think their privacy was threatened? As it turns out, cameras were almost universally deemed to be irrelevant to all aspects of every participant's day-to-day life. In fact, when asked about their security, residents living in direct view of the well publicized cameras almost never actually mentioned them. Their insecurity was caused by social indifference, by the felt absence of either community or police help in times of need. It was also caused, predictably, by visible signs of disorder, such as discarded needles and graffiti. Finally, it was also caused by random, unpredictable behaviours taking place in their own buildings or anywhere on the street, regardless of the presence of cameras. The obvious conclusion is that CCTV is disconnected from the reality of the street and that an increased police reliance on CCTV is perceived as a progressive disconnection of the police from the reality of city life: to these respondents, 'policing through the lens' (Leman-Langlois 2003) is policing the irrelevant.

Benoît Gagnon, in Chapter 4, tackles two of the new buzzwords in the media and the specialized literature: 'cybercrime' and 'cyberwar'. Comparing US and Chinese government cyberspace presence, he concludes that both are moving towards a militarization of their approach. This implies and, in fact, rests on, an increasingly nationalized view of what takes place on the web: both powers present cyberspace as territorial, 'national' space where government sovereignty can be asserted. In both cases there is also an obvious intensification of government presence in cyberspace, especially through military institutions. As a part of the national infrastructure – in fact, an important, underlying part, since it allows most of the other elements to be connected together – any form of 'misuse' or 'misbehaviour' on the web can be perceived as a threat to national 'cybersecurity'. Though of course the precise manner in which national security is conceived of differs profoundly between China and the USA, the result is the same: a rapidly increasing desire to control cyberspace.

Chapter 5 gives a fascinating glimpse into the structuring of part of what has been called the 'surveillant assemblage:' how the police, the justice system and private enterprises network and organize to control online activities identified as dangerous, immoral or damaging. As described by Johnny Nhan and Laura Huey, the assemblage is fraught with problems of various kinds: unreconcilable legal requirements, inter- and intra-agency rivalries and epistemological differences regarding the nature of crime, public police intervention and public morality – not to mention the simple lack of resources allocated to agencies tasked with fighting cybercrime.

Chapter 6 attempts to chart entirely new territory: crime and punishment in virtual societies. The example presented by Jennifer Whitson and Aaron Doyle is the computer realm of Linden Lab's *Second Life*. Still mostly considered to be games or simple hobbies by much of social science, online worlds are in fact nothing less than massive social experiments where many of the fundamental objects of sociology and criminology, such as rules, deviance and human agency, are reconfigured in real time. Group and individual dynamics are observable and accessible, social relations are restructured, new forms of deviance are identified, prevention and repression activities take shape. Politics, financial interests and legal pressures both in-world and out-world (the 'real world') influence this continuously richer reality, as courts, the police and the media begin to pay attention to what is happening. Though the future of 'second lives' of every type is difficult to predict with any degree of accuracy, one can reliably predict substantial growth and probably the progressive enmeshment of virtual lives with aspects of the real world. It remains to be seen whether this entanglement will make the virtual more concrete, or if it will reveal what we take as concrete as constructed, artificial and virtual.

In Chapter 7, Stéphane Leman-Langlois considers the development of the concept and discourse of 'privacy' online and in virtual worlds. It is the author's contention that privacy is being progressively redefined by our online activities, where much of our enjoyment of various cyberworlds – from the simple search field and results on Amazon.com to more complete realities, such as Second Life – is dependent on our willingness and ability to share information about ourselves with various known and unknown entities. One can better understand this change by thinking of privacy as a new form of currency, exchangeable for various goods, services, information, entertainment and what amounts to simple comfort in existing and acting online. If this assessment is correct, identity and privacy will lose any reference to a private inner sanctum, a sphere of intimacy to be kept secret or shared only with immediately present, trusted persons. A 'right to privacy,' therefore, will move closer to a right to property, where personal information is withheld only until a benefit is offered in exchange. This has several interesting implications for surveillance and control online, of course. One of the more obvious is that, since information flows are far from equivalent – some are personal and 'worth' something only when combined and aggregated while others from multinational corporations depend on profitability – all breaches of privacy/information property rules are unlikely to be policed equally.

In Chapter 8, Frédéric Lemieux describes how various criminal intelligence outfits have adopted complex IT systems in order to gather, store, manage, analyse and communicate information about crimes and criminals. This is technopolicing at its purest: all those involved believe in the power of technology and information to control crime. New bureaucratic policing management styles, themselves heavily tipped towards the centrality of information (we are, after all, in the 'information society'), have adopted policing styles sharing the same traits. Intelligence-led policing (ILP) is the prototype of such styles and, of course, was only thinkable when adequate computing power permitted the efficient and timely production of immediately, concretely usable ('actionable') information. Though information management was always at the centre of police (or other) investigations and to a lesser degree helpful in determining general, abstract, organizational missions and medium and long-term priorities, the idea that *all* police work, including patrol, should be 'intelligence led,' is rather new. It has also caused a minor revolution in such organizations through the introduction of expert analysts and their high-tech tools. However and predictably, the *actual* crime reduction effects of that revolution remain difficult to detect.

The impact of technology and science on the conduct of investigations, recent media attention notwithstanding, has rarely been analysed. Jean-Paul Brodeur, in Chapter 9, remedies this situation with a study of a police force's use of forensics and other technologies to solve homicides. In order to construct an empirically based theory of the criminal investigation process, Brodeur first deconstructs the typical assumptions and definitions commonly associated with investigation and finds that they are mostly tautological, founded in semantics rather than empirical observation. In reality, 'solving cases' involves many individuals who are not police investigators, and investigators do far more than investigate. The high tech of scientific investigation, so dear to Hollywood writers, mostly comes in when every other way to solve the case has failed – only to fail equally, though far more expensively.

Chapter 10 describes a society where citizenship is a matter not of legal and national belonging, with rights and responsibilities, but of a quantity of benefits one qualifies for. David Lyon explains how, for political, economic and bureaucratic reasons, individuals are increasingly asked to demonstrate that they actually qualify for those benefits – the spectres of freeloaders and crooks are routinely mobilized in public discourse to account for the inefficiencies of state and private bureaucracies. Sorting out the freeloaders (those who benefit without deserving, such as immigrants) and the crooks (those who actively find ways to abuse the system) has become a major focal point of state bureaucracies, and technocrats have enthusiastically embraced every new scheme marketed with the promise of sorting the deserving citizens from the others. National ID card systems, radio frequency idntification (RFID) chips, new, exotic types of biometrics and various yet-to-be-released panaceas are adopted everywhere without serious concern for various questions relating to their actual performance or their total, global costs (including indirect costs to consumers, travellers, etc.). Their social and political costs and, more abstractly, their cultural costs – for instance, how they reconfigure our understanding of citizenship – are, of course, usually not even conceived of or, if they are, they are deemed entirely secondary to efficiency matters.

The final chapter, by Peter K. Manning, offers what may appear, at first, as an opposite picture of that given by Lyon. Manning shows that, in reality, policing through surveillance remains focused on traditional, if not outdated, conceptions of police work. Surveillance on a higher plane, such as described by Lyon and elsewhere in this book, remains impossible in practice. The practical full realization of surveillance on a grand scale may actually never be possible, limited by failing technologies, petty power struggles, lack of interest, information incompatibility, legal hurdles and many more such obstacles. The chapter ends with a description of what the police actually do, which illustrates artfully the unbridgeable gap between surveillance and late-modern policing. That said, the question may not be whether or not 'total information awareness' is possible. If it appears to be possible, a critical mass of key politicians, bureaucrats, police officers will pursue it. This belief is changing how policing is being done through, for instance, new models such as ILP.

Together, the chapters from Lyon and Manning show us the future as a dysfunctional utopia: dreams of total surveillance structuring a progressively more fragmented control.

References

Brin, D. (1998) *The Transparent Society*. New York, NY: Perseus Books.

Byrne, J. and Rebovich, D. (eds) 2007) *The New Technology of Crime, Law and Social Control*, Monsey, NY: Criminal Justice Press.

Gibson, W. (1984) *Neuromancer.* New York, NY: Ace Books.

Kraska, P. (1999) 'Militarizing criminal justice: exploring the possibilities', *Journal of Political and Military Sociology*, 27: 205–15.

Leman-Langlois, S. (2003), 'The myopic panopticon: the social consequences of policing through the lens,' *Policing and Society*, 13: 43–58.

Mann, S., Nolan, J. and Wellman, B. (2003) 'Sousveillance: inventing and using wearable computing devices for data collection in surveillance environments', *Surveillance and Society*, 1: 331–55.

Simon, J. (2007) *Governing through Crime: How the War on Crime Transformed American Democracy and Created a Culture of Fear*. Oxford: Oxford University Press.

Wilson, J. and Kelling, G. (1982) 'Broken windows: the police and neighbourhood safety', *The Atlantic Monthly*, March: 28–39.

Chapter 2

Crime and lawfulness in the age of all-seeing techno-humanity

David Brin

Introduction

Ten centuries ago, at the previous millennium, a Viking lord commanded the rising tide to retreat. Not a deluded fool, King Canute aimed in this way to teach flatterers a lesson – that even sovereign rulers cannot halt inexorable change. A thousand years later, we face tides of technology-driven transformation that seem bound only to accelerate. Waves of innovation may liberate human civilization or disrupt it more than anything since glass lenses and movable type. Critical decisions during the next few years – about research, investment, law and lifestyle – may determine what kind of civilization our children inherit. Especially problematic are many information-related technologies that loom on the near horizon – technologies that may foster tyranny or else empower citizenship in a true global village.

Typically – in an era when the most commonly abused drug is indignation – we are told, often and passionately, that Big Brother may abuse these new powers. Or else our privacy and rights will be violated by some other group: perhaps a commercial, aristocratic, bureaucratic, foreign, criminal or technological elite. Because one or more of these power centres might use the new tools to *see better*, we're told that we should all be very afraid. Indeed, our only hope may be to squelch or suppress or fiercely control the onslaught of change. For the sake of safety and liberty, we are offered one prescription: we must limit the power of others to see.

Half a century ago, amid an era of despair, George Orwell created one of the most oppressive metaphors in literature with the telescreen system used to surveil and control the people in his novel, *Nineteen Eighty-four*. We have been raised to a high degree of sensitivity by Orwell's self-preventing prophecy, and others like it. Attuned to wariness, today's activists preach that any growth in the state's ability to see will take us down a path of no return, towards the endless hell of Big Brother.

But consider. The worst aspect of Orwell's telescreen – the trait guaranteeing tyranny – was not the fact that agents of the state could use it to see. The one thing that despots truly need is to avoid accountability. In *Nineteen Eighty-four*, this is achieved by keeping the telescreen aimed in just one direction, by preventing the people from looking back.

Shall we automatically assume that the best way to prevent tyranny is to prevent the powerful from seeing the powerless? That seems, at best, a frail hope and perhaps impossible to achieve. Fortunately, there is an alternative proposal, seldom heard but offering a different path. Instead of seeking shelter in obscurity, we might choose to face the inevitable head on, with both courage and confidence. While a flood of new discoveries and devices may seem daunting, it should not undermine the core freedoms or values of a calm and knowledgeable citizenry. In any event, none of those who bemoan science-driven progress has shown how to stop even one of the new technologies, let alone reverse a rising tide.

A world of data

Consider a few examples: radio frequency identification (RFID) technology will soon replace the simple, passive bar codes on packaged goods, substituting inexpensive chips that respond to microwave interrogation, making every box of toothpaste or razor blades part of a vast, automatic inventory-accounting system. Wal-Mart announced in 2003 that it will require its top-100 suppliers to use RFID on all large cartons, for purposes of warehouse inventory-keeping. But that is only the beginning. Inevitably, as prices fall, RFID chips will be incorporated into most products and packaging. Supermarket checkout will become a breeze, when you simply push your trolley past a scanner and grab a printout receipt, with every purchase automatically debited from your account. Does that sound simultaneously creepy and useful? Well, it goes much farther. Under development are smart washers that will read the tags on clothing and adjust their cycles accordingly, and smart medicine cabinets that track tagged prescriptions, in order to warn which ones have expired or need refilling. Cars, desks and computers will adjust to your preferred settings as you approach. Paramedics will be able to download your health status – including allergies and dangerous drug conflicts – even if you are unconscious or unable to speak.

Of course there is a downside. A wonderful 1960s paranoia-satire film, *The President's Analyst,* offered a prophetic warning against implanted devices, inserted into people, that would allow them to be tracked by Big Business and government. But who needs implantation when your clothing and innocuous possessions will carry cheap tags of their own that can be associated with their owners? Already some schools, especially in Asia, are experimenting with RFID systems that will locate all students, at all times. There will be fun to be had, for a while, in fooling these systems with minor acts of irreverent rebellion. Picture kids swapping clothes and possessions, furtively, in order to leave muddled trails. Still, such measures will not accomplish much over extended periods. Tracking on vast scales, nation and worldwide, will emerge in rapid order. And if we try to stop it with legislation, the chief effect will only be to drive the surveillance into secret networks that are just as pervasive, only they will operate at levels we cannot supervise, study, discuss or understand.

Wait, there's more. For example, a new Internet protocol (IPv6) will vastly expand available address space in the virtual world. The present IP, offering 32-bit data labels, can now offer every living human a unique online address, limiting direct access to something like ten billion web pages or specific computers. In contrast, IPv6 will use 128 bits. This will allow the virtual tagging of every cubic centimetre of the earth's surface, from sea-level to mountain top, spreading a multidimensional data overlay across the planet. Every tagged or man-made object may participate, from your wristwatch to a nearby lamp-post, vending machine or rubbish bin. Every interest group will find some kind of opportunity in this new world. Want to protect forests? Each and every tree on earth might have a chip fired into its bark, alerting a network if furtive loggers start transporting stolen hardwoods. Or use the same method to track whoever steals your morning paper. Not long after this, teens and children will purchase rolls of ultra-cheap digital eyes and casually stick them on to walls. Millions of those 'penny-cams' will join in the fun, contributing to the vast IPv6 datasphere. This new Internet protocol will offer many other benefits – for example, embedded systems for data tracking and verification (for an illustration, see Brin 2004). Over the long run, these systems may help to empower citizens and enhance mutual trust ... or else the expanded powers of vision may embolden tyrants. Much will depend on whether or not we panic.

In the mid-1990s, when I began writing *The Transparent Society* (Brin 1998), it seemed dismaying to note that Great Britain had almost 150,000 charged-couple device (CCD) police cameras scanning public streets. Today, they number in the millions. In the USA, a similar proliferation, though just as rapid, has been somewhat masked by a different national tradition – that of dispersed ownership. As pointed out by University of California, San Diego, researcher, Mohan Trivedi, American constabularies have few cameras of their own. Instead, they rely on vast numbers of security monitors operated by small and large companies, banks, markets and private individuals, who scan ever-larger swathes of urban landscape. Nearly all the footage that helped solve the Oklahoma City bombing and the DC Sniper Episode – as well as documenting the events of 9/11 2001 – came from unofficial sources.

This unique system – based on largely voluntary accordance by the citizen-owners of distributed sensors – can be both effective and inexpensive for state agencies, especially when the public is inclined to co-operate, as in searches for missing children. Still, there are many irksome drawbacks to officials who may want more pervasive and direct surveillance. For one thing, the present method relies on high levels of mutual trust and goodwill between authorities and the owners of those cameras, whether they be convenience-store corporations or video-cam-equipped private citizens. Moreover, while many crimes are solved with help from private cameras, more police are also held accountable for well documented lapses in professional behaviour. This tattle-tale trend began with the infamous beating of Rodney King, more than a decade ago, and has continued at an accelerating pace. Among recent events were some that shook America's stature in the world, such as the exposure of vicious prisoner abuse by jailers at Abu Ghraib Prison, in Iraq, ranging all the way to simple disgust over the tormenting of live birds by slaughterhouse workers for Pilgrim's Pride (suppliers to Kentucky Fried Chicken). Each time the lesson is the same one: that professionals should attend to their professionalism, or else the citizens and consumers who pay their wages will find out and – eventually – hold them accountable (those wishing to promote the trend might look into Project Witness (http://www.witness.org/), which supplies cameras to underdogs around the world).

Will American authorities decide to abandon this quaint social bargain of shared access to sensors under dispersed ownership? As the price of electronic gear plummets, it will become easy and cheap for our professional protectors to justify and purchase their own, dedicated systems of surveillance, like those already operating in Britain, Singapore and elsewhere. Systems that 'look down from above' 'surveillance' without any irksome public involvement. On the other hand, authorities might simply use our networks without asking. A decade ago, the US government fought such activist groups as the Electronic Frontier Foundation, claiming a need to unlock commercial-level encryption codes at will, for the sake of law enforcement and national defence. Both sides won apparent victories. High-level commercial encryption became widely available. And the government came to realize that it doesn't matter. It never did.

Networks of seeing machines

Driven partly by security demands, a multitude of biometric technologies will identify individuals by scanning physical attributes, from fingerprints, retinal and iris patterns, faces and voices to brain waves and possibly unique chemical signatures. Starting with those now entering and leaving the USA, whole classes of people will grow accustomed to routine identification in this way. Indeed, citizens may start to demand the *more* extensive use of biometric identification, as a safety measure against identity theft. When your car recognizes your face, and all the stores can verify your fingerprint, what need will you have for keys or a credit card?

Naturally, this is yet another trend that has put privacy activists in a lather. They worry, with some justification, about civil liberties implications when the police or FBI might scan multitudes (say, at a sporting event) in search of fugitives or suspects. Automatic software agents will recognize individuals who pass through one camera view, then perform a smooth handoff to the next camera, and the next, planting a 'tail' on dozens, hundreds or tens of thousands of people at a time (illustrated in Brin 2001a). Without a doubt, this method *could* indeed become a potent tool for some future Big Brother. Yet, should that legitimate and plausible fear be addressed by reflexively blaming technology, the routine habit of neo-luddites, or by finding ways that technology may work *for* us, instead of *against* us? Suppose you could ban or limit a particular identification technique (mind you, I've seen no evidence that it can be done). The sheer *number* of different, overlapping biometric approaches will make the whole thing fruitless. In fact, human beings fizz and froth with unique traits that can be spotted at a glance, even with our old-fashioned senses. Our ancestors relied on this fact, building and correlating lists of people who merited trust or worry from among the few thousands they met in person. In a global village of ten billion souls, machines will do the same thing for us by prostheticly amplifying vision and augmenting memory.

With so many identification methodologies working independently and in parallel, our children may find the word 'anonymous' impossibly quaint, perhaps even incomprehensible. But that need not mean an end to freedom, or even privacy. Although it will undoubtedly mean a redefinition of what we think privacy means.

But onwards with our scan of looking technologies. Beyond RFID, IPv6 and biometrics there are smart cards, smart highways, smart airports, smart automobiles, smart televisions, smart homes … and so on. Note that the shared adjective may be premature. These systems will provide improved service long before anything like actual 'artificial intelligence' comes online. Yet, machinery need not be strictly intelligent in order to transform our lives. Moreover, distributed 'smart' units will also gather information, joining together in cross-correlating networks that recognize travellers, perform security checks, negotiate micro-transactions, detect criminal activity, warn of potential danger and anticipate desires. When these parts fully interlink, the emerging entity may not be self-aware, but it will certainly know the whereabouts of its myriad parts.

Location awareness will pervade the electronic world, thanks to ever-more sophisticated radio transceivers, Global Positioning System (GPS) chips and government-backed emergency location initiatives like Enhanced-911 in the USA and Enhanced-112 in Europe. Mobile phones, computers and cars will report position and unique identity in real time, with (or possibly without) owner consent. Lives will be saved, property recovered and missing children found. But these benefits aren't the real reason that location awareness and reporting will spread to nearly every device. As described by science-fiction author, Vernor Vinge, it is going to happen because the capability will cost next to nothing as an integrated part of wireless technology. In future, you can assume almost any electronic device will be trackable, although citizens still have time to debate who may do the tracking.

The flood of information has to go some place. Already, databases fill with information about private individuals, from tax and medical records to credit ratings; from travel habits and retail purchases to which movies they recently downloaded on their TiVo personal video-recorder. Yahoo's HotJobs.com recently began selling 'self' background checks, offering job-seekers a chance to vet their own personal, financial and legal data – the same information that companies might use to judge them. Data aggregators like Acxiom Corporation, of Arkansas, or ChoicePoint, of Georgia, go even farther, listing your car loans, outstanding liens and judgments, any professional or pilot or gun licences, credit checks and real estate you might own – all of it gathered from legal and open sources.

One online dating service hopes to help its love-seekers avoid the sleazily married by filtering philanderers. True.com, which already screens for felons, recently expanded its partnership with database provider Rapsheets.com to review public records and to verify a user's single status. If a would-be Romeo turns out to be a married Pinocchio, the user is thrown out of the cyber-circle (of course, people seeking extramarital bliss have other options: Yahoo Inc. and Microsoft Corp's MSN even have online chat groups dedicated to the 'married and flirting', Yahoo! 2004).

On the plus side, you'll be able to find and counter those rumours and slanderous untruths that can slash from the dark. The ability of others to harm you with lies may decline drastically. On the other hand, it will be simple for almost anybody using these methods to appraise the background of anyone else, including all sorts of unpleasant things that are inconveniently true. In other words, the rest of us will be able to do what elites (define them as you wish, from government to aristocrats to criminal masterminds) already can.

Some perceive this trend as ultimately empowering, while others see it as inherently oppressive. For example, activist groups from the American Civil Liberties Union (ACLU) to the Electronic Privacy Information Center call for European-style legislation aiming to seal the data behind perfect firewalls into separate, isolated clusters that cannot cross-link or overlap. And, in the short term, such efforts may prove beneficial. New database filters may help users find information they legitimately need while protecting personal privacy ... for a while, buying us time to innovate for the long term.

But we must not fool ourselves. No firewall, program or machine has ever been perfect, or perfectly implemented by fallible human beings. Whether the law officially allows it or not, can any effort by mere mortals prevent data from leaking? (And just *one* brief leak can spill a giant database into public knowledge, for ever.) Cross-correlation will swiftly draw conclusions that are far more significant than the mere sum of the parts, adding up to a profoundly detailed picture of every citizen, down to details of personal taste.

The following is a related titbit from the *Washington Post* (18 July 2004):

> Minnesota entrepreneur Larry Colson has developed WebVoter, a program that lets Republican activists in the state report their neighbors' political views into a central database that the Bush-Cheney campaign can use to send them targeted campaign literature. The Bush campaign has a similar program on its Web site. And here's Colson's response to anyone who feels a privacy qualm or two about this program: '[It's] not as if we're asking for Social Security number and make and model and serial number of car. We're asking for party preference … Party preference is not something that is such a personal piece of data.'

That statement may be somewhat true in today's America. We shrug over each others' harmless or opinionated eccentricities. But can that trait last very long when powerful groups scrutinize us, without being scrutinized back?

Tools and toys of late-modern life

The picture so far may seem daunting enough. Only now add a flood of new sensors. We have already seen the swift and inexpensive transformation of mere mobile phones into a much more general, portable, electronic tool by adding the capabilities of a digital camera, audio recorder and personal digital assistant (PDA). But have we fully grasped the implications, when any well e-quipped pedestrian might swiftly transform into an *ad hoc* photojournalist – or Peeping Tom – depending on opportunity or inclination?

On the near horizon are wearable multimedia devices with displays that blend into your sunglasses, along with computational, data storage and communications capabilities woven into the very clothes you wear. The term 'augmented reality' will apply when these tools overlay your subjective view of the world with digitally supplied facts, directions or commentary. You will expect – and rely on – rapid answers to queries about any person or object in sight. In essence, this will be no different from querying your neuron-based memories about people in the village where you grew up. Only we had a million years to get used to tracking reputations that way. The

21

new prosthetic memories will prove awkward, at first. Today we worry about drivers who use mobile phones at the wheel. Tomorrow will it be distracted pedestrians, muttering to no one as they walk? Will we grunt and babble while strolling along, like village idiots of yore?

Maybe not: having detected nerve signals near the larynx that are preparatory to forming words, scientists at NASA Ames Research Center lately proposed subvocal speech systems – like those forecast in my 1989 novel, *Earth* – that will accept commands without audible sounds. Potentially useful in spacesuits, noisy environments or to reduce the inevitable babble when we are all linked by wireless, all the time. Making this trend more general, volition sensing may pick up an even wider variety of cues, empowering you to converse, give commands or participate in far-away events without speaking aloud or showing superficial signs.

Is this the pre-dawn of tech-mediated telepathy? Advertising agencies are already funding research groups that use position emission tomography (PET) scans and functional magnetic resonance imaging (fMRI) to study the immediate reactions of test subjects to marketing techniques and images. 'We are crossing the chasm' said Adam Koval, chief operating officer of Thought Sciences, a division of Bright House, an Atlanta-based advertising and consulting firm whose clients include Home Depot, Delta Airlines and Coca Cola, 'and bringing a new paradigm in analytic rigor to the world of marketing and advertising.' Those who decry such studies face a tough burden, since all the test subjects are volunteers, though it is eerie to imagine a future when sensitive devices might scan you as a passer-by. Will you be better able to protect yourself if these technologies are banned, and thus driven underground, or regulated, with a free market that might offer us all pocket detectors, to catch scanners in the act?

Meanwhile, the trends continue outside our brains. Microsoft recently unveiled Sensecam, a camera disguised as jewelry that automatically records scores of images per hour from the wearer's point of view, digitally documenting an ongoing daily photo-diary. Such 'Boswell machinery' may go far beyond egomania. For example, what good will your wallet do to a mugger when images of the crime are automatically broadcast across the web? Soon, cyber-witnessing of public events, business deals, crimes and accidents will be routine. In movie parlance, you will have to assume that everybody you meet is carrying a 'wire'.

Meanwhile, you can be sure that military technologies will continue spinning off civilian versions, as happened with infrared night vision. Take 'sniffers' designed to warn of environmental or chemical dangers on the battlefield. Soon, cheap and plentiful sensors will find their way into neighbourhood storm drains, on to lamp-posts or even into your home taps, giving rapid warnings of local pollution. Neighbourhood or activist groups that create detector networks will have autonomous access to data-rivalling local governments. Of course, a better informed citizenry is sure to be more effective ... and far more noisy.

The same spin-off effect has emerged from the military development of inexpensive unmanned aerial vehicle (UAV) battlefield reconnaissance drones. Some of the 'toys' offered by Draganfly Innovations can cruise independently for more than an hour along a GPS-guided path, can transmit 2.4-Ghz digital video, then return automatically to the hobbyist owner. In other companies and laboratories, the aim is towards miniaturization, developing micro-flyers that can assist an infantry squad in an urban skirmish or carry eavesdropping equipment into the lair of a suspected terrorist. Again, civilian models are already starting to emerge. There may already be some in your neighbourhood.

Cheap, innumerable eyes in the sky. One might envision dozens of potentially harmful uses, hundreds of beneficial ones and millions of others ranging from the irksome to innocuous, all leading towards a fundamental sea change in the way each of us relates to the horizon that so cruelly constrained the vision and imagination of our ancestors. Just as baby boomers grew accustomed to viewing far-away places through the magical – though professionally mediated – channel of network television, the next generation will simply assume that there is always another independent way to glimpse real-time events, either far away or just above the streets where they live.

Should we push for yet another unenforceable law to guard our backyards against Peeping Toms and their drone planes? Or perhaps we'd be better off simply insisting that the companies that make the little robot spies give us the means to trace them back to their nosy pilots. In other words, looking back may be a more effective way to protect privacy.

Conclusion: looking back

One might aim for reciprocal transparency using new technology. For example, Swiss researcher Marc Langheinrich's (2002) PDA application detects nearby sensors and then lists what kind of information they're collecting. At a more radical and polemical level, there is the 'sousveillance movement', led by University of Toronto Professor, Steve Mann (Mann *et al.* 2003). Taking a play off 'surveillance' (overlooking from above), Mann's coined term suggests that we should all get in the habit of looking *from below,* proving that we are sovereign and alert citizens down here, not helpless sheep. Mann contends that private individuals will be empowered to do this by new senses, dramatically augmented by wearable electronic devices. Recent events, especially the courage and resiliency of private citizens in the face of terror (Brin 2001b), suggest that Mann may turn out to be right.

We have skimmed over a wide range of new technologies, from RFID chips and stick-on pennycameras to new Internet address protocols and numerous means of biometric identification, from database mining and aggregation to sensors that detect chemical pollution or the volition to speak or act before your muscles get a chance to move. From omni-surveillance to universal localization. From eyes in the sky to those that may invade your personal space. Note a common theme. Every device or function that's been described here serves to enhance some human sensory capability, from sight and hearing to memory. And while some may fret and fume, there is no historical precedent for a civilization refusing such prosthetics, when they became available. Such trends cannot be boiled down to a simple matter of good news or bad. While technologies of distributed vision may soon empower common folk in dramatic ways, giving a boost to participatory democracy by highly informed citizens, you will not hear that side of the message from most pundits, who habitually portray the very same technologies in a darker light, predicting that machines are about to destroy privacy, undermine values and ultimately enslave us. In fact, the next century will be much too demanding for fixed perspectives. Agility will be far more useful, plus a little healthy contrariness. When in the company of reflexive pessimists – or knee-jerk optimists – the wise among us will be those saying 'yes, but ...'

Orwell's metaphors were so powerful, so transforming of our attitudes, that his novel is the archetype of what I've called the 'self-preventing prophecy', having girded us to vow our lives in effort to prevent take-over by some controlling elite, armed with new, oppressive technological powers. And yet, the most fearsome thing about Orwell's telescreen-equipped state apparatus was not the power of vision but the restricted nature of the vision: the fact that it flowed only one way, providing information to – but never about – the monsters in command.

This has tremendous pertinence here and now. In an era featured by fear of terrorism, we are frequently told that there is a fundamental choice to be made in a tragic *trade-off* between safety and freedom. While agents of the state, like then Attorney General John Ashcroft, demand new powers of surveillance – purportedly in order better to protect us – champions of civil liberties (e.g. the ACLU) warn against surrendering traditional constraints on what government is allowed to see. For example, they decry provisions of the Patriot Act that open broader channels of inspection, detection, search and data collection, predicting that such steps take us on the road to despotism.

While they are right to fear such an outcome, they could not be more wrong about the specifics. As I discuss in greater detail elsewhere (Brin 2007), the very idea of a trade-off between security and freedom is one of the most insidious and dismal notions I have ever heard – a perfect example of a devil's dichotomy. We modern citizens are living proof that people can and should have both. Freedom and safety, in fact, work together, not in opposition. Furthermore, I refuse to let anybody tell me that I must choose between liberty for my children and their safety! I refuse, and so should you.

As we've seen throughout this chapter, and in a myriad other possible examples, there is no way that we will ever succeed in limiting the power of elites to see and know. If our freedom depends on blinding the mighty, then we haven't a prayer. Fortunately, that isn't what really matters, after all. Moreover, John Ashcroft clearly knows it. By far the most worrisome and dangerous parts of the Patriot Act are those that remove tools of *supervision,* allowing agents of the state to act *secretly*, without checks or accountability. Ironically, these are the very portions that the ACLU and other groups have most neglected. In comparison, a few controversial alterations of procedure for search warrants are pretty minor. After all, appropriate levels of surveillance may shift as society and technology experience changes in a new century. The Founders never heard of a wire tap, for example. But our need to watch the watchers will only grow. It is a monopoly of vision that we need to fear, above all else. So long as most of the eyes are owned by the citizens themselves, there will remain a chance for us to keep arguing knowledgeably among ourselves. Debating and bickering, as sovereign, educated citizens should.

It will not be a convenient or anonymous world. Privacy may have to be redefined much closer to home. There will be a lot of noise. But we will not drown under a rising tide of uncontrolled technology. Keeping our heads, we will remain free to guide our ships across these rising waters. To choose a destiny of our own.

References

Brin, D. (1989) *Earth*. New York, NY: Bantam.

Brin, D. (1998) *The Transparent Society*. New York, NY: Perseus Books.

Brin, D. (2001a) *Kiln People*. New York, NY: Tor Books.

Brin, D. (2001b) 'The value – and empowerment – of common citizens in an age of danger', *Futurist.com* (www.futurist.com/archives/society-and-culture/value-and-empowerment/).

Brin, D, (2004) *2020 Vision: Journalism the Day After Tomorrow* (http://www.ojr.org/ojr/workplace/1078288485.php).

Brin, D. (2007a) http://www.futurist.com/portal/future_trends/david_brin_empowerment.htm.

Brin, D. (2007b), *A Dangerous World: Transparency, Security and Privacy* (http://www.davidbrin.com/privacyarticles.html).

Langheinrich, M. (2002) 'A privacy awareness system for ubiquitous computing environments', in G. Borriello and L. Erik Holmquist (eds) *4th International Conference on Ubiquitous Computing (Ubicomp 2002)* (LNCS No. 2498). Springer-Verlag.

Mann, S., Nolan, J. and Wellman, B. (2003) 'Sousveillance: inventing and using wearable computing devices for data collection in surveillance environments', *Surveillance and Society*, 1: 331–55.

Washington Post (2004), 'Minn. GOP asks activists to report on neighbors' politics', 18 July: A17–18.

Yahoo! (2004) 'Yahoo! news', 1 August.

Chapter 3

The local impact of police videosurveillance on the social construction of security

Stéphane Leman-Langlois

Introduction

The use of closed circuit television (CCTV) in public spaces has given rise to a sizeable amount of literature, which generally falls into four broad categories. First, many authors have looked at the effects of increased surveillance on various aspects of civil society. The main concern has been to evaluate (or simply to criticize) the real, potential or imagined impacts of videosurveillance on privacy. Privacy, of course, is a somewhat slippery concept and is particularly difficult to define objectively. Consequently, this area of analysis has suffered from inadequate model specification and has generally dealt with normative perspectives.

The second category, located inside the 'crime science' programme, involves numerous efforts to measure the effect of videosurveillance on local and aggregate crime rates. Analyses and meta-analyses abound, but a definitive conclusion has yet to be reached. Cameras appear to work extremely well as a deterrent or as a response tool, but only under a relatively complex set of conditions. The most obvious but, surprisingly, often overlooked of these conditions is that the devices must be installed properly and be operational, on a purely technical level. Cameras stuck in dense foliage, lenses obscured by birds' nests and cobwebs, monitors that are not actually monitored and defective recording apparatuses are far from uncommon. Another, less glaring condition is the architecture of the area being watched, especially whether it is a relatively closed or open space: cameras do not appear to be effective crime-reducers in wide-open spaces (Welsh and Farrington 2002).

The third category of videosurveillance literature is modest by comparison and includes studies of the uses made of camera images by operators and the social organization of surveillance work (Norris and Armstrong 1999; Leman-Langlois and Brodeur 2005; Mackay 2006; Fussey 2007). Cameras, like all other forms of technology, are neutral in purely technical terms but do not exist in neutral space (Marx 2006). In the real world, individuals, organizations, industries and governments use cameras in politically and socially structured ways. They establish priorities and target specific spaces and populations in support of specific agendas. In return – and this key point is often neglected – technology modifies these priorities and agendas according to its capabilities, availability and the way it transforms our knowledge of the social environment.

The last category is the one I am interested in this chapter and has to do with the way ordinary people react to the transformation of surveillance, not in terms of legalistic or moralistic views of privacy or rights but in terms of their understanding of what this transformation means to their security – to their freedom from artificial, humanly created threats, including those involving state actions and attitudes towards ordinary citizens. There are few precedents for research in this area, with the notable exception of Ditton (2000). Ditton's research focused on perceptions of security in areas under videosurveillance but among respondents who did not live in areas under camera surveillance. In that population, perceptions of security and fear of crime remained unchanged by the installation of cameras. Unfortunately, his research did not deal with the fundamental question of whether all citizens have the same understanding of security and of the specific functions of security cameras. A psychometric study by Brooks (2005) assessed the felt risk ('dread' and 'familiarity') associated with the presence of cameras themselves. He found that the sampled population of respondents living near a camera system identified a certain level of risk associated with the presence of cameras, but found the risk acceptable when measured against the perceived benefits. The statistics do not explore why people felt that cameras represented a risk and which benefits they were most happy with. In fact, the author notes that his respondents had, on the whole, 'given very little thought to the issue' (Brooks 2005: 27).

Direct and indirect (of one's family, for instance) exposure to an open police videosurveillance system may be a mere by-product of the system itself, whose installers and operators may have different goals in mind. The indecisiveness of the context is largely due to the conception of deterrence one favours. If deterrence is aimed at all citizens, who are assumed to be equally capable of crime, generalized and conscious exposure is an intended feature of the system. If only the 'rabble' must be deterred, the experience of law-abiding citizens is inconsequential. Though of course installers, monitors, politicians, bureaucrats, the police and other officials have their own conception of what camera exposure is intended to achieve, I am interested in the way local citizens construct their own. This subject has a number of interesting sociological aspects, as well as a practical one: substantial research has shown the extent to which people's feeling of insecurity or 'fear of crime' is the result not of actual, tangible crime but of various *symbols* of criminality (graffiti, general decrepitude, disorderly youths, insufficient lighting, etc.), as well as their general knowledge and understanding of crime, which are usually constructed from news and fiction presented in the mass media. Yet, little thought has been given to visible cameras as a potential symbol of either security or *omnipresent danger*, in which case they would have the opposite effect.

Since the summer of 2004, the Montreal police department (Service de la police de la ville Montréal – SPVM) has run a very limited videosurveillance pilot project in an area of the south-east downtown core consisting of a roughly eight-block area, as shown in Figure 3.1 (the actual area and camera placement have changed over the years; the map shows the 2007 installation). In the summer of 2007, a second project was introduced a few blocks away and will be studied at a later stage of this research. Both projects involve fewer than 10 cameras each, placed in areas where criminal activity (destruction of property, theft and drug dealing) was thought to be most intense (see also Chapter 11 for police understanding of 'high crime' areas). Both areas are diverse in nature, with bars and clubs, shops, theatres, cinemas and dwellings. In order to reach the various populations living in the targeted areas effectively, my team first mapped out the presence of *all* cameras in plain view from the street. Most of these are privately operated and directed at specific commercial entrances or premises, although a few seem to cover short stretches of pavement and street. I purposefully chose to ignore the privately owned cameras, which are omnipresent in every area of town, and concentrated on the much publicized presence of police cameras, which are accompanied by signs warning pedestrians of their presence. The findings presented below fully support this choice.

Police-operated cameras are easily recognizable: they are all encased in the same high-quality polycarbonate shells, equipped with wireless network antennas and mounted on public lighting poles. Each police camera was photographed and a short video of their approximate field of vision was recorded in order to identify the buildings and pavements within view. I then used Google Earth to create a mosaic of the area in order to identify simplified and approximate 'security fields' that corresponded to the likely *perceived* intensity or frequency

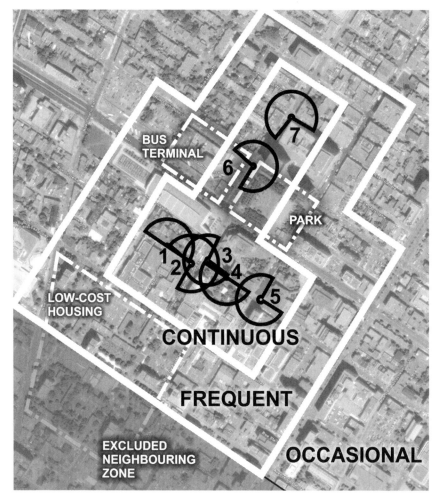

Figure 3.1 The Montreal video surveillance pilot project area

of surveillance, which I assumed to be proportional to camera proximity (shown in Figure 3.1). The researchers then used the resulting map to recruit citizens to participate in the study according to where they resided and/or worked.

The first field corresponds to the area situated directly under police cameras, where surveillance cameras are almost continuously visible. Individuals residing or working in this area must walk under the cameras every day. This is a largely commercial area, with few dwellings, a large library and several buildings owned by a large university. The second field, surrounding the first, includes premises whose occupants would most probably have to walk regularly in the first field (for instance, when running various errands). This has more dwellings, including a vast low-cost housing project, more commercial establishments and more buildings of the same university. The last field was outside the perimeter, where presence within the police videosurveillance project area was occasional at the most (Figure 3.1 also shows an excluded, neighbouring zone belonging to our second observation site).

This chapter presents analysis and conclusions resulting from data obtained during four focus group sessions held in our first research site (a total of 25 participants). Participants were grouped according to the location of their residence or place of work, and the meetings were held at a standard conference room in one of the buildings owned by the above-mentioned university (to which this researcher is not affiliated). Upon arrival, participants were asked to fill out the customary agreements and to locate their place of work or residence on a photographic map resembling that of Figure 3.1 (without camera placements or zone identifications).

Most meetings lasted between 60 and 90 minutes and were recorded on high-quality digital video and later transcribed. I acted as moderator and kept my interactions with the group to the absolute minimum (I followed a pre-established standardized interview guide). In most cases I intervened only at the very end of the meetings to ask directly whether the participants knew where the police cameras were located. Since the main objective of this research is to discover the place videosurveillance occupies in citizens' conceptions of public order and security, I started each group interview with an open question about security ('Do you feel secure in your neighbourhood?') rather than addressing the object of police cameras directly (although participants were aware that the research concerned camera use in their area).

The results were sorted with Nvivo qualitative analysis software and were organized into three main conceptual categories, corresponding to the next sections of this chapter. The first section looks at the representations of crime and policing that were held by these groups. The second section presents the participants' views of the more abstract subject of disorder and the signs by which it may be recognized. The presence and effect of videosurveillance are then discussed in relation to the first two themes. There then follows an analysis of the results.

Crime and policing

One of the main conventional aspects of security is, of course, a general, abstract risk of criminal victimization. Our groups had more concrete, manifest examples of such risk: the continuous presence of recognizable criminals – individuals known to have committed crimes in the past or continuously, openly committing crimes in the present. To our groups, crime is a common, almost daily occurrence, mostly taking the form of various drug offences.

As expected, all the focus groups immediately pointed out that their area has the highest number of individuals from various marginalized groups in the city. These include vagrants (some of whom are psychologically disorganized), the obvious presence of street-gang members, dealers and clients in visible drug commerce, disaffected youths, runaways arriving daily at the nearby bus terminal and unruly visitors from outside the neighbourhood who come for the quite active nightlife. Interestingly, the vagrants, runaways, idle youths and even the 'squeegees' (who make money by washing car windows at traffic lights) are generally well tolerated by the groups. Although these visually identifiable categories of individuals are often associated with disorder, incivility and other irritants in the criminological and policing literature, they seem to cause little concern in the neighbourhood. The respondents are more fearful of specific individuals they see regularly on the street. One participant had been attacked by a vagrant and slightly wounded by a knife, only to see his aggressor back on the street some days later. This was discussed by the group as a good example of what creates insecurity: dangerous, usually disorganized individuals left to fend for themselves by a shoddy, broken 'system' (usually the criminal justice system, but social service agencies were also singled out as dysfunctional). Older participants did tend to be fearful of beggars, thinking they might be attacked if they did not give them money.

Shop owners and their employees noted that the marginalized masses have a propensity towards petty crimes, mostly shoplifting. One fast-food restaurant owner spoke of unruly behaviour by drunks and junkies, including the use of his toilet as a shooting gallery. In shops and restaurants, confronting unwanted customers was an important source of insecurity, but it was noted that the risk of open conflict and violence was difficult to associate with particular types of individuals. While junkies and drunks might comply with simple demands to leave the premises, well dressed patrons might also blow up, especially late at night.

Despite this, one group comprising residents and workers directly under the cameras spontaneously agreed that the excitement of living downtown came with some less desirable aspects one just had to accept. Another felt that, in some aspects at least, this area, as well as downtown Montreal in general, was more secure than in the 1970s. Generalized group opinion is that crime also exists in other areas of town, as well as in smaller communities elsewhere, and that their area is not exceptional in this respect. One particularly vocal participant underlined that crime is equally present everywhere and felt personally insulted by any mention of danger in his neighbourhood. Most participants agreed that, in this particular area of town, the immediate, uncontrolled aggressiveness shown by some individuals is relatively rare.

Police action against all forms of identified crime or misbehaviour is universally seen as insufficient. Groups noted that police officers are slow to respond and do not take complaints seriously – most have adopted the habit of heavily exaggerating the events taking place when calling 911. (One exception was the story of our wounded participant: his call to the police was immediately responded to when he threatened to retaliate with an iron bar.) A common belief is that the police often purposefully wait for fights to be over before arriving on the scene in order to avoid open conflict and danger to themselves. Some noted that, since police services are distributed according to the number of calls received, the best course of action for citizens is to call as often as possible and to exaggerate the report to mobilize police response and increase the allocated resources. Otherwise, groups noted that increases in police presence are consistently directed at the control of squeegees or vagrants in the park and bus terminal, instead of directed at patrolling areas where 'real crimes' occur or at responding to emergency calls. A restaurant owner noted the near-absence of the police in places where day-to-day incivilities and petty crimes take place. Another recalled an instance where repeated calls to 911 concerning a drunk who had passed out on his premises were simply ignored by the emergency services. One police tactic that received special scorn was the issuing of tickets to vagrants. It was denounced as petty, useless and costly to the taxpayer, since penniless vagrants might end up in jail for defaulting on their multiple fines. One group was amused with a story of five police cars being burglarized and vandalized while in the car park at the local police station.

Some of our participants had been or were still themselves in low-intensity 'gangs' and reported having been harassed by the police while occupying some of the spaces in the area under study. They had had their picture taken by police officers, had been asked to identify themselves, had been frisked, had their premises searched or were forced to disperse or to vacate semi-abandoned structures. Their conclusion was that, once they had left, elements from outside were able to come in and use the space for much more serious criminal activity, with no regard for the safety or quality of life of local residents: 'Police are afraid of real criminals; instead they concentrate on residents and their kids' (participants 0211d and 0211h). Parents agreed that exaggerated control over children's activities, combined with the disappearance of many non-criminal opportunities for 'hanging out' and 'being kids', were the reason many children join criminal gangs or experiment with drugs to occupy their free time. This is a crucial but often ignored element in the study of community efficacy and local, informal social control. Gangs in such studies are usually seen as homogeneous and characterized by undesirable criminal activities. In fact, the presence of gangs of local youth may be a factor of social organization rather than a symptom of disorganization.

Insecurity comes from the knowledge that extremely aggressive behaviour could break out at any moment and that no help would come. Police support is hopelessly slow, and privately installed cameras are inadequate either to prevent or to repress crime (because of faulty installation, low quality and other technical problems). For their part, because of the level of aggressiveness among wrongdoers, participants feel that security and order are not their personal responsibility. Shop owners and employees, in particular, believe that any confrontation with thieves or other delinquents inside their place of work or in public areas could put their lives in danger. In one group in particular, a number of incidents of extreme violence involving knives, handguns and even a Molotov cocktail were reported. Most of these, it was said, had occurred within metres of surveillance cameras, some in plain view. (Note that the field of view of the police cameras is impossible to ascertain from the ground.)

Paradoxically, police action is sometimes linked to increased danger rather than security. Participants did not fear police officers or police strategies, but the massive raids that were occasionally organized against gang members in the seedier bars and clubs trigger violence and unpredictability and were considered to be comparable with gang fights.

One group of low-cost housing project residents noted that social peace had been better maintained by strong gangs in the 1970s than by the police today. Some were nostalgic for an era where ordinary residents were actually protected by gangs who worked hard to make sure they didn't attract police attention. Their conflicts were solved with fists, not with guns, added a few respondents. A second group of residents from the same area discussed a series of incidents that had taken place in their buildings over the years, such as men with knives roaming the hallways and one knife attack against security personnel (who are not allowed, by law, to carry weapons). Participants who lived outside the low-cost housing area were surprised at the stories of violence that took place there, and few people had equivalent narratives. All agreed that the presence of youth gangs and the displacement of crack dealers to that area were the main causes of increased violence. Residents from other areas also noted that a camera installed in a previous 'crackhead' hangout had pushed them 'on my doorstep, which is no fun at all when I get out with my stroller and my baby' (participant 1107e).

Disorder and symbols of disorder

Groups were quick to note that, without necessarily representing an immediate danger, many forms of symbolic disorder, such as groups of youths loitering on street corners, especially if they have dogs, can be frightening to many people, even when they did not feel afraid themselves. Shop owners, especially, see such visual threats as bad for business, as they tend to scare customers away. Dishevelled squeegee kids in front of restaurants also scare customers away. Employees of the nearby Quebec National Library (the very large light-grey building located near the centre of Figure 3.1) identified beggars and other loiterers monopolizing 'their' benches as major irritants to themselves and their visitors. It is believed that women are particularly likely to be affected by various types of undesirable behaviour, including insistent begging, rowdiness, fights, dog fights and impolite, inappropriate (especially sexual) or aggressive talk from street kids. At the same time, groups noted that dress and attitude are not reliable predictors of behaviour: more conventionally dressed and behaved individuals have been known to solicit sexual gratification from female citizens, while dishevelled vagrants may show respectful, even helpful behaviour. Quite a few participants knew vagrants and other regulars by name.

One park at the centre of the study area has been identified as problematic and happens to be well outside the range of most of the cameras (illustrated in Figure 3.1). Participants underlined the difficulty, and even occasional danger, linked to crossing this park, even though it is only a city block in size and mostly open, with few places to hide: a textbook 'defensible space'. In my repeated visits to the area, police presence in the park was obvious: on one occasion there were two police cars with four officers inside, in addition to three separate foot patrols nearby. Considering the limited size of the park, this is rather heavy presence. In winter the park is far quieter, as snow and ice reduce access.

Another space was the subject of conflicting evaluations of risk: a newly refurbished alley located behind the National Library was considered to be a very dangerous place by some, while others thought it was quite safe. Two young women, in two separate groups, said they used it almost everyday, one after local bars close at 03:00 (she worked in one of the establishments). The architectural features of either spaces were never mentioned. Those who felt the spaces to be highly dangerous did not refer to a lack of lighting, a wealth of hiding places or some other material characteristic. Danger was associated either with the presence of many dangerous individuals or with the fact that the area was deserted.

Most of the residents and workers who have to cross the park or other spaces known to be sites of harassment, aggressive begging, mugging or other forms of violence have found a way to live in the area. It consists of a combination of partial avoidance and ignoring or responding calmly or with humour to the unwanted approaches of vagrants, beggars and prostitutes. In fact, most of that section of the population are spoken of with respect and even, at times, appreciation. A few of our participants told stories of vagrants intervening and defusing potentially violent situations involving junkies. Conversely, our groups were shocked by stories of well-off citizens beating up or otherwise mistreating vagrants and street kids.

As already briefly mentioned, one of the most often emphasized sources of insecurity is the indifference of other members of the public when help is needed; some participants realized that this conduct was understandable, given their own refusal to get involved in social control activities for fear of getting hurt. Groups evoked a series of news items about current and less current events (one recalled the Kitty Genovese incident, in 1964 – though with the wrong date and name) in order to depict a rather uncaring social context. Passers-by are said to avoid people calling for help, possibly because of their own fear of violent retaliation but more probably because they are simply too busy. There were many stories of harassment or even extortion where fellow shoppers or subway passengers pretended not to see what was happening. Yet it is not possible to draw any generalization about this theme. The indifference and inaction of others in times of need were the most frequently mentioned source of insecurity, but this idea had to coexist with the notion that crowded streets are more secure than deserted ones. At the same time, stories of persons attacked in plain view of passers-by were common (in particular a recent murder committed in broad daylight on the busiest street of the area).

One of the most reliable physical symbol of disorder is the presence of used syringes on pavements or in back alleys. Many participants, however, noted the near disappearance of the needles after the April 2007 opening of a new location for a needle exchange and drug treatment centre in the area (named 'Cactus'; see cactusmontreal.org). This was taken as further proof that solutions to everyday problems are not provided by those in charge of security, but by various other actors.

One final visual indicator of social difference – ethnicity – was sometimes a flashpoint of our discussions (in part because they were held during a highly visible series of public consultations on the matter commissioned by the government of Quebec). Not all groups mentioned it, but some of the citizens living in the low-income housing zone, where ethnic make-up has changed profoundly in the last 20 years, were preoccupied by their new minority status. This change was insignificant to some and a source of insecurity to others.

Surveillance and security: effect of proximity to cameras

Cameras were said to have had an effect on open drug deals in most areas where our participants identified a problem, although some respondents disagreed. This effect, however, was hard to pinpoint in our sessions. Some groups emphasized the displacement of dealing to other areas and saw this as immediately beneficial to the quality of life in their neighbourhood. Others, who lived in the 'receiving' area (notably the low-cost housing development seen in Figure 3.1), were extremely unhappy with having a new crowd of dealers and purchasers on their doorsteps. A few claimed they still regularly saw drugs being sold in plain view of the cameras. Here a class distinction was clearly visible: the low-cost housing group agreed that videosurveillance had been demanded by enterprises whose shopfront was on one of the 'problem' streets and that it had been efficient at clearing the rabble from *these* doorsteps – by pushing it over on to neighbouring blocks. Class was also openly referred to by respondents to account for discrepancies between their area and the western part of the downtown core, where the marginalized are few, street crime is low, streets are clean and no police cameras have been installed. They see the creation of that consumer paradise as a direct cause of many of their problems. The western part is described as richer and more attractive to better-off, middle-class visitors. Some think that police strategy has been deliberately to chase all unseemly characters out of that area and into their own, where opposition is not organized and citizens have less political weight.

In previous years, dealers sold mainly marijuana and other lighter drugs; this was seen as, at worst, a nuisance. Some even noted that this first wave of dealers, mostly affiliated with biker gangs, had had a beneficial effect on overall security: rather quiet and polite themselves, they imposed a form of social control on other elements, such as unruly street kids, in order to avoid police attention on their block. Over time, however, crack became the merchandise of choice, filling a gap created by massive police arrests of bikers in 2001. With crack came a very different kind of dealer and clientele: more violent and more likely to harass passers-by, potential clients and employees going about their business. This is where videosurveillance had the most identifiable effect on the life of group participants, by reducing the presence of crack dealers and consumers in some areas.

Groups were divided on the overall impact of public or private videosurveillance on crime, but most tended to explain poor results in terms of insufficient or incorrect implementation, which is a typical feature of technological solutions (Leman-Langlois 2003). People who are either afraid for themselves or for their children, or older parents, would like to see more cameras. At the same time, groups are in near complete agreement that, for the time being, the presence of cameras does not enhance their own security in any way. Most are aware that cameras could be instrumental in solving crimes they may fall victim to but believe that any preventive effect they might have remains imperceptible. They feel that their only purpose is to reassure the general public about security in the downtown core (Manning, in Chapter 11, makes a comparable observation for the city of Boston) and point out that there are always sufficient dead angles where invisible attacks are possible. Many groups doubted that anyone was actually monitoring the feeds: 'is anyone actually being paid to watch the cameras?' (participant 0211d, adult male living in low-cost housing). Others concluded that whether or not actual human beings are monitoring the images makes little difference: 'I think they simply will not move their ass for anything they may see on their monitor' (participant 0211e, adult female living in low-cost housing). There was general agreement that the mandate and powers of those watching – if they exist – are unclear. Some compared the situation with what they knew of London's videosurveillance system, certain that the latter is well monitored and far more efficient in reducing crime.

The extent to which police or security guards on the beat are being replaced by cameras is a subject of disagreement. It was often noted that cameras lack the immediate capacity to react to incidents, and in fact may lower the police's ability to respond by allowing the reassignment of police officers to areas where there are no cameras. At the same time, the invulnerability of high-perched, remote-controlled eyes was seen as a way to reduce crime against the police and guards: 'cameras do not get stabbed' (participant 3110a, older woman living in low-cost housing, where two private security guards had been assaulted in the previous months).

Interestingly, when directly asked about camera placement, many participants admitted only extremely fuzzy knowledge about where the cameras were. They know a police videosurveillance system has been in place in area 1 for a few years, but are mostly oblivious of its presence. It is not surprising, then, that conventional concerns about privacy were almost never spontaneously raised by our groups and, when they were, they were systematically held to be less important than two positive aspects of videosurveillance: the identification of wrongdoers and the deterrence of crack dealers. In one case the feeling of being watched was identified by a participant as a factor that might exaggerate overall insecurity. Another one described the possible multiplication of cameras, in conjunction with the disappearance of actual police officers on the beat, as having a 'big brother' effect, where the few secretly watch the many. Yet this was not accompanied by a clear normative judgement. In one of the groups the collective discourse held, simultaneously, that cameras were too few to have a preventive effect, that more are needed *and* that constant surveillance of everyone is an annoying side-effect. One of our groups agreed that one effect of the presence of cameras might even be counterproductive, noting the expressive function of criminality: cameras may be *helping* criminals express themselves by making their crimes more visible, encouraging those who want to defy the system or prove their toughness. A parallel was drawn with crimes recorded by the criminals themselves, which sometimes are shown on TV or on YouTube.

Paradoxically, the effect of police camera surveillance increases with distance. Residents and workers who live under the cameras credit them with leading to mild decreases in crack dealing and very little else. Those living in 'frequent' and 'occasional' surveillance areas see a much more pronounced – albeit negative – effect, in that they force unwanted individuals into their area.

Discussion

It should first be pointed out that the atmosphere in all the focus groups was relaxed and civil. All participants spoke at some length of their experiences or discussed those of others with humour and detachment – or at least resignation – but generally with a sense of irony. The consensus was that police videosurveillance, as well as any other types of cameras, has no connection with what is happening 'on the street' in terms of security and insecurity. One participant called them a way to mock or dupe the local population (participant 1107d, resides and works in the area). Most were convinced that cameras could help elucidate crimes after they happen but felt that, since the system's response to crime was disorganized, this did not actually remove dangerous people from the street. And even in cases where it did, there was a nearly infinite supply of marginalized and criminalized individuals ready to replace them, some coming 'by the busload' at the nearby terminal from all corners of Quebec and Canada. In short, cameras are simply *irrelevant* to life and security in the area. One interesting fact is that most participants in the groups had only a vague idea of where cameras had been installed – some did not know at all and showed only passing interest in the matter.

In fact, the main factor of insecurity, which was mentioned by nearly every participant in every group, is the utter detachment, absence of care or unwillingness to help in any way that they perceived as a universal characteristic of modern urban life. Without necessarily realizing the link between the two discourses, a majority of our respondents admitted readily that they wouldn't get involved in social control activities either, for fear of violent retaliation from unpredictable individuals. They explained inaction by *others* as largely the result of egoism or laziness, while their own inaction was justified by this ever-present danger. There is no way to ascertain the extent to which this concern with a lack of involvement would be redirected towards crime, criminals, or the marginalized if the feeling of community was somehow restored, or if insecurity was actually significantly reduced.

Though this research does not offer a psychometric or other attempt at measuring the *intensity* of the insecurity felt by individuals in this area of town, we noted that actual counter-actions or changes of behaviour caused by fear of crime were astonishingly few. Some respondents reported that they avoided some streets or dark alleys, or the infamous park; some workers said they kept various objects that they could use to defend themselves. Others said they had stopped painting over graffiti, since the taggers usually came back within hours. In general, the consensus was that people engaged in normal daily activities had little to fear and that, though irritating and uncivil behaviours were common, they did not translate into fear or insecurity. Shop and restaurant owners and employees had their own, specific problems to deal with, since they must undertake local social control activities on their premises ('minding their own business' is an entirely different concept for them) and thus expose themselves to retaliation. All agreed that calling the police was, in most cases, counterproductive, since the wait was too long and in the end nothing would be done.

The discrepancy between the 'insecurity talk' (stories of crime and disorderly behaviour) and the lack of actual countermeasures can be explained in a number of ways. First, there is a tendency in such groups towards a type of one-upmanship where better, more extreme stories are recalled and retold. This leads to an over-representation of serious crimes and a lack of stories that may have a more social, communitarian tone. The subject, announced at the beginning of each session, also tipped the balance towards narratives of insecurity and danger. Secondly, most of the irritants reported were not actual physical threats to those telling the stories, and therefore could not be linked to anything other than mild avoidance strategies. Actions threatening personal security were presented as occasional, unpredictable events directed at people who were 'at the wrong place at the wrong moment', where 'nothing can be done'. Serious crime appeared less as a strategic obstacle to be dealt with and more as an omnipresent, latent risk, or perhaps an unavoidable result of fate. Accordingly, attitudes towards personal security were not defeatist or pessimistic but sarcastic and ironic. This attitude was also prevalent when the subject was the security effect of cameras, whether private or police operated.

In terms of the personal effects of surveillance, our participants were far, far less eloquent. We might conclude that they have not given these questions much thought, since their list of higher-priority problems is already very long. However, since the general impression was that cameras were inefficient, that there was perhaps no one monitoring the feeds and that the police made no apparent anti-crime use of the cameras, it may be that any possible effect on privacy was evaluated in the same way. In other words, whether or not the police actually use their videosurveillance system for prevention, investigation or other objectives (they do, of course), the fact is that, from the point of view of ordinary people, the relationship between surveillance and any subsequent intervention or consequence is wholly undetectable. If this is the case, cameras will *always* appear to be useless to those on the street. Attempting to counter this perception is one reason crime footage is routinely given by the police to the media, in hopes of projecting a message of efficiency and positive social value (Doyle 2003; Leman-Langlois 2003). The idea that videosurveillance is useless and inadequate probably may apply to any idea that it might represent an invasion of privacy.

To a large extent, our respondents thought the SPVM's strategy was to 'police cleanliness', mostly on behalf of a few commercial enterprises, through, for instance, issuing tickets to vagrants instead of policing 'real crime'. Nearly all police strategies described by our groups were judged negatively, on a scale varying from useless to counterproductive, with videosurveillance at the useless end. Only a few participants, who were involved in some form of co-operation with the police, claimed that police presence and action seemed to have a preventative effect, although they were unable to point to any specific example, other than videosurveillance having caused some crack dealers to move away.

Conclusion

This chapter began by questioning the role of videosurveillance in social representations of security. I presented this general problem as encompassing typical police concerns about crime, about broad concerns with what it means to feel secure or safe and concerns about whether videosurveillance can be seen as a threat in itself, in concrete, political, legal or moral terms. A few of our respondents noted that cameras had a negative impact on their ability to feel free to use the public street any way they chose, but they had great difficulty in articulating why and were incapable of giving clear examples of this phenomenon. (This is not surprising, given its highly complex, abstract nature.) A few others were under the impression that, in some cases at least, the presence of cameras actually triggered crimes or less serious misbehaviour. But the broad consensus was that, on the whole, cameras have no effect one way or the other on them.

They also had no effect on crime, incivilities and other irritants, other than displacement to less visible areas and inside premises. This created something of a class divide in our groups. While a few noted a decrease in open drug dealing, others were quick to complain that their area had been taken over by the same thugs. The cameras are situated on a commercial street adjacent to a low-cost housing project, whose residents now feel under siege. Furthermore, police interventions are also different in the two areas (see Chapter 11). On the commercial street, it may be qualified as 'mild,' including camera surveillance and foot patrols, while in the project it consists of harassing local youths and conducting massive raids in targeted apartment buildings where crack dealers are suspected to live.

One obvious conclusion is that videosurveillance, as a tool of the technopolice, is not working, as seen from the street: 1) it has not affected citizens' evaluations of the dangerousness of their neighbourhood – in fact, in some ways it has made it worse; 2) citizens link camera presence to the appearance of widely disapproved police strategies, such as youth harassment, ticketing of vagrants, spectacular, loud raids and generalized physical absence; 3) videosurveillance has reduced citizens' confidence in the ability of the police to counter crime; 4) videosurveillance addresses virtually none of our respondents' sources of insecurity because it operates at the wrong level; and 5) videosurveillance use makes clear the disconnection between police services and citizens' daily lives and overarching concerns.

This is not to say that videosurveillance, as a police tool, is likely to be abandoned. The logic of technology, it seems, is far stronger than negative findings. This is true even when the findings are part of the same logic of surveillance. For instance, statistical evaluations of the effect of videosurveillance on crime have shown that it is useless in some settings (Welsh and Farrington 2002), yet cameras continue to be installed in those settings. Findings based on an entirely different level of investigation – such as those presented here – are unlikely to be judged relevant by those in charge, regardless of the number of times they are replicated.

One can make three very reliable predictions for the future. First, videosurveillance will continue to be seen as a clever, cheap, efficient way to police the city. Secondly, privacy advocates will continue to produce an almost entirely irrelevant discourse about rights to privacy and big brothers. Thirdly, citizens living and working in the areas where the new panaceas of technopolicing are adopted will continue to be dissatisfied by the services they are offered.

References

Berg, B. (2007) *Qualitative Research Methods for the Social Sciences* (6th edn). Boston, MA: Pearson Education.

Brodeur, J.-P. (2003) *Les Visages de la Police*: Montréal: Presses de l'Université de Montréal.

Brodeur, J.-P. and Leman-Langlois, S. (2004) 'La surveillance totale', *Cahiers de la Sécurité intérieure*, 55: 61–90.

Brooks, D. (2005) 'Is CCTV a social benefit? A psychometric study of perceived social risk', *Security Journal*, 18: 19–29.

Chan, J. (2003) 'Police and new technologies', in T. Newburn (ed.) *Handbook of Policing*. Portland, OR: Willan Publishing.

Coleman, R. and Sim, J. (2000) '"You'll never walk alone". CCTV surveillance, order and neo-liberal rule in Liverpool city centre', *British Journal of Sociology*, 512: 623–39.

Ditton, J. (1999) *The Effect of Closed Circuit Television Cameras on Recorded Crime Rates and Public Concern about Crime in Glasgow. Scottish Office Central Research Unit Main Findings*, 30. Edinburgh: Scottish Office Central Research Unit.

Ditton, J. (2000) 'Crime and the city public attitudes towards open-street CCTV in Glasgow', *British Journal of Criminology*, 40: 692–709.

Doyle, A. (2003) *Arresting Images*. Toronto: University of Toronto Press.

Fussey, P. (2007) 'An interrupted transmission? Processes of CCTV implementation and the impact of human agency', *Surveillance and Society*, 4 (http://www.surveillance-and-society.org/criminaljustice.htm).

Leman-Langlois, S. (2003) 'The myopic panopticon: the social consequences of policing through the lens', *Policing and Society*, 13: 43–58.

Leman-Langlois, S. and Brodeur, J.-P. (2005) 'Les technologies de l'identification', *Revue internationale de Criminologie et de Police technique et scientifique*, 1: 69–82.

Mackay, D. (2006) 'The changing nature of public-space CCTV', *Security Journal*, 19: 128–42.

Markova, I. (2003) 'Les focus groups', in S. Moscovici (ed.) *Les Méthodes des sciences humaines*. Paris: Presses Universitaires de France.

Marx, G. (1988) 'La société de sécurité maximale', *Déviance et Société*, 12: 147–66.

Marx, G. (2006) 'Mots et mondes de surveillance : contrôle et contre-contrôle à l'ère informatique', *Criminologie*, 39: 43–62.

Marx, G. (2007) 'Rocky bottoms: techno-fallacies of an age of information', *International Political Sociology*, 1: 83–110.

Morgan, D. (2004) 'Focus groups', in S.N. Hesse-Biber and P. Leavy (eds) *Approaches to Qualitative Research: A Reader on Theory and Practice*. Oxford, Oxford University Press.

Nock, S.L. (1993) *The Costs of Privacy: Surveillance and Reputation in America*. New York, NY: Aldine de Gruyter.

Norris, C. and Armstrong, G. (1999) *The Maximum Surveillance Society: The Rise of CCTV*. New York, NY: Berg.

Nunn, S. (2001) 'Police technology in cities: changes and challenges', *Technology in Society*, 23: 11–27.

Poster, M. (1990) *The Mode of Information: Poststructuralism and Social Context*. Chicago, IL: University of Chicago Press.

Sampson, R. and Raudenbush, S. (2001) 'Disorder in urban neighborhoods — does it lead to crime?', in *National Institute of Justice Research in Brief*. Washington DC: US Department of Justice.

Skogan, W. (1990) *Disorder and Decline*. New York, NY: The Free Press.

Welsh, B. and Farrington, D. (2002) *Crime Prevention Effects of Closed Circuit Television: A Systematic Review*. London: Home Office Development and Statistics Directorate.

Williams, K. and Johnstone, C. (2000) 'The politics of the selective gaze: closed circuit television and the policing of public space', *Crime, Law and Social Change*, 34: 183–210.

Wilson, J. and Kelling, G. (1982) 'The police and neighborhood safety: broken windows', *Atlantic Monthly*, 249: 29–38.

Chapter 4

Cyberwars and cybercrimes

Benoît Gagnon

Introduction

February 2000. A hacker launched a series of highly publicized denial-of-service cyber attacks against large commercial websites, including Yahoo!, Amazon.com, Dell Inc., E*TRADE, eBay and CNN. The hacker's codename: Mafiaboy. The US Federal Bureau of Investigation (FBI) and the Royal Canadian Mounted Police (RCMP) acted quickly after intercepting a discussion in an Internet relay chatroom where someone claimed responsibility for the hack. They arrested a 16-year-old-boy in April 2000.

Mafiaboy was brought to court on 58 charges. After a high-profile trial, on 12 September 2001, the Montreal Youth Court sentenced him to eight months of open custody, one year of probation, restricted use of the Internet and a small fine. According to the prosecutors, the case sent 'a strong message to hackers that they will get caught if they do things like that' (McCarthy 2001). From the court's perspective, the sentence was meant to demonstrate that the justice system was both present and effective in cyberspace. Unfortunately, events elsewhere in the world entirely eclipsed the decision.

May 2007. The Estonian government was targeted by a massive denial-of-service attack after a monument honouring the Russian Second World War dead was moved despite intense opposition from the Russian ethnic minority. The government's networks were literally buried under bits of information, and the economy began to suffer from the resulting paralysis of government web-based activities. Russian hackers were believed to be responsible for the denial-of-service attack. Eventually the Estonian government, having exhausted its own capabilities, officially requested NATO's help in defending its computer infrastructure against the continuing cyber attacks, and Russia was identified by analysts as the most probable origin of the cyber attack. Although the Russian government was not officially accused of launching, participating in or facilitating the attack, Silver Meikar, a member of the Estonian Parliament who followed information technology issues in Estonia, told the press that 'there are strong indications of Russian state involvement. I can say that based on a wide range of conversations with people in the security agencies' (Finn 2007). An instant media frenzy occurred and experts quickly labelled the Estonia–Russia incident 'the first cyberwar' (Landler and Markoff 2007).

Interestingly, the latest information concerning these attacks shows that the Russian government was in no way involved, the attacks did not originate on Russian sovereign territory and they were not the work of Russian hackers as originally suspected (Poulsen 2007). As in the Mafiaboy case, a teenager was the sole suspect in the attack. He had no connection with Russia, nor was he an ethnic Russian. Further, it is quite possible that the fact that the attack coincided with the Russian memorial controversy was purely fortuitous. Of course, since 'the attacks were botnet-driven and launched from servers all over the globe, it's impossible to state definitively that only a single individual was involved' (Hruska 2008).

As Baudrillard might have concluded, the Estonian cyberwar never happened. The reaction of the security authorities, however, is interesting: military response was considered the proper reaction to a problem that had until then been considered to be a form of cybercrime. Few details are available about the specific methods used by NATO and Estonia to solve the crisis. What we do know is that the nations that are part of NATO have demonstrated interest in expanding their cyberwar operational capabilities and increasing their collective military presence in cyberspace. Estonia, for its part, employed the computer capabilities of its military, as well as suggesting that a NATO 'cooperative cyber defence centre of excellence' be set up, which is certainly indicative of the trend towards an increased military response (NATO 2007).

The two incidents discussed above are not linked, but they provide information about the structure and deployment of various cybersecurity agencies. In the first case, police agencies acted on behalf of the state to respond to a cybercrime. In the second case, military organizations were mobilized to respond to what was seen as an act of cyberwar, and responded by using tactics similar to cybercrime.

This chapter has two objectives. First, it shows that the fight against cybercriminality is becoming increasingly militarized. A description of current trends in cybersecurity in the USA shows that cybersecurity agencies are clearly preoccupied with 'national security', in which military or military-like institutions play a key role. Secondly, it describes how cybersecurity agencies are fighting cybercrime and prosecuting its authors while planning and committing cybercrimes themselves. One example is the use of network-enabled attacks against other countries or against their own citizens that are justified by 'raison d'état'. Acceptance of this contradiction is apparent in the cybersecurity discourse held at various levels of government, in which recourse to criminal tactics is justified to protect national cybersecurity.

The chapter is divided into three sections. The first covers the evolution of the Internet from a military-controlled communications toolbox to a tool in the civilian environment and then the slow return of an increasing military presence and a remilitarization of the Internet. This remilitarization is closely associated with a Cold War worldview. The second section covers US cybercrime control strategy. Specifically, it shows how US cybersecurity agencies are blurring the boundaries between the fight against cybercrime and the conduct of cyberwar. In the national cybersecurity mindset, it is becoming increasingly likely that such agencies will choose to fight cybercrime with military tactics and with the help of institutions traditionally seen as responsible for military responses rather than crime-fighting. The third section discusses the response of Chinese authorities when faced with web-based invasions in their country, largely through comprehensive monitoring of all Internet-based activities of their citizens. There, too, the national interest is held to justify official cybercrime.

The evolution of the web and the US security environment

The USA is one of the most interesting countries to look at with regard to the evolution of cybercrime and cyberwar. One reason for this is that 70 per cent of the US population has access to Internet facilities: with 210 millions users, it is one of the most wired countries in the world (Central Intelligence Agency 2008; Internet World Stats 2008). The importance of web activities in the USA has led authorities to develop strategic doctrines about the Internet, its possibilities and the potential threats that might emerge from it. Finally, because so much of the early work on the Internet took place in the USA, we can easily trace the influence of the Internet in US security policy.

Childhood: the Internet

It is well known that the Internet was created as part of the structure President Dwight D. Eisenhower referred to as the 'military industrial complex'. In the late 1960s, the Defense Advanced Research Projects Agency (DARPA, known as ARPA at the time of the birth of the Internet, as in 'Arpanet') was involved in the development of the first computer network. Joseph Carl Robnett Licklider, one of the founding fathers of the Internet, wanted to connect different computers to facilitate information exchange (see Waldrop 2002). The project led to the creation of the TCP/IP protocol, which permitted a 'conversation' between two or more computers. Such networks rapidly became the norm and spread quickly through US government organizations and universities. But computer network science found its greatest supporters in the US military. The possibilities of computer networking capabilities were recognized quite early by the military. For instance, command and control in military operations could be revolutionized by linking hardware across space. Some hybrid military–civilian organizations like NASA (North American Security Association) also took advantage of these new capabilities. However, the military monopoly on computer networks did not last long. As computer science took off in universities worldwide, computer networks appeared in different countries, giving scientists unprecedented power to communicate. In order to benefit from academic research on computer networking, the military had to relinquish its monopoly over the networks it had developed.

Adolescence: the World Wide Web

The adolescence of cyberspace began with the arrival of commercial Internet service providers (ISPs) ISPs, combined with the availability of hypertext and graphic-friendly World Wide Web standards (invented in Europe in 1989), clearly marked the beginning of a massive democratization of the Internet. From this point on, a large proportion of computer users could connect to a worldwide network and access information in a user-friendly format. As ISPs increased, a growing number of private entities chose to be present on the web, leading to the end of the short-lived oligopoly of academia and the

49

military in cyberspace. The original centre of power divided into a sea of new players, each with new levels of power inside the web. Corporations, co-operative movements, small communities and even individuals can exert more influence than ever before through the web. In the information society, this also means new forms of power outside the network. The result of this multiplication of actors was the emergence of what is known as cyberspace, or virtual community, as Benedikt (1992: 85) called it: 'The earliest cyberspaces may have been virtual communities, passage points for collection of common beliefs and practices that united people who were physically separated. Virtual communities sustain themselves by constantly circulating those practices.' As a space for shared practices, knowledge and exponentially growing social networks, cyberspace quickly attracted the attention of governments and their institutions of control – especially US security agencies, who began to rethink their position towards the web.

Adulthood: cyberspace as strategic space

The various security doctrines that have been developed around cyberspace tend to see this new space as increasingly important from a strategic point of view. This has led to new ideas about the role of the military in cyberspace. Military institutions have started to think about cyberspace as another potential theatre of operations, a space where strategic dominance must be achieved. This is cogently illustrated by the writings of Robert J. Bunker, particularly in a paper published in *Parameters*, a leading journal on US strategy:

> Humanspace represents the traditional physical dimension of the human senses within which military forces operate ... Cyberspace, on the other hand, represents not only the electromagnetic spectrum, but also that dimension in which military forces seek refuge for defensive purposes. Forces that enter this dimension are removed from the human sensing based battlefield and are thus invulnerable to attack; at the same time, they retain the capacity to attack military forces that exist in humanspace ... Cyberspace may be considered dominant over humanspace. For this reason, the goal of the Army in future war, beyond that of securing assigned politicomilitary objectives, will be that of total cyberspace dominance – not just digital battlespace dominance. (1996: 4).

From a strategic standpoint, cyberspace has become a new space for the projection of state power and dominance – a drastic change of position.

The near future: old models in new environments

The web is prone to rapid, unpredictable change, but two new trends can be identified in relation to national cybersecurity: the implementation of a Cold War strategic model and, consequently, a push for increased nation-state sovereign power in cyberspace. The persistence of Cold War principles and worldview can be clearly seen it the White House's *National Strategy to Secure Cyberspace*:

> In the 1950s and 1960s, our Nation became vulnerable to attacks from aircraft and missiles for the first time. The federal government responded by creating a national system to: monitor our airspace with radar to detect unusual activity, analyze and warn of possible attacks, coordinate our fighter aircraft defenses during an attack, and restore our Nation after an attack through civil defense programs. Today, the Nation's critical assets could be attacked through cyberspace. The United States now requires a different kind of national response system in order to detect potentially damaging activity in cyberspace, to analyze exploits and warn potential victims, to coordinate incident responses, and to restore essential services that have been damaged (White House 2003: 19).

The document calls for new methods to counter cyberspace threats but does so with direct reference to the Cold War period. The fact that this mindset continues to influence the development of policy has definite consequences. For instance, it has led the US government and its security agencies to develop a nationalistic view of cyberspace, apparent in the title of the publication quoted above. The strategy is set out in the same territorial, sovereign, nation-state language that dominated Cold War doctrine, but the space it refers to is strictly virtual, non-national, flexible and dynamic. Though computers as physical things are situated on sovereign territory and geographically locatable, the cyberspace they support does not share their location in any meaningful way. The construction of a state-centric view of the Internet and its threats – the key phrase 'national cyberspace' is repeated more than 40 times in the document – is indicative of the US attempt to extend the idea of the nation-state to uncharted, and obviously not too well understood, territory. The document also makes a point of 'delimiting cyberspace' in social and cultural terms, stressing the difference between 'us' and 'them', between *our* cyberspace and *their* cyberspace. Introduced as a 'framework for the contributions that we all can make to secure our parts of cyberspace' (White House, 2003: viii), it assumes that we need to secure our cyberterritory against threats from other entities affirming their sovereignty over other cyberterritories (or, worse, over the same one).

Blurring the line of cyberwar and cybercrime

The USA and the fight against cybercrime

Considering the number and importance of US agencies involved in some form of cybersecurity, one can safely say that the USA is a world leader in the fight against cybercrime. Many key institutions are involved in countering various forms of cybercrime: the Department of Justice (DoJ), the (FBI), the Department of Homeland Security (DHS), the Department of Defense (DoD), the Federal Trade Commission (FTC) the Federal Inspectors General (FIG) and a host of other state and local law enforcement organizations. There is also a significant contribution from the private sector, through different 'public and private partnerships' (see Table 4.1).

Table 4.1 offers a quick snapshot of the vast number of cybersecurity actors in the USA as of January 2008, a (non-exhaustive) list that makes clear the importance of cybercrime in the US security agenda. The history of cybercrime, peppered with notorious cases such as that of Kevin Mitnick – the only hacker whose name has been listed as one of the ten most-wanted criminals in the USA – demonstrates that cybercrime can be considered a high-level threat to national security, even if no physical danger is involved. (At the height of its chase, the FBI put Mitnick, a computer geek, on its top-ten list alongside drug traffickers, murderers and terrorists.) Another clue that cybercrime has been elevated to the level of a national security threat is the fact that the US government has decided to include the DoD as one of the key players in its strategy to counter it.

There have been other points of policing and military convergence. The war on drugs has been one, from as early as the 1980s. Counterterrorism is certainly another, as terrorism comprises both national security and criminal aspects. With cyberspace becoming a virtual site for high-tech national security concerns, cybercrime and cybersecurity are bound to become the third point of police/military convergence, where future 'cyberwars' will be fought. Cyberwarfare programs are being introduced as necessary steps to defend the US interest in imminent cyberwars and cyber terrorism, but are also useful against lesser crimes, like hacking, defacing and denial-of-service.

US cyberwar: legitimizing cybercrime as warfare

The USA is probably the only nation in which security authorities have publicly admitted the use of cyberweapons in recent conflicts. In fact, the amount of publicly available information regarding US cyberwarfare is unusually large when compared with what other countries are prepared to reveal.

We can pinpoint the advent of cyberwar to the 1991 USA–Iraq Gulf war. In planning its operations, the US military realized that understanding and efficiently exploiting the opposition's IT vulnerabilities was key to gaining strategic domination (Harshberger and Ochmanek 1999: 170). At the time, military cyberweapons had not yet been devised, but their potential – as well as the possibility that they might be used to exploit US military vulnerabilities – became painfully obvious when, sometime before the launch of the operation, 34 military computer systems were penetrated by teenagers in the Netherlands, who managed to steal information on various weapons, including the Patriot missile system. It would be a few years, however, before the first actual, concerted cyber attack, which occurred in 1997 in Sri Lanka and was designed to further the cause of the Tamil Tigers (Havely 2000). The USA used cyberweapons for the first time only in 1999, during its operations in Kosovo. Little is known about the methods and cyberweapons used during that conflict, but a leaked report from an army memorandum mentions they were highly efficient. It concludes that, if they had been applied more thoroughly, cyberwarfare tools and strategies could have significantly shortened the war in Kosovo (Knight 1999). When accounts like these are combined with official documents such as training manuals, research reports and policy statements, the use of cyberwar as part of military strategy and government policy becomes clear.

Table 4.1. Key actors involved in countering cybercrime in the USA

Administrations	Organizations	Sub-organizations	Responsibilities
Department of Justice (DoJ)	Criminal division	Computer Crimes and Intellectual Property Section (CCIPS) Child Exploitation and Obscenity Section (CEOS) Fraud Section	Supporting the department's Computer Crime Initiative in combating cybercrime (data) thefts, intrusions, cyber attacks, child abuse, etc.)
	US attorneys' offices	Computer Hacking and Intellectual Propety (CHIP) units	Co-ordination of investigations, prosecutions and other cybercrime matters
	FBI Cyber Division	Computer Intrusion Section Cybercrime Section Information Sharing and Analysis Section	Leading federal agency in investigation cybercrime
	FBI field offices	Computer Intrusion Program Computer crime task forces Regional computer forensics laboratories Computer analysis response teams	Investigation cybercrime within their region of responsibility
Department of Homeland Security (DHS)	Secret Service	Electronic crimes special agents Electronic Crimes State and Local Program Electronic crime task forces Criminal Intelligence Section National Computer Forensic Institute	Investigation of cybercrimes (data theft, etc.) that represents a threat to the US economical infrastructure

Administrations	Organizations	Sub-organizations	Responsibilities
	National Cybersecurity Division	Law Enforcement and Intelligence Section; US Computer Emergency Readiness Team (US-CERT); Cyber Cop portal; Strategic Initiatives Branch	Considered the national focal point for addressing cybersecurity issues and co-ordinating national cyberstrategy
	Immigration and Customs	Cybercrimes Center; ICE field offices	Investigation and prosecution of domestic and transborder cyber criminal activities
Department of Defense (DoD)	Defense criminal and counter-intelligence investigative organizations	Department of Defence Criminal Investigative Service (DCIS); Air Force Office of Special Investigation (AFOSI); Naval Criminal Investigative Service (NCIS)	Represents the leading enforcement agencies in the DoD for the investigation of cyber criminal activities
	DC3	Defense Computer Forensics Laboratory; Defense Computer Investigations Training Program; Defense Cybercrime Institute	Performs forensics activities for the defence criminal and counterintelligence investigative organizations

continued over

Administrations	Organizations	Sub-organizations	Responsibilities
	Joint Task Force – Global Network Operations	Global network operations	The detection and deterrence of cybercrime activities that could disrupt the DoD Global Information Grid (GIG)
Federal Trade Commission (FTC)	Bureau of Consumer Protection	Advertising practices Consumer and business education Enforcement Financial practices Marketing practices Planning and information Privacy and identity protection	Filing civil enforcement actions either in federal district court or administratively enforcing matters related to cybercrimes
Federal inspectors general	Affiliated to different departments and organizations		Preventing, detecting and investigating cybercrime within their respective agencies
State and local law-enforcement organizations		Numerous state and local organizations involved in fighting cybercrimes	Address cybercrime through efforts to share information, improve expertise and facilitate cybercrime prosecutions both nationally and locally
Private sector entities	Private institutions that focus on protection and detection efforts	Internet service providers (ISPs) Security vendors Software developers Computer forensics vendors	Development and implementation of technology systems to protect against computer intrusions, Internet fraud and spam and, if a crime does occur, to detect it and gather admissible evidence for an investigation

Administrations	Organizations	Sub-organizations	Responsibilities
Public and private partnerships	Internet Crime	FBI	A platform to receive
	InfraGard	Federal, state and local law	Protecting physical and cyber-based critical infrastructure assets by sharing information and analysis.
	The National	DHS	Providing cybersecurity awareness and education resources for the home user, small business, and education
	National	FBI	Providing a venue to share critical confidential information about cyberincidents and to share resources.
	Electronic	US Secret Service (USSS)	Creating strategic alliances among various stakeholders.

Sources: Federal Trade Commission (2007), General Accounting (Office 2007).

From 'defence' to 'operations'

What is particularly interesting about the use of cyberweapons by the USA is the way it has been institutionalized and the way the nature of this institutionalization has changed over a short period of time. In 1998, a new military unit was created: 'the Department of Defense recognized a growing cyber threat and in response created the Joint Task Force-Computer Network Defense [JTF-CND], which achieved initial operational capability on 30 December 1998 and full operational capability by June 1999' (US Strategic Command 2007). Initially, the JTF-CND was designed to protect the computer networks of the US military, and its mission included domestic cybersecurity responsibilities and occasional deployment abroad when military computers needed protection in remote theatres of operations. Soon, however, the missions of the JTF-CND were adjusted, as was its name: 'In the fall of 2000, in accordance with DoD doctrine, JTF-CND became the Joint Task Force-Computer Network Operations [JTF-CNO]' (US Strategic Command 2007). The name change is not simply cosmetic. The new JTF-CNO implies a change in the mission and in the way government can use the unit. With the substitution of 'operations' for 'defense,' we can expect cyberweapons to be mobilized for offensive purposes.

This change coincided with a change in the way the Internet was perceived. In 2002, under a new plan for unified command, JTF-CNO was aligned under the US Strategic Command – USSTRATCOM (US Strategic Command 2007). The USSTRATCOM is one of nine unified commands in the DoD in charge of US space operations – and nuclear weapons. In other words, cybersoldiers are now integrated into a service in charge of the most powerful weapons of modern warfare, giving a new status to cyberwarfare. Not only is it now among the key elements of the US line of defence but it will also be one of the most secretive. So secretive, in fact, that National Security Presidential Directive 16 (NSPD-16), the order outlining the way offensive cyber operations should be used in military deployment, is kept completely secret (Graham 2003; Federation of American Scientists 2007). After land, sea, airspace and extra-atmospheric space, the US military now projects its power into cyberspace – the new 'strategic space', considered almost as important as its more traditional counterparts

One last, but crucial, aspect of US cyberweaponry is its globalization. In April 2004, JTF-CNO was modified by USSTRATCOM in order to join a Global Information Grid (GIG) network, to allow it to fulfil new a new mission of 'Global Network Operations [GNO], combining the disciplines of enterprise systems and network management, network defense, and information decision management' (US Strategic Command 2007). The director of the Defense Information Systems Agency (DISA) was given command of the newly renamed JTF-GNO.

The continuously changing nature (and name) of the JTF-XXX is illustrative of the new era. The continual bureaucratic rearrangement of the taskforce betrays an ever more pressing desire to show that cyberwarfare is taken seriously and that the military has improved its cyberwar readiness. It also indicates that the USA is prepared to respond to cybercrime with cyberwar. This includes making full use of all available cyberweapons, regardless of their peacetime legality. For example, in a context of open conflict the military apparatus could launch a denial-of-service attack against the opposing forces, just as soldiers may commit murder during battle, for *raison d'état*.

China: behind the Great Firewall

China is an interesting example of a state using cybercrime-like activities in its national cybersecurity strategy. Much like the USA, China is actively developing its cyberarsenal. Some analysts (e.g. Tkacik 2008) claim that China is well versed in cyberwarfare and that it could easily cripple the national infrastructures of its potential enemies:

> Chinese PLA cyberwarfare units have already penetrated the Pentagon's unclassified NIPRNet (Unclassified but Sensitive Internet Protocol Router Network) and have designed software to disable it in time of conflict or confrontation. Indeed, Major General William Lord, Director of Information, Services and Integration in the Air Force's Office of Warfighting Integration, admitted that 'China has downloaded 10 to 20 terabytes of data from the NIPRNet already' and added, 'There is a nation-state threat by the Chinese' (Tkacik 2008: 11).

The mindset behind the development of this kind of strategy is like that which predominates in the USA. However, the Chinese case is actually more informative about an entirely different aspect of cyberwar: the Chinese government's use of clearly illegitimate – if not illegal – methods in order to control its own population. The main element of this control is the surveillance of activities on the web to protect its citizens from 'disturbing' contents. Chinese cybersecurity organizations have put in place tight controls over telecommunications using two approaches: one industrial and one legal.

On the industrial side, restricting Internet usage was fairly straightforward: in China, cyberspace is available only through companies with close government ties. From the start, state-owned companies such as China Unicom, China Mobile, China Netcom, JiTong and China Railway Telecom were used to build the national Internet infrastructure (Hachigian 2001: 119–20). Through these companies, and with new private–public partnerships, the Chinese government and the Chinese Communist Party (CCP) have managed to control most potential Internet threats. This state-controlled portion of cyberspace, however, is a technological monster that scares away most neophyte computer users. For example, basic Internet access is burdened with an intricate system of rules meant to facilitate state control:

> Physical access to the Internet is controlled by the Ministry of Information Industry (MII), the main regulatory organ of the telecommunications sector, and is provided by seven state-licensed Internet access providers (IAPs) (with three more IAPs under construction), each of which has at least one connection to a foreign Internet backbone. IAPs peer at three Internet exchange points (IXPs) run by the state. IAPs grant regional Internet service providers (ISPs) access to backbone connections (OpenNet Initiative 2008).

This is only the tip of the iceberg of Chinese rules, procedures and restrictive structures on the Internet. This extraordinary complexity is repeated in the laws governing cyberspace in China. Internet regulation in China is a multifaceted response to a myriad of requirements and prohibitions issued by different state organizations and agencies: 'at least a dozen entities have authority over Internet access and content in some form. These rules frequently overlap and restate prior provisions. Conforming to these requirements is made more difficult by the broad, sweeping definitions that many regulations employ' (OpenNet Initiative 2005: 8).

One of the key regulations available to the Chinese cybersecurity agencies was established in 1997. Known as the 'Computer Information Network and Internet Security Protection and Management Regulation', it attempts to regulate three aspects of Internet activities in China:

- It forces ISPs to record all the information they have on their users at the China Internet Network Information Center.
- It requires third-party actors interested in the Chinese 'web market' to submit to government control and surveillance.
- It establishes a list of websites that are considered a threat for China. Consulting those sites is illegal (Abbott 2001: 102).

Since 2000, Chinese attempts to control cyberspace have expanded. To summarize, China's current regulation strategies on the web can be divided into three broad types:

- Regulations applicable to Internet access and web-based services, which dictate the way users should act online – including, but not limited to, what is internationally defined as cybercrime.
- Regulations regarding content: what can be accessed and how providers should behave with regards to allowed and disallowed content.
- Regulations protecting state secrets, including 'confidential information in areas ranging from social development, to technology, to international relations, to the national defense and economy' (OpenNet Initiative 2005: 3–4).

As stated by Human Rights Watch (2006), the key content restriction provision is Article 19, which forbids:

- violating the basic principles as they are confirmed in the constitution;
- jeopardizing the security of the nation, divulging state secrets, subverting of the national regime or jeopardizing the integrity of the nation's unity;
- harming the honour or the interests of the nation;
- inciting hatred against peoples, racism against peoples or disrupting the solidarity of peoples;
- disrupting national policies on religion, propagating evil cults and feudal superstitions;
- spreading rumours, disturbing social order or disrupting social stability;
- spreading obscenity, pornography, gambling, violence, terror or abetting the commission of a crime;
- insulting or defaming third parties, infringing on the legal rights and interests of third parties;

- inciting illegal assemblies, associations, marches, demonstrations or gatherings that disturb social order;
- conducting activities in the name of an illegal civil organization; and
- any other content prohibited by law or rules.

Paradoxically, though the restrictions are both extremely broad and extremely strict, providing the Chinese government with wide-ranging powers to invade citizens' privacy and dictate their behaviour, some privacy rights are provided for in the regulatory structure. One important one is the protection of personal information against potential abuse from industrial partners. Victims of data disclosure have the right to sue for damages. Abuse of personal information in the form of interference with individual affairs is equally prohibited. Interfering with electronic mail is a criminal offence. The Chinese regulatory position towards the web and web-based activities appears almost schizophrenic: one part of it tries to respond to the demands of globalized markets, while the other it is still burdened with the requirements of its rigid, totalitarian regime.

What is particularly inconsistent in the Chinese government's actions is that it is systematically eavesdropping on its population, something its own laws and regulations explicitly forbid. There are, right now, more than 30,000 government employees systematically reading emails, watching website content, spying on blogs, bulletin boards, Internet forums and chatrooms, making sure that the 120 million Chinese Internet users (10 per cent of the population) are protected against 'offensive' content – including, of course, any disparaging information on China's regime and its government (Boyd 2004). (This is about the same number of employees that NASA has.) The inconsistency is also apparent in the government's position on hacking and pirating (not to be confused with *piracy*) While the Chinese government forbids those activities, it does not hesitate to engage in them on a wide scale when this is considered 'necessary' for the protection of state interests. One of the best known examples of this are the tactics used in late 1999 to tame Falun Gong, a sect that was believed to be subversive. To restrict Falun Gong's availability on the web, its website was crippled by a series of denial-of-service attacks (Deibert 2002: 149; Morais 2006).

Conclusion

There are three conclusions to be drawn from a consideration of the trends discussed in this chapter. The first concerns the (re-)militarization of cyberspace. Although born into the military family, the Internet swiftly shifted towards civilian organization and guardianship. At the apex of this change, the military almost completely lost its ability to conduct significant activities in cyberspace. With the new millennium, however, military organizations are trying to regain their strategic capacity in cyberspace. Secondly, we are witnessing a militarization of the fight against cybercrime. The trends that are apparent in the USA are probably the best example of this. The shifting balance between the DoD and DHS as to which one should be responsible for cybersecurity is a good indication of the direction in which the government is moving in its fight against cybercrime. Finally, cybersecurity organizations are increasingly willing to commit cybercrimes in order to meet their objectives, even when there are clear regulations strictly forbidding such activities.

Interestingly, these trends are present both in the USA and China, countries that are otherwise very different. The USA currently exercises 'cyberhegemony' over the web, but China is closing in. However, in many ways the changing of the guard, if and when it happens, may not be so large a change. Whatever happens, the two counties are such important players in cyberspace that it is highly probable they will influence the way that other states structure their future presence in cyberspace. In that future, judging by current trends, we can be certain that the militarization of the web is going to continue and that committing cybercrimes for cybersecurity purposes will become the norm.

References

Abbott, J.P. (2001) 'Democracy@Internet.Asia? The challenges to the emancipatory potential of the net: lesson from China and Malaysia', *Third World Quarterly*, 22: 99–114.

Bambauer, D., Deibert, R., Palfrey, J., Villeneuve, N. and Zittrain, J. (2005) 'Internet filtering in China in 2004–2005: a country study', *Berkham Center for Internet and Society at Harvard Law School Research Publication*, 10: 1–59.

Benedikt, M. (ed.) (1992) *Cyberspace First Steps*, Cambridge, MA: MIT Press.

Boyd, C. (2004) 'Bypassing China's net firewall', *BBC News* (http://news.bbc. co.uk/2/hi/technology/3548035.stm).

Bunker, R.J. (1996) 'Advanced battlespace and cybermaneuver concepts: implications for force XXI', *Parameters*, 26: 108–20.

Central Intelligence Agency (2008) *Rank Order – Internet Users* (https://www. cia.gov/library/publications/the-world-factbook/rankorder/2153rank. html).

Deibert, R.J. (2002) 'Dark guests and great firewalls: Chinese Internet security policy', *Journal of Social Issues*, 58: 143–59.

Elgin, B. and Einhorn, B. (2006) 'The great firewall of China', *BusinessWeek* (http://www.businessweek.com/technology/content/jan2006/ tc20060112_434051.htm?campaign_id=rss_tech).

Fallows, J. (2005) 'Success without victory', *The Atlantic Monthly*, January– February: 80–90.

Federal Trade Commission (2007) *About the Bureau of Consumer Protection* (http://www.ftc.gov/bcp/about.shtm).

Federation of American Scientists (2007) *National Security Presidential Directives* (http://www.fas.org/irp/offdocs/nspd/index.html).

Finn, P. (2007) 'Cyber assaults on Estonia typify a new battle tactic', *Washington Post*, (http://www.washingtonpost.com/wp-dyn/content/ article/2007/05/18/AR2007051802122.html?referrer=THREATLEVEL).

General Accounting Office (2007) *Cybercrime: Public and Private Entities Face Challenges in Addressing Cyber Threats* (http://www.gao.gov/new.items/ d07705.pdf).

Graham, B. (2003) 'Bush orders guidelines for cyber-warfare', *Washington Post*, 7 February: A1.

Hachigian, N. (2001) 'China's cyber-strategy', *Foreign Affairs*, 80: 118–33.

Harshberger, E. and Ochmanek, D. (1999) 'Information and warfare: new opportunities for US military forces', in Z.H. Khalilzad, and J.P. White (eds) *The Changing Role of Information in Warfare*. Santa Monica, CA: RAND Corporation.

Havely, J. (2000) 'When states go to cyber-war', *BBC News* (http://news.bbc. co.uk/1/hi/sci/tech/642867.stm).

Hruska, J. (2008) 'Student behind DoS attack that rekindled bad soviet memories', *ArsTechnica* (http://arstechnica.com/news.ars/post/20080124- student-behind-dos-attack-that-rekindled-bad-soviet-memories.html).

Human Rights Watch (2006) 'How censorship works in China: a brief overview' (http://www.hrw.org/reports/2006/china0806/3.htm).

Internet World Stats (2008) *Top 20 Countries with the Highest Number of Internet Users* (http://www.internetworldstats.com/top20.htm).

Knight, W. (1999) 'Cybercrime navy reports on Kosovo conflict "cyber-soldiers"', *ZDNet* (http://news.zdnet.co.uk/internet/0,1000000097,2074242,00.htm).

Landler, M. (2007) 'Digital fears emerge after data siege in Estonia', *The New York Times* (http://www.nytimes.com/2007/05/29/technology/29estonia. html?_r=1&oref=slogin).

Landler, M. and Markoff, J. (2007) 'In Estonia, what may be the first war in cyberspace', *International Herald Tribune* (http://www.iht.com/articles/2007/05/28/business/cyberwar.php).

Littman, J. (1996) *The Fugitive Game: Online with Kevin Mitnick*. London: Little Brown.

McCarthy, K. (2001) 'Mafiaboy given eight months', *The Register* (http://www.theregister.co.uk/2001/09/13/mafiaboy_given_eight_months/).

Morais, R.C. (2006) 'China's fight with Falun Gong', *Forbes* (http://www.forbes.com/2006/02/09/falun-gong-china_cz_rm_0209falungong.html).

NATO (2007) 'Military committee chairman visits Estonia', *NATO* (http://www.nato.int/ims/news/2007/n070715e.html).

OpenNet Initiative (2005) *Internet Filtering in China in 2004–2005: A Country Study* (http://www.opennetinitiative.net/studies/china/).

OpenNet Initiative (2008) *China (including Hong Kong)* (http://opennet.net/research/profiles/china).

Poulsen, K. (2007) 'Estonia "Cyberwar" wasn't', *Wired* (http://blog.wired.com/27bstroke6/2007/06/estonia_cyberwa.html).

Privy Council Office (2004). *Securing an Open Society: Canada's National Security Policy* (http://www.pco-bcp.gc.ca/default.asp?Language=E&Page=InformationResources&Sub=Publications&Doc=NatSecurnat/natsecurnat_e.htm).

Tkacik Jr, J.J. (2008) 'Trojan dragon: China's cyber threat', *Executive Summary Backgrounder*, 2106, 1–12.

US Strategic Command (2007) 'Joint task force – global network operations', *US Strategic Command* (http://www.stratcom.mil/fact_sheets/fact_jtf_gno.html).

Waldrop, M. (2002) *The Dream Machine: J.C.R. Licklider and the Revolution that Made Computing Personal*. New York, NY: Penguin Books.

White House (2003) *The National Strategy to Secure Cyberspace*. Washington, DC: White House.

Wired News Report (2001) 'Prison urged for Mafiaboy', *Wired* (http://www.wired.com/politics/law/news/2001/06/44673).

Chapter 5

Policing through nodes, clusters and bandwidth

Johnny Nhan and Laura Huey

Introduction

Historically, the nature of policing has been intricately tied to territory and the need to secure defined spaces (McCormick and Visano 1992; Ericson 1994; Ericson and Haggerty 1997; Herbert 1997). With technological advances, however, the real world has been simulated in a digital world of wires, ill-defined 'cyber' spaces and truly disembodied subjects. The result has been a significant change in our thinking about what constitutes 'the world'. This is particularly so for the police: cyberspace has forced a challenge to this institution's understanding of the meaning of territory (Huey 2002). The cyber-world, with its ability to amplify crime across time and space, has required law enforcement agencies to reassess policing roles and techniques in the light of new, extra-territorial spaces. The result has been the development of new forms of police 'expert knowledge', as well as increasing public–private partnerships through which police agencies harness the expert knowledge of other institutions (Ericson 1994).

It has been suggested that the net effect of the expansion of public policing through the increasing patchwork of security-based alliances, both in cyberspace and in the real world, is the creation of a 'security quilt' (Ericson 1994: 153). Although the security quilt analogy has some merit for describing the overall effects of the provision of multi-layered security services, it is conceptually inadequate for the task of tracing relationships between institutional actors and provides little to our understanding of both the static factors and dynamic shifts that structure relations. In this chapter we employ Johnston and Shearing's (2003) 'nodal governance' model to map the relations between four sets of institutional actors who are primary agents in the prevention of and response to what has been identified as 'cybercrime'. Under this theoretical framework, the analogy of the patchwork quilt is replaced with that of the computer network: security provision is seen as the result of variously dependent and interdependent networks consisting of interconnected 'nodes', or institutional actors (Johnston 2006). These nodes form a security network when they choose to pool knowledge and resources in order to manage common threats. Through exploring the structure of nodal relations, what we seek to do is to enhance understanding of the mechanisms through which cyberspace is presently governed.

In the pages that follow, we draw on empirical data collected in California for a research project on inter-jurisdictional cybersecurity in order to begin the process of mapping the relations between four nodal clusters or sets of institutional actors. These clusters include law enforcement, government, private industry and the public. After examining each cluster in turn, internodal relationships that we have identified as critical relations within the governance of cyberspace are explored in order to offer a preliminary assessment of the nature and level of communication – 'bandwidth' – that can occur between clusters. Through exploring network relations between the industry–police nodal clusters, what are revealed are both patterns of co-operation and conflicts based on divergent policy objectives and institutional worldviews. The chapter concludes with future considerations.

Method of inquiry

Our work is informed by data drawn from four sources: observation of the meetings of a public task force on cybercrime; online public surveys of attitudes and practices of online users; relevant primary and secondary documents; and 50 interviews conducted between 2005 and 2007 with representatives from law enforcement, the film industry and the information technology sector.

Twenty-two members of the law enforcement community were interviewed.[1] Participants from this cluster are members of interagency computer and high-tech crimes units established in California. These specialized units are composed of officers, detectives, federal agents and special state and county prosecutors, whose function is to investigate and prosecute cases brought forward by agencies and companies within their unit's jurisdiction, often working directly with corporate victims from various industries.

Though the private industry nodal cluster consists of a wide range of economic interests potentially vulnerable to online crime – including banks, insurance companies and major retailers – we have limited our focus to two industries that appear to be disproportionately impacted by cybercrime: the film and information technology fields. The tech sector, consisting of computer hardware and software companies, was selected because of its vulnerability as a target for hacking, software piracy and intellectual property theft,[2] its pivotal role in developing the technologies and standards of the Internet and computer network security, and for its historically complex relationship with law enforcement. The information technology sector is represented in this study through interviews with 18 IT technicians, network administrators, network architects and software engineers from public companies in both the hardware and software fields. The film industry was selected because of its vulnerability to piracy, its strong relationships with law enforcement and for its members' willingness to engage in legal action. Individuals in the film industry group are largely security supervisors and specialists, some with law enforcement backgrounds. These experts are highly involved with criminal investigations on matters affecting their organizations. Eight participants from this category were interviewed.

As our focus is on regional security networks in the State of California, two key informants from the State of California's Office of Emergency Services (OES) were interviewed. OES has oversight of cybercrime task forces under the Governor's Office of Criminal Justice Programs (OCJP). Within the parameters of the present study, it was deemed impracticable for us to conduct public surveys. Therefore information on the public cluster was derived from existing studies of citizen online behaviour and security practices. A number of surveys from both professional organizations and research groups were consulted, including several conducted by the Pew Internet and American Life Project (Fox *et al.* 2000; Fox and Lewis 2001; Fox 2005). To learn more about the volume and content of reports to US law enforcement of online victimization among online users, we consulted the Internet Crime Complaint Center's[3] (IC3) 2005, 2004 and 2003 annual reports. Symantec, one of the leading developers of security software, also produces bi-annual reports on current Internet security threats and their impact on user groups who report victimization. The most recent Symantec reports were also reviewed (Symantec, 2005a, 2005b, 2006).

Our third data source consists of primary and secondary documents analysed in order to provide an understanding of some aspects of the social, political, economic and geographical nature of cyberpolicing. Document sources include both hard-copy text and web-based materials, such as industry reports, news articles, annual legislative reports, task-force literature and forensics studies. Legislative reports provided insight into the bureaucratic mechanisms that affect state-level cybercrime policies, as well as highlighting issues that legislative bodies find important.

Nodal governance

Nodal governance is a model that views security as a conscious product of series of interconnected social networks between actors (Johnston and Shearing 2003). This model draws extensively on network theory, analogizing social relations as 'networked relations' (Castells 1996, 1998, 2000). With some sense of irony, we employ the nodal governance model, and thus social network theory, to analyse social relations that structure the provision of security on computer networks.

To assist the reader in understanding the analogy on which we are drawing, we first offer a brief primer on the operation of computer networks. The Internet is a decentralized network of smaller networks (subnets) that connect different sources of information (hosts) through a series of communication lines and multiple connection switching elements (routers). Network communication is facilitated through the use of an Internet protocol, which sends packets of information for the purpose of universal resource sharing. Each subnet contains computer systems and databases that provide data-processing services and store unique information. For example, some subnets host email services and store user mail, address books and so on. The speed of information passed along is determined by the bandwidth or channel capacity (throughput) of the communication line. Information sent from one host to another host on a different subnet can take multiple paths, so routers are used to determine the most efficient path, depending on network conditions. On a computer network, a node is a device that can receive and/or send data.

Shearing and Johnston's nodal governance model relies on the treatment of human relations as analogous to the functioning of a computer network. Security is seen as a collective action: groups of actors with overlapping interests joining together to form structured relationships that result in security networks. In analysing these relations, the primary unit of analysis is the node: in social relations, a node is an actor or entity with embedded mentalities, technologies and resources (Wood 2006). Each node within a given network contributes to the overall provision of security through the pooling of resources in pursuit of individual and common goals. Although power can be diffused across a given network (Drahos 2004), nodes wield differential degrees of power and influence on other actors in a network. The degree of influence depends on the nature of isometric relationships. More powerful nodes have greater access to political, economic, cultural, social and symbolic resources, or capital, that can be used to negotiate security outcomes, and thus are able to exert more influence in the setting of a network's goals, standards and rules (Dupont 2004, 2006).

As the ability to mobilize forms of capital is critical to both the operation of a given security network and the ability of a node to influence collective agenda setting, policies and security outcomes, some brief discussion of these five forms is necessary. Following Dupont's (2006) schema, political capital is defined here as an actor's relative proximity to or distance from governmental power and the ability to influence the machinery of government to achieve outcomes. Economic capital refers to the ability of an actor to command financial resources that can be used to secure outcomes. Cultural capital pertains to an actor's unique knowledge of a particular field. Social capital is the strength and direction of an actor's relations in the social field and their ability to exercise social connections to produce outcomes. Finally, symbolic capital refers to the authority that an actor commands by virtue of the honour or prestige conferred on them through their activities. It is through analysis of how actors negotiate, purchase, demand, give or receive capital that we can understand the nature of relations within a given security network (Wood 2006; Huey forthcoming).

In this chapter, we examine the cybersecurity work of nodes in aggregate form – that is, as nodal clusters. We define clusters as bodies of nodes (or actors) that appear externally to function as a single entity because they share common features – primarily parallel operating functions and similar worldviews. It should be underlined that, while we find clusters to be a useful conceptual tool for analysing relations between multiple groups within and across networks, they should not be understood as homogeneous groups. Nodes within a given cluster may share similar worldviews, but may also differ in relation to institutional agendas, structure, technologies, tactics and access to resources. For the purposes of this chapter, we have identified four clusters: state/government, law enforcement, private industry and the general public.

Government

This nodal cluster is composed primarily of federal and state bodies, with varying degrees of assistance provided by regional administrative entities and local governments. Wielding greater access to political, social, symbolic and economic forms of capital within security networks than other actor groups, this cluster serves to bridge nodes, acting as a central point of contact, information and resources router. With its ability to command significant resources and power within security networks, the government node can facilitate predictable and reliable conditions for efficient communication and information sharing, as well as setting policies and funding priorities that can have major impacts on the development of responses to cybercrime. For these reasons, nodes directly involved with Internet-related infrastructure security, such as software development and network communications companies, often have embedded policy-level relationships with US federal and state governments.

Analogous to a computer network stack, the cluster of government nodes consists of hierarchical layers of authority, each with differing jurisdictions and functions. In the California high-tech security network, the allocation of funding and resources flows from state government to task-force jurisdictions consisting of individual counties and municipalities. The California State government, represented by the OES, takes recommendations for funding and policy for computer crime enforcement from a state-legislated steering committee. This committee consists of representatives from federal, state, county and local law-enforcement agencies and various private industry sectors. Quarterly meetings serve to inform OES members of emerging crimes and the specific needs of different industry sectors. A senior emergency services administrator explained the government's function within security networks in the following terms: 'the state serves as a "resource broker". One of the services we provide is being a bridge linking task forces, state agencies, office of privacy protection, consumer affairs, *et cetera*. All state agencies make a concerted effort to work with each other.'

In California, there are currently five regional task forces with fixed jurisdictions. Each task force operates as an independent body, forming *ad hoc* relationships with external agencies and private entities when assistance is needed. Within regional networks, government nodes operate as routers that receive information (cultural capital) from law enforcement, private industry and the public (typically through complaints to law enforcement) and, in turn, channel public funds and resources through law enforcement to combat cybercrimes. An annual report is submitted by the high-tech crimes division of the law enforcement community to the OES for performance review and projected future budgets. This report contains aggregate statistics on the numbers of crimes investigated, arrests made, cases filed, convictions, victims and estimated total monetary loss by victims. Annual reports, as well as direct input from the steering committee, give the OES a snapshot of computer crime in the state. Success for state-level cybercrime initiatives is evaluated on the basis of consistent revenue growth in affected sectors, crime report statistics and reduced numbers of industry complaints.

Because of a greater access to four of the forms of capital – political, economic, social and symbolic – nodes in the government cluster typically wield greater degrees of influence within and across security networks. The state can also exert influence on network relationships through the implementation of legislation and regulations. For example, in 2002 the US federal government enacted the Sarbanes-Oxley Act 2002[4] ('Sarbox') as a means of bolstering the integrity of corporate governance following the corporate accounting scandals of the early 2000s. The Act, requiring public companies to implement more transparent accounting practices and reporting procedures, has generated considerable resistance in the private sector, on a number of grounds. One computer security expert expressed his frustration with the law's impact on business functions, stating: 'non-technical people are drafting laws and not involving enough technical people.' Another expert explained that

> Sarbox was initially a kick in the ass for company IT personnel and it really did divert resources to compliance issues. It was considered a 'shakedown' of companies, in which a lot of shadier businesses went out of business because of it. For legitimate businesses that had good record keeping in place, it was more of a nuisance. Now it's just a matter of paperwork and following protocol and policy. The initial shock was the greatest and now everything seems to be functioning okay.

Despite the enormous financial resources that the state as a whole can bring to bear in response to cybercrime, it is not without system capacity limits. Indeed, one major structural obstacle frequently facing government agencies is a lack of funding. As was pointed out by interviewees, the network of five task forces is inadequate to cover the entire state, leaving nearly the entire central region of California without services. These enforcement gaps are described by one state administrator as 'blank spots'. Further, in California the five regional task forces are funded as a 'line-item' in the annual state budget. This means that task-force funding is subject to review each year. In addition to the possibility of being cut by the Governor, the static nature of its line-item status virtually guarantees budget problems. One senior administrator explained: 'Every year the cost of business goes up and there are no automatic mechanisms that increase funds … unless there's an action by the Governor or legislature, the dollar amount stays the same.' This deficit is often shifted to participating county and local agencies, where cybercrime initiatives typically compete for funding with traditional policing programmes.

In sum, the ability of actors in the government cluster to exercise relative levels of legislative authority, to provide political legitimacy to projects and ability to access needed resources can assist in the establishment of new nodal relationships, as well as strengthening existing ones. In addition, the state can function as a regulatory negative feedback mechanism that facilitates internodal functioning. However, as we have documented above, the ability of state agencies to command resources is not without limit. We would further add that the various levels of government also have very different legislative powers; thus, for cybersecurity networks to operate effectively, the significant involvement of local, regional, state and federal is critical.

Law enforcement

Public law enforcement in the USA is a layered patchwork of federal, state and local agencies with overlapping jurisdictions. Local municipalities and county sheriffs, representing approximately 76 per cent of the total law-enforcement body, handle the majority of law- enforcement functions in the USA. State law-enforcement bodies consist of approximately 7 per cent of the national total, whereas federal law enforcement comprise about 11 per cent of available law enforcement (Reaves and Hickman 2002). Federal law enforcement generally deals with interstate and national security-related crimes, while state and local agencies handle regional needs.

Throughout the 1990s, the increasing sophistication of cybercrimes, the increasing cost of damages to cybervictims and the often evoked possibility of crippling cyberterrorism attacks justified an expansion of the role of federal, state and local law-enforcement agencies in the policing of online crime (National Infrastructure Advisory Council 2003). Federal computer crime task forces began to appear. The US Secret Service became the first agency to start a collaborative task force to address specifically address computer and other high-tech crimes in 2002. Subsequently, the California state legislature authorized funding to start its own regional task forces.

California State law-enforcement agents with regional cybercrime task forces are responsible for a number of policing functions in the digital world, including investigating cyberfrauds, child pornography and various modes of theft, tracking organized crime online and conducting multi-jurisdictional investigations related to software and hardware piracy, among other online crimes. Regional cyber-task forces also provide technical expertise to local law-enforcement agencies in relation to such issues as obtaining search warrants in computer crime cases, the recognition and investigation of high-tech crimes and the preservation of digital evidence. Other efforts are directed at providing information and assistance to the private sector. For example, various task forces offer 'loss prevention assistance' to technology industries, as well as 'outreach training' to other area businesses (Northern California Computer Crimes Task Force 2007). Given that much of the policing and governance of cyberspace occurs in the private sector, the question was posed to law enforcement personnel as to why cyberpolicing task forces remain necessary. In response, a member of one such agency explained that private sector cybersecurity actions are frequently derived from a 'profit-centric' worldview, and thus may be antithetical to the best interests of the larger society. Thus, we were told, 'task forces like this [are] going to be necessary because you're not going to slow down the tide; it's going to get worse'.

In relation to cybersecurity issues, the police agents interviewed clearly recognized the need for law enforcement agencies to build effective policing networks. As one police investigator advised: 'building relationships is key.' Regional task-force members revealed that they are keen not only to build relations with external (non-law enforcement) agencies but also with other police organizations. For example, a prosecutor attached to one of the task forces advised that the following question is considered when developing new strategies for combating cybercrimes: 'if we do respond to [certain situations] will it facilitate growth of an appropriate response in the law enforcement community for this type of situation?' To increase network connections across law enforcement at local levels, regional task-force members offer 'educational' services. As an interviewee explained: 'We try to get as many agencies to participate in this as possible. It serves the whole community well to do this because the more people come here to get this training experience and they go back to their agencies, it spreads to other agencies.'

Some cases are brought to a task force as a result of embedded relations with nodes in the private sector. For example, a task-force supervisor advised that '[a couple of organizations] are the only ones able to call us directly with cases. The reason they have this luxury is they have members on the [steering] committee'. However, more often cases are the result of *ad hoc* relations and/or contingent circumstances, as the following quotation from a task-force member indicates:

> I'll get a call from a company rep asking for [the previous investigator who held his position] and I'll tell them he's been transferred out of the unit. They'll just get all my information and before you know it, another company will call asking for me, being referred by so and so … they come looking for me.

What private companies and the general public are typically seeking when they contact law enforcement agents are those forms of capital that law enforcement agencies have ready access to: investigative forensic capabilities and the power to arrest culprits. Indeed, the ability to access police forensic expertise is appealing to film and recording industries, members of which are more likely to report crimes as a result. The desire of private actors to access police investigative resources is not surprising. Computer forensics is a time-consuming enterprise that requires a significant level of expert knowledge. Kay (2006) makes a similar point: 'computer forensics is not a task to be undertaken lightly by just any IT worker … it calls for specialized skills and careful, documented procedures.' Further, as a software engineer noted, 'Forensics is *very* expensive.' Thus some companies prefer to 'pass the buck' to law enforcement. However, this is hardly a universal position. One tech company studied started its own in-house forensic work. The result was that it is now less willing to call on the regional cybersecurity task force for assistance. Some individuals interviewed believe that this move may represent the beginning of a growing trend. Other interviewees disagree, pointing out that the cost of in-house forensic work to companies cannot be justified when looking at a corporation's bottom line.

For the public and some members of private industry (although not all), law enforcement involvement in the policing of cyberspace is also seen as both necessary and desirable because of the unique position of police agents as agents of the criminal justice system. This power is understood as a deterrent to would-be perpetrators, as well as an incapacitating factor for those who have been arrested. These reasons provide potential incentives for the public and corporations to report crimes committed against them, and for the latter to expend time and energy working with law enforcement on both individual cases and larger security initiatives.

While law enforcement nodes offer network partners access to capital in the form of criminal sanctions and forensics investigations, the role of public policing agencies in a security network is also subject to system capacity limits, including financial funding and resource allocations issues. However, law enforcement agencies can provide critical human skills (such as forensic and investigative abilities), economic and technological resources (largely in the form of access to existing labs and other equipment) and the state-sanctioned power of arrest, each of which makes this nodal cluster a significant cog in the cybersecurity machine.

Private industry

The private industry cluster is composed of a large variety of private businesses, each with its own unique enterprise goals and security needs. These security needs are often handled internally through preventative policy measures (i.e. requiring frequent user-password changes), as well as with security technologies (i.e. anti-virus software). However, increased losses due to computer intrusions and various forms of data theft, along with federal and state laws requiring businesses to report cybersecurity breaches, have forced some private companies to network with law enforcement and other government agencies to a greater extent than had occurred previously (Gordon *et al.* 2006).

For the purposes of the present study, we selected representatives from two industries under heavily publicized assault from various forms of technocrime: the film and IT sectors. The primary goal of nodes in each of these business sectors is the protection of intellectual property (IP). Concerns typically centre on the need to prevent the piracy of physical mediums such as optical disks ('hard goods') and digital IP items (e.g. computer software and movie files ('soft goods')). One security expert noted that high-quality unauthorized replicating plants and piracy distribution networks 'pose the greatest threat' to the computer software and other industries. Another engineer explained that such piracy networks are often highly organized criminal networks.

It is important to remember that most of the vast technological resources of the Internet infrastructure are privately owned and operated (Powner and Rhodes, 2006). Each private industry node actively monitors network activity, scanning for potential threats. A network security expert explained:

> legitimate businesses have the daunting task of securing their networks in addition to [undertaking] daily functions ... businesses must secure all ports of entry and be vigilant in monitoring activity and safeguarding. The attacker, on the other hand, needs to know only one thing and know it extremely well.

Thus, as major stakeholders whose financial survival depends largely on uninterrupted information flow, industry nodes have become the greatest source of knowledge about both cyber threats and cybersecurity. As actors in regional cybersecurity networks, private companies have access to a significant form of cultural capital: knowledge about crime and its commission, which is critical to the development of effective security efforts.

As we discuss in further detail in the section that explores inter-nodal relations between law enforcement and private industry clusters, there are significant differences in how members of the tech and film sectors typically function in the security networks studied. However, what each subcluster shares is a business-oriented worldview that treats security as necessary to the goal of protecting profits and minimizing losses from compromised IP and private information. As hackers are often affronted or challenged by boasts of strong security practices, nodes in the tech sector often prefer to rely on discrete internal policies and practices to stop threats. Arrests are viewed as doing little to stop or curtail network attacks; rather, the worry is that the overly aggressive use of law enforcement and legal actions may trigger a public backlash, followed by increased criminal activity. As a software engineer made evident, many tech companies are wary of responses that may hurt their bottom line: 'no [company] wants to say "we're screwed".'

While members of the tech sector tend to rely on discrete internal detection and prevention methods, representatives of the film industry, on the contrary, often prefer to work with external law-enforcement agencies in the hopes that publicized major arrests will have deterrent effects. Further, for nodes in this cluster, arrests that lead to the shutting down of pirate distribution sites such as p2p networks, 'topsites'[5] and reproduction facilities, are seen as the best means of attacking piracy.

By necessity, industry nodes have built private security infra-structures based on technology and knowledge acquired through the analysis of detected incidents of victimization. This form of cultural capital is vital to the operation of cybersecurity networks, particularly as methods of attack seem to be increasingly more sophisticated, and that securing virtual borders is becoming more difficult and expensive. However, the willingness of private industry to pool resources is not without limitations. While some nodes in private industry have recognized that the need to expand security networks is paramount, other groups continue to view such collaborative efforts with a degree of suspicion and scepticism.

The general public

The general public nodal cluster embodies a broad spectrum of individuals and groups who play significant roles in the framework of cybersecurity. The public functions in Internet security networks in four non-mutually exclusive forms: as potential victim, unknowing instruments of crime, perpetrators of crime and as a first line of defence against cybercrimes. Participants in this cluster range from casual computer end-users to organized international criminal groups with differing levels of knowledge.

The general public is the largest and most frequent target of online crime (Symantec 2006). Crimes targeting home users include identity theft, online auction and other frauds, computer intrusions, destructive viruses and phishing schemes (Fox *et al.*, 2000; O'Brien 2004; IC3 2005). The sheer volume of victimization experienced by the public has overwhelmed the capacity of law enforcement and the criminal justice system, which have responded by setting minimum loss thresholds in determining which cases to pursue.

The public cluster is also the biggest potential instrument of crime. For instance, individual users can be employed, unknowingly, to exploit vulnerabilities in corporate servers. This can occur when the security features of computer systems have not been updated, leaving them vulnerable to remote use, often in order to disable company websites and databases or to interrupt Internet traffic altogether. Armies of such remote-controlled computers, or 'botnets', as a security administrator explained, complicate forensic investigations: 'they serve as the middle man … making it *very* difficult to find out who's in charge.' End users are also frequently exploited in order to propagate malicious worms when they unknowingly open email attachments that execute unauthorized code. According to one software engineer, the CodeRed worm, in 2001, was a 'wake-up call to the security industry', having 'basically shut down parts of the Internet'. Such exploits create entryways into secure databases that store sensitive information. As a county prosecutor summed the situations: 'you find that people are becoming, for lack of a better term, unwitting participants to the crime. We get these gullible victims.'

Members of the public also knowingly function as technocriminals. To nodes in the private industry cluster, the biggest monetary threat to film and software companies is piracy. One film industry security supervisor described piracy as 'the next-generation of white-collar crime', caused by 'the ease of crime, low risk, and high rewards'. Illegal file sharing is seen as particularly harmful to the film industry, especially when major movies are distributed online before release dates at retailers. To address the public's role in these crimes, members of private industry have adopted 'public education' campaigns in an attempt at changing normative perceptions that file sharing is acceptable behaviour. As one film industry Internet security expert explained: 'It's an issue of legitimacy; to win the "hearts and mind" and convince people it's easier to buy than to steal. The public and industry needs to get to that point but right now it's not there yet and that can be a permanent solution [to piracy].'

The public node can also serve as a frontline defence against cybercrime through engaging in self-protective measures that limit the ability of cyberpredators to exploit online vulnerabilities. Some recent studies have suggested that users are becoming less trusting online and are increasingly assuming responsibility for reducing criminal victimization through the adoption of precautionary measures (Fox *et al.* 2000; Fox 2005). However, members of the public do not simply choose to assume that responsibility willingly. The phenomenon can be read as part of a larger trend in criminal justice, in which individuals are increasingly 'responsibilized' into becoming educated 'risk managers' who look after their own self-interests (O'Malley and Palmer 1996; Ericson *et al.* 2000). In cyberspace, this responsibilization is enforced through a general message not to rely on the police for cyberprotection. As one federal agent explained, it is up to the public not to be 'low-hanging fruit', or easy targets.

Despite the fact that increasing numbers of online users in the public cluster are willingly taking precautions to reduce the threat of their own victimization, the public is frequently perceived as indifferent to the part they play in increasing the risk of victimization to private industry. One of the primary goals of security representatives in the industries we examined is to change this perceived indifference to a willingness to assume some responsibility for protecting corporate interests (or 'making the public active partners in the prevention of Internet crime', as both industry and law enforcement officials term this form of responsibilization). However, little has been done actively to encourage a wider breadth of public participation in the variety of forums where issues concerning local, regional and federal cybergovernance are decided. For example, while the public is permitted to attend and voice their views at state-level steering committee meetings in California, there is virtually no community presence in the meetings or formal seat for community representatives. Thus, the goal of increasing public participation in the creation of *digital defensible spaces* in the online environment is currently not being realized because members of the public do not see themselves as community stakeholders but, rather, as the self-interested individuals they have been responsibilized into becoming.

As is evident from the workings of the open-source community, end users in the public cluster have their own forms of capital to bring to cyberspace security networks. In particular, actors in this cluster have access to cultural capital – unique knowledge and expertise as end users involved in a wide variety of cyberactivities – that can translate into practicable information for developing security measures and focusing online investigations. For instance, end users are frequently among the first to detect criminal activities online. However, for as long as the perception remains that the public have little to contribute to or to gain from defeating cybercrime, many will continue to feel little incentive to report.

Internodal relations

An analysis of internodal relationships reveals structural variables and inter-institutional dynamics that affect a given security network's ability to respond to Internet-based security threats. In this section, we explore internodal communications, or 'bandwidth', by focusing on network relations between regional law enforcement and nodes in the private industry cluster. Our selection of these relations for examination is based on the fact that these two clusters currently share a major portion of the burden of policing cyberspace at local, regional, national and international levels. In the paragraphs that follow, we identify five key factors that affect relations between these two clusters: 1) the fit between the security goals of nodes in different clusters; 2) institutional mistrust; 3) intranodal structural supports and constraints that affect internodal communications; 4) jurisdictional issues; and 5) demands for limited public police resources.

The first factor we have identified is the compatibility of the goals sought by various nodes in a network. For example, a core institutional mandate in law enforcement subculture has traditionally been defined as 'catching bad guys'. For members of the film industry who see their security needs being met through the apprehension and incapacitation of criminal threats, the forensic capabilities of law enforcement agencies are viewed as valuable, desirable forms of cultural and symbolic capital worth negotiating for. This results in the appearance of strong partnerships between nodes in these two clusters, as well as active participation by film industry nodes at regional steering committee meetings. For the technology sector, relations with law enforcement are viewed as significantly weakened as a result of divergent goals. One tech sector security professional explained: '[our industry] enforce laws as standards and policy. This is only a means to an ends; for law enforcement, enforcement is the ends.'

Despite recent increases in cybercrime reporting by tech sector nodes (which might realistically be attributed to the enforced compliance scheme set out in the Sarbanes-Oxley Act), links between this subcluster and law enforcement remain tentative, *ad hoc* and limited. Interviews with individuals in the tech sector reveal that such relations are attributable to issues related to institutional mistrust. Companies that have developed technologies through extensive research and development are often reluctant to share information with external actors. As one software engineer explained: 'we want to make a buck. We're not going to pass info to [the government or police] that we use to make a dollar.' The unwillingness of nodes in the tech sector to share information freely is also manifest in the use of encryption tools that no longer provide 'back door' access to law enforcement. While such back-door methods were meant to allow law enforcement access in the course of investigations (Akdeniz and Walker 1999), today the trend by companies is to place no such compromises in security. Members of the tech sector further advised that they would only work with specific individual contacts in law enforcement, who were viewed as competent and trustworthy in their handling of sensitive information. A police investigator reported that regional task forces have 'extremely limited' relations with members of the banking industry for similar reasons. He further added that, '[banks] only cooperate with cops that they trust. They will never allow someone to take a look at their system'.

Institutional mistrust is not a one-way street. Members of police agencies are also often reluctant to share information with counterparts in the tech sector. This point is particularly evident in the experiences of an IT security professional who complained of having a history of federal law-enforcement agents refusing to share information: 'in the 20 years, I had one occasion out of hundreds [of security incidents].' The explanation for this exception, he reasoned, was that he had developed a 'personal rapport' with a particular agent.

A third factor – structural supports and constraints within a given node – can also have significant impacts on internodal relations. For example, the size of an organization or other body may facilitate or impede communications between nodes and across clusters. Smaller organizations often complain that the larger institutions they network with on security matters are frequently slow in disseminating critical information. In relation to information sharing across a computer security intelligence network, a security engineer noted that 'I'll submit information that I think is important and maybe two days later I'll get an email with a warning with something I've dealt with two days earlier'. Complex bureaucratic procedures within organizations can also create pressures on internodal relations. One detective explained the stress on victimized businesses caused by law-enforcement reporting procedures:

> For a hacking case, the [case routing] process takes about a week. In the meantime the [victim] is calling and the case is in limbo. Sometimes, I get a call from the victim and I have no idea what [the victim] is talking about since I haven't received the case. In which case, I have to call the station and have them fax me the case. [The company] just wants someone working on their case.

The result of impediments to reporting crimes can be the fostering of a sense of unwillingness on the part of victims to report future crimes.

Issues related to police jurisdictional boundaries are another commonly identified factor. Various informants repeatedly advised that jurisdictional issues relating to the organization of law enforcement operate to inhibit the building of security networks and strong relations within. For example, at the federal level the Federal Bureau of Investigation (FBI), which incorporates computer crimes within its national security mandate, has taken a lead role in handling interstate and international cases. Thus, if a case originates outside local or regional law-enforcement jurisdictions, regional task forces refuse it on jurisdictional grounds. As a regional investigator noted: 'if [a case] is overseas, you can forward it to federal authorities. If they don't pick it up, the case is done. Bottom line is local law enforcement doesn't go out of the country.'

The fifth factor affecting relations between law enforcement and private industry nodes are tensions caused by competing demands for limited law-enforcement services. Public outcries against online predators result in external demands that law enforcement agencies focus their efforts on violent crimes. Such external demands can couple with internal pressures: the police occupational culture has historically prioritized violent over economic offences. This is manifest in a view prevalent among members of the law enforcement community that cyberpolicing efforts should be focused on dealing with 'serious crimes'. This attitude was recently illustrated at a meeting where a task-force supervisor advocated a reprioritization of his organization's caseloads. His proposal was on the ground that 'my community is concerned about child exploitation'. Another supervisor supported this amendment, noting that the reality of caseloads for his task force is that 'ten out of eleven phone calls are not coming out of industry but from law enforcement'. Further, this officer warned: 'you don't want a situation where while we're waiting for [industry] to call, we're sitting on our thumbs when children are being molested and killed.'

The reaction to such views in private industry is frustration. One industry representative said in response to the call for expanding the regional police task force's cyberpolicing roles to include child pornography cases:

> on behalf of people with lesser crimes, we don't want to at the end of the day feel like we're going to lose out … Adding additional scope is making it harder. We do have difficulties [getting cases investigated] sometimes. We're already taking a backseat to things like identity theft.

The gap between what members of the law enforcement and industry clusters see as regional cyberpolicing priorities places serious strains on internodal relations in these particular regional networks. A California emergency services co-ordinator warned that, if such divisions are not addressed, the result could be a permanent rupture in relations.

Concluding remarks

In the complex borderless Internet environment, where time and space are rendered insignificant, a layered defence security model involving multiple nodes is necessary to create what we term, borrowing from Jane Jacobs (1961) and Oscar Newman (1973), 'digital defensible spaces'. Using Internet communications as an example, the Internet protocol serves as a universal link between subnets with different assets that can operate as one (a form of social cohesion based on interdependence). In similar fashion, a security network can establish a single protocol for information and resource sharing – a pooling of resources leading to defensible cyberspaces.

In this chapter, we have attempted a preliminary analysis of how existing regional security networks currently operate to provide cybersecurity. Mapping California's cybersecurity networks has provided an excellent opportunity for understanding the adaptation of law enforcement and other actors to information and risk-based strategies applied to an information-based medium. What has been revealed is that inherent structural barriers and power struggles in the security field are the main sources of bandwidth limitation. In addition, a lack of leadership from figures and institutions in the government nodal cluster, and ignorance and apathy on the part of the public, we argue, can create additional limits on the potential effectiveness of cybersecurity networks. Further, there are clearly significant differences in relation to how different nodes perceive given acts – for example, theft of data could be treated as a 'crime' to be dealt with by law enforcement or as a nuisance that is simply the 'cost of doing business' and thus to be treated as an internal security matter. These differences in worldview clearly affect how nodes in networks will respond to cyberthreats, and these responses have clear implications for the larger issue of cybersecurity. This is all very worrisome. To build effective security networks to police the borderless Internet environment, significant numbers of actors in each of the clusters must be willing to participate fully in order to increase internodal bandwidth and thus strengthen the density and/or centrality of nodal relationships in the security field (Dupont 2006).

In sum, creating a defensible space at the intersection between the cyber and the physical involves reliance on networks that are proactive and responsive to both virtual and real harms. Such networks require actors who are not only willing to share their respective capital in pursuit of common security goals but also able to expand their capacities and overlap security functions where necessary. In relation to the regional security networks examined, it would appear that significant structural variables and barriers exist that affect the capacity of various clusters to protect Californian residents and industries from computer crimes.

Notes

1 To increase confidence in the reliability of the data collected, multiple interviews were conducted with key participants from each cluster.
2 A University of Maryland study found that computers are hacked on average every 39 seconds (Ramsbrock *et al.* 2007). The CSI/FBI computer security survey estimates total losses from computer security incidents at over $52 million in 2006 (Gordon *et al.* 2006).
3 The IC3, formerly the Internet Fraud Complaint Center, is a joint project between the US FBI and the US National White Collar Crime Center. IC3's mandate is to accept and refer complaints of online criminal victimization to local and/or regional law enforcement.
4 Public Company Accounting Reform and Investor Protection Act 2002 (Pub. L. No. 107–204, 116 Stat. 745).
5 Topsites are high-speed underground servers that list the most-wanted movies for pirating. These sites often limit access to a network of 'elite' users whose sole purpose is to propagate stolen media as quickly as possible (Howe 2005).

References

Akdeniz, T. and Walker, C. (1999) 'Whisper who dares: encryption, privacy rights, and the new world disorder', in *Proceedings from the 9th Annual Conference of the Internet Society.* San Jose.
Castells, M. (1996) *The Information Age: Economy, Society and Culture. Vol. I. The Rise of the Network Society.* Oxford: Blackwell.

Castells, M. (1998) *The Information Age: Economy, Society and Culture. Vol. III. End of Millennium.* Oxford: Blackwell.

Castells, M. (2000) 'Materials for an exploratory theory of the network society', *British Journal of Sociology*, 51: 5–24.

Drahos, P. (2004) 'Intellectual property and pharmaceutical markets: a nodal governance approach', *Temple Law Review*, 77: 401–24.

Dupont, B. (2004) 'Security in the age of networks', *Policing and Society*, 14: 76–91.

Dupont, B. (2006) 'Power struggles in the field of security: implications for democratic transformation', in J. Wood and B. Dupont (eds) *Democracy, Society and the Governance of Security*. New York, NY: Cambridge University Press.

Ericson, R. (1994) 'The division of expert knowledge in policing and security', *British Journal of Sociology*, 45: 149–75.

Ericson, R., Barry, D. and Doyle, A. (2000) 'The moral hazards of neo-liberalism: lessons from the private insurance industry', *Economy and Society*, 29: 532–58.

Ericson, R. and Haggerty, K. (1997) *Policing the Risk Society.* Toronto: University of Toronto Press.

Fox, S. (2005) 'The threat of unwanted software programs is changing the way people use the Internet', *The Pew Internet and American Life Project* (http://www.Pewinternet.org).

Fox, S. and Lewis, O. (2001) 'Fear of online crime: Americans support FBI interception of criminal suspects' email and new laws to protect online privacy', *The Pew Internet and American Life Project* (<http://www.Pewinternet.org>).

Fox, S., Rainie, L., Horrigan, J., Lenhart, A., Spooner, T. and Carter, C. (2000) 'Trust and privacy online: why Americans want to rewrite the rules', *The Pew Internet and American Life Project* (http://www. Pewinternet.org).

Gordon, L., Loeb, M., Lucyshyn, W. and Richardson, R. (2006) '2006 CSI/FBI Computer Crime and Security Survey', *Computer Security Journal*, 22: 1–21.

Herbert, S. (1997) *Policing Space: Territoriality and the Los Angeles Police Department*. Minneapolis, MN: University of Minnesota Press.

Howe, J. (2005) 'The shadow Internet', *Wired*, 13: 155–9.

Huey, L. (2002) 'Policing the abstract: some observations on policing cyberspace', *Canadian Journal of Criminology*, 44: 243–54.

Huey, L. (forthcoming) '"When it comes to violence in my place, I am the police!" Exploring the policing functions of community service providers in Edinburgh's Cowgate and Grassmarket', *Policing and Society*.

Internet Crime Complaint Center (2003) *Internet Crime Report* (http://www.ic3.gov).

Internet Crime Complaint Center (2004) *Internet Crime Report* (http://www.ic3.gov).

Internet Crime Complaint Center (IC3) (2005) *Internet Crime Report* (http://(www.ic3.gov).

Jacobs, J. (1961) *The Death and Life of Great American Cities*. New York, NY: Random House.

Johnston, L. (2006) 'Transnational security governance', in J. Wood and B. Dupont (eds) *Democracy, Society and the Governance of Security*. New York, NY: Cambridge University Press.

Johnston, L. and Shearing, C. (2003) *Governing Security: Explorations in Policing and Justice*. New York, NY: Routledge.

Kay, R. (2006) 'QuickStudy: computer forensics', *Computer World Security* (http://www.computerworld.com/action/article.do?command=viewArticleBasic&articleId=110497).

McCormick, K. and Visano, L. (eds) (1992) 'Regulating an urban order: policing pathologies in the carceral city', in K. McCormick and L. Visano (eds) *Understanding Policing*. Toronto: Canadian Scholars Press.

National Infrastructure Advisory Council (2003) *National Strategy to Secure Cyberspace*. Washington, DC: Government Printing Office (http://www.whitehouse.gov/pcipb/cyberspace_strategy.pdf).

Newman, O. (1973) *Defensible Spaces: Crime Prevention through Urban Design*. New York, NY: Macmillan.

Northern California Computer Crimes Task Force, (2007) NC3TF website (http://www.nc3tf.org/).

O'Brien, T. (2004) 'Identity theft is epidemic. Can it be stopped?' *The New York Times*, 24 September (http://www.newyorktimes.com).

O'Malley, P. and Palmer, D. (1996) 'Post-Keynesian policing', *Economy and Society*, 25: 137–55.

Powner, D. and Rhodes, K. (2006) *Internet Infrastructure: Challenges in Developing a Public/Private Recovery Plan. Testimony before the Subcommittee on Federal Financial Management, Government Information, and International Security, Senate Committee on Homeland Security and Government Affairs* (GAO-06-863T). US Government Accountability Office.

Ramsbrock, D., Berthier, R. and Cukier, M. (2007) 'Profiling attacker behaviour following SSH compromises', in *Proceedings from the 37th Annual IEEE/IFIP International Conference on Dependable Systems and Networks*.

Reaves, B.A. and Hickman, J. (2002) *Census of State and Local Law Enforcement Agencies 2000. Bureau of Justice Statistics Bulletin*, NCJ 194066 (http://www.ojp.usdoj.gov/bjs/pub/pdf/csllea00.pdf).

Symantec (2005a) *Symantec Internet Security Threat Report, Trends for January 05–June 05*. (http://www.symantec.com).

Symantec (2005b) *Symantec Internet Security Threat Report, Trends for July 05–December 05*. (http://www.symantec.com).

Symantec (2006) *Symantec Internet Security Threat Report, Trends for January 06–June 06* (http://www.symantec.com).

US Bureau of Justice Statistics (2000) (http://www.ojp.usdoj.gov/bjs/lawenf.htm).

Wood, J. (2006) 'Research and innovation in the field of security: a nodal governance view', in J. Wood and B. Dupont (eds) *Democracy, Society and the Governance of Security*. New York, NY: Cambridge University Press.

Chapter 6

Second Life and governing deviance in virtual worlds

Jennifer Whitson and Aaron Doyle

This chapter argues that virtual worlds are an important new site of research for criminologists, a key new location in which we need to study how deviant behaviour is and could be governed. We use the online realm Second Life (SL) as our key example. Literature on 'cybercrime' (Goodman 1997; Akdeniz 2001; Finch 2002; Huey 2002) has traditionally focused on a small set of crimes, such as hacking, computer viruses and child pornography. Analysis based on this narrow set of examples is far removed from what is occurring in these new virtual worlds. Issues around governing problem behaviours have become increasingly important in these online realms, but criminologists have only just begun to research them (Wall and Williams 2007). This chapter examines how governance in SL features ideologies and practices parallel to those in the 'real world', but also resituates and reinvents those ideologies and practices. Our exploratory examination of this rapidly expanding online world reveals new variations on key criminological themes: the public and the private, freedom and security, identity and anonymity, and community and exclusion.

Introduction: game spaces as sites of criminological inquiry

Virtual worlds are computer-based simulated environments where people interact using characters called avatars. Many of these virtual worlds are referred to as massively multi-player online role-playing games (MMORPGs). Some, such as our example SL, involve the creation of virtual communities that mirror 'real world' communities, even down to the buildings and art. Recent research highlights the increasing social and economic importance of these spaces. One study of the MMORPG, World of Warcraft, found that the average participant spends 22 hours a week in the world (Yee 2006). Another study monitored online auction sites to determine the real-world value of the virtual goods being traded and found that the average hourly income of an EverQuest inhabitant was $3.42 USD and that the national GNP was $135 million USD – nearly the same, per capita, as Bulgaria's (Castronova 2003; Dibbell 2003).

Lastowka and Hunter (2003) suggest that there are three main reasons for studying virtual worlds such as SL. First, they are becoming increasingly important for social interaction. Secondly, the economic boundaries between real and virtual worlds are progressively more porous. Forms of capital flow from virtual world to real world and vice versa. Some virtual worlds even have economists on staff to advise them on monetary and fiscal policy. Finally, criminologists and law makers in particular should explore virtual worlds because they often provide a serious challenge for real-life legal systems. Determining the relationship between pixilated bodies and corporeal bodies, what constitutes harm to an avatar or if and how traditional courts should respond to potentially criminal behaviour in virtual worlds are massive and very significant questions.

The police are also increasingly recognizing the significance of such worlds. Canadian police departments are currently recruiting in SL, while the Belgian police recently established a presence in SL in response to a purported 'virtual rape' ('Belgian police patrols Second Life to prevent rape' 2007 – http://www.wtfsrsly.com/sl.php; Eustace 2007).

Despite all this, there is a paucity of research on crime, deviance and governance in these worlds (Wall and Williams 2007). Several factors may explain this neglect by researchers. These virtual worlds are commonly trivialized simply as games and entertainment that lack any significance in their own right or any substantial impact on the outside world. The speed of technological change makes it difficult for researchers to keep up with emerging virtual worlds (Castells 2001). For example, SL, created in 2003, already has over 12 million 'residents', illustrating how rapidly a new world can appear out of nowhere and assume massive social importance.[1] Researchers face other particular challenges in researching such worlds. Ideally, researchers must be willing to become 'inhabitants' themselves for substantial periods (Taylor 1999; Mortensen 2002; Ducheneaut *et al.*

2006) – a process that may be very time consuming.[2] Researchers who do interviews online must also grapple with questions about the verifiability of their online interviewees' identities and the truthfulness of their answers. Although in-person interviewers face their own challenges in claiming to confront the 'true, authentic other', these issues are compounded in virtual environments (Taylor 1999). Researchers must also grapple with the ethics of such research and with ethics boards who are not attuned to virtual worlds. Finally, the lack of criminological research on virtual worlds may also be attributed partly to the fact that many problem behaviours that take place in virtual worlds do not fit our typical definitions of crimes, or even fit the new category 'cybercrimes'. The recent term 'cybercrime' has been used generally to describe crime committed with or against computers. A number of scholars have debated whether cybercrime differs in a fundamental qualitative way from traditional crime, or whether the term simply describes substantially similar crimes in a new context, or 'old wine in new bottles' (Wall 1997; Grabosky 2001; Huey 2002; Jewkes 2002). However, the catalogue of crimes used in these theorizations is relatively limited, focusing on viruses, worms and spam, cyberterrorism and hacking, censorship and child pornography, 'phishing' and identity theft (Goodman 1997; Akdeniz 2001; Castells 2001; Levi 2001; Finch 2002; Levi & Wall 2004; Wall 2006). Most of the existing work on cybercrime also focuses narrowly on formal methods of policing and on the difficulties inherent in translating traditional policing techniques and existing laws to online spaces (Goodman 1997; Chan 2001; Huey 2002; Wall 1997, 2002).

These studies neglect many important kinds of deviant behaviours that are occurring in virtual realms. These behaviours are largely governed in various other ways besides formal policing and criminalization. The police face numerous constraints in pursuing online crime (see Chapter 5, this volume). While a few behaviours are actually criminalized, many other behaviours exist in a shadowy space where they resonate with 'real world' crimes but are, as yet, of an unclassifiable legal status. Virtual crimes range from tax evasion (earning but not declaring real-world funds from building, selling and trading online goods), intellectual property theft, illegal gaming and betting, vandalism, assault and even the rape of avatars. This fits with the more general situation regarding online behaviours that might be criminalized. While certain forms of hacking, obscene materials and online stalking have been met with criminalization, many other behaviours are ignored due to their 'esoteric' nature (Williams 2006). For example, although arguably they could be criminalized, online discussions surrounding the manufacture of explosives, racist and xenophobic behaviour and harassment largely escape the attention of the authorities. Accordingly, Williams advocates that social scientists should focus on online 'harms' instead of the narrower category of crimes: 'examining how one's behaviour on a computer network can negatively affect an individual, be it financially or psychologically, allows for a greater scope in understanding both criminal and non-criminal computer related activities' (2006: 19). Similarly, many of the behaviours in virtual worlds that we argue here are worthy of criminological attention are currently of unclear legal status. For the purposes of this exploratory chapter, we thus maintain an inclusive definition. We are not narrowly interested in 'crime'. Instead, we explore the governance of a broad range of behaviours that are or might be understood as deviant in virtual worlds, leaving aside the issue of whether some of them could be formally criminalized. This, of course, raises the key question of who decides these norms and who decides what is deviant. As we discuss, there is a key issue in SL around whether deviance is defined in terms of 'community' standards or those of the corporate owners of the world in question.

A couple of examples make clear some of the challenges in using terms and theories based on 'real world' crime and governance to address what is occurring in such online realms. A key early episode that dramatized some of the complexities around what constituted 'crime' in a virtual world was captured in technology writer Julian Dibbell's well-known article, 'A rape in cyberspace'. In the text-based virtual world LambdaMOO, an avatar took over the virtual bodies of several other characters and forced them to 'have sex with him, and with each other, and to do horrible, brutal things to their own bodies' (Dibbell 1998: 11). Furious debate arose over whether the 'hijacking' and textual representation of rape actually constituted rape – whether rape can occur without a corporeal body and how to respond to this act given that the real-world perpetrator remained anonymous. Currently in SL and other virtual worlds there is similar debate over 'child prostitution', and about whether cybersex with avatars that look like children is and should be illegal, even if the avatars are operated by real-world adults (Au 2007; Consalvo 2007).

Two recent works have begun to draw attention to virtual worlds as a site for criminological study. Williams (2006) and Wall and Williams (2007) explore the different ways in which online social spaces maintain orderly communities. Williams uses Hirschi's (1969) control theory and its concepts of attachment, involvement, belief and commitment to explain why not everyone engages in deviant behaviour in the face of the anonymity and ephemerality prevalent in virtual communities (Williams 2006). After exploring community-level responses to deviant behaviour, both formal (including real-world and virtual-world policing bodies) and informal, Wall and Williams ultimately conclude that informal measures, such as peer pressure, ostracism and shaming, are the preferred method of order maintenance in online communities (Williams 2006; Wall and Williams 2007). While Wall and Williams make an important contribution to starting criminological study in this area, we argue that we also need to pay more attention to the economic structures of such worlds and, in particular, to the central role of their corporate owners in their governance. We suggest we need to question more what 'community' actually means in such contexts. First, we argue that this examination needs to be rooted in an analysis of the unique property relations that may emerge in such worlds, as exemplified in the case of SL. Before continuing it is important to note that although we restrict our analysis to Second Life, many of the issues we discuss are common to most virtual worlds. These issues will continue to be relevant to criminological study even if the popularity of SL fades in favour of other virtual worlds.

Second Life case study

The virtual world, SL, is a valuable example for a case study exploring these issues. The remainder of this chapter explores both similarities and key differences between governance in the 'real world' and in SL, in order to draw out some important themes that future criminological researchers might take up around the public and the private, security and freedom, identity and anonymity, and community and exclusion.

An obvious key consideration is that Second Life is largely governed by a private company rather than a publicly elected government. However, this situation is not as simple as it might at first appear. In fact, SL features novel property relations between its corporate creators and the world's users – relations that somewhat problematize a conventional public–private dichotomy. Even so, as we show, the company maintains control over key processes of governance.

Many activities that take place in-world in SL are akin to real-world practices in important ways and thus defy traditional stereotypes that might lead us to dismiss SL as simply a computer 'game'. Although gamers are stereotypically depicted as young, SL 'residents' have a median age of 32, according to Philip Rosedale, former Chief Executive Officer of Linden Lab. Rosedale said residents spend an average of 40 hours a month in SL (Lazarus 2006). Many spend much more time than this in-world, as they earn real incomes by selling both real and virtual goods and services, such as avatar body modifications, online sex services and material goods (such as electronics and clothing). SL even has its own currency and currency exchange; at the time this chapter went to press, about 270 'Lindens' could be exchanged for one US dollar. Over 7,000 SL businesses are profitable, and financial transactions total over $1 million USD every 24 hours, drawing the attention of such corporations as IBM, American Apparel and Sears (Fitzgerald 2007; Kirkpatrick 2007).

Two characteristics of SL allow it to echo 'real life' more faithfully than most other virtual worlds. First, inhabitants follow no directive from the creators of the game about their ultimate objectives: there are no 'levels' to proceed through, no 'quests,' nor any way to win. Residents instead determine for themselves what they want to get out of the game space and pursue all manner of activities and interactions parallelling those in the 'real' world (thus raising the question of whether it is appropriate to refer to SL as a game at all). Secondly, inhabitants legally own the content they create, thus giving an incentive for entrepreneurship. This key feature was only added after SL had already been introduced to the public. The SL platform started as a 'blank slate' where the first visitors could build any content they so chose. However, Linden Lab discovered that without any incentive to build, the content of SL was slow to evolve and that novel content was necessary to attract new inhabitants to the virtual world. On the verge of financial ruin, Linden Lab decreed that inhabitants could own and resell virtual land in addition to owning intellectual property and having the ability to claim copyright on their designs. Hence SL became a site of innovation and entrepreneurship and experienced phenomenal growth — from just over 1,000 residents when the changes were instituted in November 2003, to 180,000 in April 2006, to over 5 million a year later (*Economist* 2006; Bell *et al.* 2007).

With such rapid population growth, SL is facing various governance challenges, a few of which will now be outlined. These challenges illustrate a tension between Linden Lab encouraging something parallelling neoliberal self-governance – exemplified in granting inhabitants ownership of their creations as well as the ability to access the source code of the world – and the lab's attempts to maintain a secure, profitable world and satisfied consumers, which ultimately require sometimes restricting citizens' freedoms. This kind of tension between freedom and security has, of course, always been central to 'real world' governance but takes distinctive forms here. After outlining the unique difficulties inherent to governance in SL, the chapter focuses on some of the techniques that Linden Lab has instituted to deal with some of these issues.

With the influx of new residents, Linden Lab faces a problem common to many real-world cities – maintaining and updating the underlying infrastructure of the world, although in this case the infrastructure is digital rather than physical. Because 'debugging' the world was overloading Linden Lab's staff, it instituted another change that would make SL revolutionary: open source code (Infoworld.com 2007; Kirkpatrick 2007). This allows anyone to access, navigate, operate and improve certain parts of the underlying digital architecture of SL, creating the potential for a self-sustaining world: in-world resident programmers can do the work that was once restricted to corporate lab employees. Rosedale envisioned that at some point in the future SL would be entirely self-sufficient and would be able to operate without the oversight of Linden Lab. This vision has interesting parallels with contemporary neoliberal governance strategies characterized by the increased privatization and deregulation of state functions (although in this case, of course, the 'privatization' involves devolution from a 'government' that is already private, Linden Lab). Tied to this are expanding risk management practices that encourage governance-at-a-distance. Key to neoliberal techniques of governance is an emphasis on responsibilization and self-reliance in response to potential risks (Garland 2001). Although the state remains the key node responsible for providing public security, it increasingly takes a 'steering' role rather than a 'rowing' one and focuses efforts on making individuals accountable for their own wellbeing. It may be argued that Linden Lab is assuming a parallel role.

Understanding the unique property relations of SL is a crucial context for an examination of how behaviour deemed problematic in the world might be governed. A key tension in SL governance occurs around the purported freedom that residents are supposed to have to shape the virtual world. Despite Linden Lab's advertised policies on open code and intellectual property, there are still considerable issues surrounding the agency and ownership of online content. Residents of SL are clearly not as free as Linden Lab portrays; this freedom has its limits, as we now discuss. Even in the situation of SL, the design and production of computer software and hardware, and by extension virtual worlds themselves, is still in large part a process of configuring its users – defining the identity of desired and potential users and setting constraints on their likely future actions (Woolgar 1991). Design decisions by the corporate owners echo and amplify a set of values, an assumption about the larger society, and reinforce certain worldviews (Johnson 1997). In virtual worlds, attempts to define and delimit users' possible actions include, for example, restricting the users' choice of their characters' gender either to solely male or female and thus excluding transgender or androgynous selections; setting constraints on which behaviours are allowed, such as forbidding gambling or sex play; or setting delimiters on players' legal rights within the game space (Taylor 2003a). Although SL has fewer delimiters than most virtual worlds, there are nevertheless very significant ones, which can be found in the end-user licensing agreements (EULAs) that residents must agree to before being allowed access to the world. These EULAs structure the relationship between SL inhabitants and Linden Lab, setting basic parameters on the conduct of both users and Linden Lab itself. Most importantly, although inhabitants may now own intellectual property rights and accumulate inventories of virtual objects that have market value, Linden Lab still reserves the right to terminate any user account, content or even SL itself, and is indemnified from any harm or litigation that would result from this termination. Consequently, there is a key tension between the terms of the EULAs that install Linden Lab as 'god' and Linden Lab's claim that SL is 'imagined, created, and owned by its residents' (www.secondlife.com).

As an aside, it is worth noting that, as a result of open code and the private ownership of intellectual property, SL is no longer solely created and owned by Linden Lab. Virtual realms like SL are not finished products created by a single author. SL continues to develop as inhabitants add new content and modify existing content and as Linden Lab releases new content: 'Rather than linear, the production model is recursive and networked. Rather than a single author (or developer team known as author) there are multiple authors' (Humphreys 2007: 83). Accordingly, a production that is shared between developers and inhabitants redefines the concept of authorship and problematizes traditional understandings of copyright and intellectual property laws.

To sum up, then, platforms such as SL are nearly entirely dependent on user-created content. This unpaid labour is an inexpensive and efficient way to respond to the demand for increased and improved content to attract new inhabitants and to keep existing inhabitants from abandoning SL. It also awards increased creative control to inhabitants, resulting in a stronger identification and emotional investment in the game space. Yet despite all this, the situation remains that, when conflicts arise between inhabitants of virtual worlds and their corporate developers, there has been little accountability on the part of companies: 'Decisions to ban players and deny them access to their communities and their own electronic identities are made without any requirement of a neutral point of view or fairness' (Humphreys 2007: 78). Inhabitants are loathe to abandon their virtual inventories, digital creations, social contacts and the countless hours they have dedicated to cultivating them, and thus see few other options than to accede to Linden Lab's dictates. Great tension thus exists between the purported freedom of SL inhabitants and their fundamental lack of autonomy and the increasing corporatization of their world (Taylor and Kolko 2003). There is a conflict between Linden Lab's corporate oversight and the desire of SL inhabitants to escape corporate governance, as exemplified by the argument made by Herman *et al.* (2006: 204).

> You have no political rights to participate in the establishment of the constitutional conditions that create the parameters of your second life. Like other consumers you are free to express grievances, but you can do so effectively only in circuits of interactivity controlled by the corporation itself. Even your continued access to these circuits is entirely at the discretion of the company. Goodwill, however, is a benevolent despot; there is always the possibility that the corporate owners of the game will continue to respond to your complaints by modifying the constitutional terms of the game's governance to meet your needs. Ultimately, though, we must ask, is this your second life or a half-life of corporate servitude in which fundamental democratic norms of political representation, accountability, and responsibility are ignored, rights of speech and assembly are truncated, and attendance to distributional inequities are unknown?

The desire of Linden Lab to create a libertarian utopia, 'giving users a freewheeling environment where they can do as they please without interference', is often at odds with its desire to deal quickly with unsavoury behaviours that mar this utopian image and consequently endanger profitability (Clark 2006). By 'designing out' certain behaviours (e.g. monitoring for foul language or prohibiting certain sex acts), Linden Lab contradicts these libertarian ideals, yet in order to attract more residents and corporate investment, it must provide a safe and welcoming environment. Linden Lab is currently struggling to strike a balance between security and liberty without becoming a virtual police state. As such, Linden Lab – in true neoliberal form – is attempting to find more ways to help users govern and police themselves instead of bearing the large costs of policing (Rose 1996, 1999, 2000; Garland 2001). In the 'real world', neoliberal governance strategies have often featured governments encouraging citizens to govern and police themselves. Such behaviours may then be augmented by a large, costly internal police force, effectively increasing the net of social control (Cohen 1985).

In addition to 'designing out' behaviours, another form of governance in SL takes the shape of written rules of conduct. Linden Lab sets detailed rules for building sizes and object restrictions, yet has only six 'community standard' rules that can result in suspension or expulsion from the world:

- *Intolerance*: defined as 'Actions that marginalize, belittle, or defame individuals or groups ... The use of derogatory or demeaning language or images in reference to another Resident's race, ethnicity, gender, religion, or sexual orientation'.

- *Harassment*: defined as 'Communicating or behaving in a manner that is offensively coarse, intimidating or threatening ... unwelcome sexual advances or requests for sexual favors, or [any behaviour that is] otherwise likely to cause annoyance or alarm'.

- *Assault*: defined as 'shooting, pushing, or shoving another Resident ... creating or using scripted objects which singularly or persistently target another Resident in a manner which prevents their enjoyment of Second Life'.

- *Disclosure*: defined as 'Sharing personal information about a fellow Resident – including gender, religion, age, marital status, race, sexual preference, and real-world location beyond what is provided by the Resident in the First Life page of their Resident profile is a violation of that Resident's privacy. Remotely monitoring conversations, posting conversation logs, or sharing conversation logs without consent are all prohibited in Second Life and on the Second Life Forums'.

- *Indecency*: 'Content, communication, or behavior which involves intense language or expletives, nudity or sexual content, the depiction of sex or violence, or anything else broadly offensive must be contained within private land in areas rated Mature (M).'

- *Disturbing the peace*: defined as 'Disrupting scheduled events, repeated transmission of undesired advertising content, the use of repetitive sounds, following or self-spawning items, or other objects that intentionally slow server performance or inhibit another Resident's ability to enjoy Second Life' (Linden Lab 2007a).

Linden Lab embeds an Abuse Reporter function in residents' help menus to allow for the immediate reporting of potential community standard violations. A liaison team monitors the real-time information 24-hours a day, seven days a week and responds to each individual event, generally issuing a warning but also suspensions and banishments. Yet it is very significant that the interpretation, adjudication and enforcement of 'community' standards are in the hands of Linden staff. While Linden Lab reports that serious disruptive incidents are resolved nearly immediately and overall response times have been reduced from days to hours, the community reaction has tended to be that this governance process lacks transparency, fails to respond adequately to each report and is too lenient (Linden Lab 2007b; Ludlow and Wallace 2007). Thus critics may charge that 'community standards' actually reflect Linden Lab's ideals rather than the standards of any wider community.

Behaviours that violate the norms of SL – both those endorsed by Linden Lab and those followed by the majority of inhabitants – may broadly be separated into four categories. There are deviant behaviours against virtual persons (e.g. assault, stalking, harassment, etc.), there are violations against property (e.g. infringing on intellectual property rights, illegally copying property, vandalism, etc.), there are economic violations (e.g. illegal gambling, tax evasion and fraudulent market dealings) and there are violations against the world itself (e.g. hacker attacks that act to slow or crash the server).

In addition to the tensions we have discussed around the public and the private, and around freedom and security, SL also offers new variations on the important criminological themes of identity and anonymity. The dialectic between anonymity and identity is central to governance issues in SL, especially in response to the category of deviant behaviour that is deemed to harm virtual persons. Many argue that the increased anonymity enabled by information communication technologies (ICTs) such as SL encourages irresponsibility (Poster 2003) and potentially criminal behaviour (Sandywell 2006). The

Internet provides a distance 'both spatially and symbolically that enables a differentiation to be made between transactions carried out online and the equivalent transactions in real life' (Finch 2002: 96). People use the Internet to experiment with alternative identities, and its purported anonymity allows for 'exit options' if one's reputation online gets unpleasant (Castronova 2003). For example, if one's reputation in SL becomes 'tainted', SL could be abandoned for another similar world, or one could just re-enter SL under a new name (although both options mean that any accumulated virtual goods must be abandoned, a crucial point for many users). Anonymity makes it difficult for Linden Lab to apply sanctions to violators, as it does not yet require proof of identity[3] for users, although an age-verification process using a social insurance number, driver's licence or passport is currently being introduced. Linden Lab employees estimate that hundreds of people have been kicked out, and some have been banished more than once (Clark 2006).

According to Grabosky (2001), anonymity in such contexts may often be an illusion, as there is frequent surveillance online and true identities may be traced back through Internet service providers. Online spaces lend themselves very well to the built-in capturing, analysis and dissemination of data. The full extent of information Linden Lab can access regarding user identities remains unclear. Indeed, what 'privacy' can and should mean in such a context is also still inchoate (see Chapter 7, this volume).

Regardless of this, apparent or assumed anonymity can be a key contributing factor to normlessness in virtual worlds. When the Internet was in its infancy new users were initiated into the mores by older users, but with the expansion and rapid transformation of the Internet – as exemplified by the dramatic growth of SL in just several years – this is becoming increasingly difficult to accomplish. Poster (2003: 535) argues that the ease of 'disappearance' online requires a different type of moral obligation:

> The virtual invokes the ethical duty to maintain one's identity. Continuity of subject position in the virtual is an ethical requirement that makes no sense in real life … The mechanisms of interpellation and misrecognition operate just as surely in the virtual as in the real. If one insists on ethical terms, it might be said that virtual ethics entails a different, perhaps deeper type of obligation. The moral imperative might be 'act so that you will continue to maintain the identities you have constructed in relations with others'.

Although there is evidence to suggest that few gamers act as anything other than themselves when they play games (Williams *et al.* 2006), part of the attraction of worlds such as SL is to leave one's real life, body and name behind. Encouraging residents to follow Poster's precepts may therefore be a difficult undertaking.

Gary Marx has made arguments both in support and in opposition to identifiability that can be applied to SL. Marx (2001: 319) argues that human sentiments and social needs favour identifiability because:

> It is more difficult to do ill to others when we know who they are and must face the possibility of confronting them. Mutual revelation is a sign of good faith that makes it easier to trust (not unlike the handshake, whose origin reportedly was to show that one was not carrying a weapon). It is a kind of free sampling of one's inner worth or an early showing of part of one's hand. It also makes possible reciprocity, perhaps the most significant of social processes.

Being able to verify the identities of those we interact with aids in relationship building and fosters accountability and consequently more socially approved behaviours. Yet, at the same time, there are benefits of anonymity as well. Anonymity encourages attention to what people say and do rather than to their physical appearance, class or age, for example. This anonymity also can protect one's time and person from unwanted intrusions and guard one's reputation and personhood by keeping one's business and behaviour private. In addition, anonymity enhances games and encourages experimentation and risk taking as there are few consequences or risk of embarrassment since one's identity is protected (Marx 2001). Anonymity also promotes identity exploration, which can have therapeutic effects in terms of providing a relatively consequence-free space to work out real-world problems (Turkle 1995). There are further reasons to advocate anonymity, given recent fears of identity theft (Whitson and Haggerty 2007, forthcoming). Linden Lab's computers were hacked in 2006, potentially giving the hackers access to the real names and addresses of as many of 650,000 residents, opening them up to real-world stalking and other dangers (Lazarus 2006). This anonymity is taken very seriously by Linden Lab, as evidenced by the fact that one of the six cardinal sins that can result in banishment is disclosing other's personal information, remotely monitoring conversations or even sharing conversation logs without consent (Linden Lab 2007a).

In an attempt to find a balance between identifiability and anonymity, Linden Lab has invited experts to attend discussions on possible further avenues of governance, in addition to those we have already discussed. Potential additional solutions include conferring some form of citizenship to SL residents wherein certain privileges could be revoked for misbehaviour. Other possibilities include the creation of 'validated' or 'trusted' accounts where residents can selectively choose not to see or hear users who may lack certain certifications (Clark 2006), although the resulting kind of 'class' system would cut against the egalitarian ideals some have for SL. According to Rosedale, some groups have started up Better Business Bureau-style associations to deal with anti-social players, while Linden Lab itself may encourage the publication of blacklists of known rule-breakers (Holaan 2006). Grassroots solutions, including the vigilante justice and shaming practices described by Wall and Williams (2007), have their drawbacks. Thus, in contrast to libertarian ideals, there is also a desire expressed in these community forums for an 'official' and 'legitimate' authority to mete out punishments, as well as for a structured system to respond to and contest erroneous claims. It remains to be seen to what extent SL may eventually evolve towards such a formal justice system.

Meanwhile, Linden Lab's attempts to make SL self-governing are related to governance strategies that have been embraced in an increasingly privatized and deregulated society in the 'real world'. In this neoliberal vision, a 'real' government, just like Linden Lab, is 'an address to which [citizens] are unlikely to send their complaints and stipulations. They have been told, repeatedly, to rely on their own wits, skills and industry, not to expect salvation from on high' (Bauman and Vecchi 2004: 46). In this way again, SL might be seen as an experiment in a form of neoliberal governance, a site in which to discover whether an economically stable society can flourish with minimal government interference, at least in this virtual context. This experiment hinges in large part on fostering identity and community in a society fragmented by technology. Virtual worlds are at the cutting edge of broader shifts in what constitutes community in late modernity. ICTs, such as the Internet and the operating platform of SL itself, allow for social interactions that take place simultaneously over long distances (Giddens 1990). Increased personal mobility combined with the technological capacity to interact with others via 'bodiless' – i.e. electronically mediated – protocols inevitably means that distant strangers interact more frequently and that traditional notions of geographically based communities are dissolving. Technologies such as SL negate face-to-face interaction and encourage the abstraction of identity into binary flows, sign-on names and user IDs. New social relationships are increasingly focused on networked individualism wherein the growing distance between citizens and the state fosters individual withdrawal from the social sphere in favour of social networks such as those encouraged in SL that are built on the basis of individual affinities, interests and values (Castells 2001).

One potential solution to SL's governance problems is tied to community building in order to promote reputation formation. As claimed by Linden Lab (2007c):

> Ultimately, any sustainable community relies on social norms, with the threat of disdain and ostracism, to encourage individuals to act responsibly. We're proud that the Second Life community has historically risen to the challenge of dealing with disruptive individuals without overweening regulation, and we plan to continue to apply a light touch, fostering more sophisticated community norms rather than instituting heavy-handed crackdowns.

Yet even this communal ideal is not without substantial problems. In some ways, the original spirit of SL fits Sennett's (1971) 'new anarchism'. According to Cohen (1985: 217), Sennett envisions:

> a new kind of urban confusion and tolerance for diversity and disorder. He constructs a genuine utopian vision, precisely opposite to that of the planners, crime controllers and environmental designers. Cities should be made *more* disorderly; there should be contact without sameness; we should actually look for and create places with a high level of tension and unease; people should be made to confront each other through various forms of non-violent contact; centralized social-control bodies, pre-planning and zoning should all be removed.

Yet, contrary to Sennett's vision and despite the SL ideals of libertarianism and 'new anarchism', there is a final form of governance also emerging in SL that we will now discuss: creating areas of inclusion and exclusion.

As with crime in the 'real' world, many forms of deviant behaviours targeting virtual persons (e.g. stalking, harassment, assault, rape, identity theft, etc.) can be tied to anonymity and the lack of community supervision and restraint characteristic of modernity (Bauman 2002). One purported solution for these crimes resides in re-establishing identity and self-regulating communities, albeit in an online form. The creation of community in SL is a difficult task given that residents share no common history, geography or goals and only interact through artificial and intensely mediated environments. It could be argued that any community established in SL would be a 'simulated' one – just as residents replicate homes, temples and sex online, they feign that they have created a cohesive and persistent community – although all communities are in some sense 'imagined'.

For both Williams (2006) and Wall and Williams (2007), online communities play a substantial role in governance. They state that community members prefer the use of vigilante justice, peer pressure and ostracism in terms of order maintenance, and specifically focus on shaming as a method of governance: 'Essentially the virtual offender's moral conscience is considered to be a far more effective deterrent against further deviance than any formal form of governance' (Wall and Williams 2007: 404). Yet the threat of disdain and ostracism is not always effective, and any effects of shaming in virtual environments may sometimes be nebulous and fleeting. Wall and Williams recognize that, 'given the unique characteristics of the online environment – anonymity, ephemerality of interaction and disinhibition – it is questionable whether vigilante-style regulation, which is dependent upon shaming (whether reintegrative or disintegrative), will be any more effective than organized forms of proximal (online) policing' (2007: 406). Accordingly, acts of ostracism and public ridicule may be rooted less in shaming, and more in 'the alleviation of the feelings of those harmed. The chief concern is to protect the community's integrity and to expel anyone that threatens its solidarity, while simultaneously repairing the harm done via a process of retribution' (Wall and Williams 2007: 408). While Wall and Williams focus on social bond theory and shaming to explain the role of community in governance practices, very different theoretical approaches to 'community' may also be fruitful. It is our belief that the role of the community in crime control in such realms should also be analysed in terms of gated communities and 'securitization of habitat' (Rose 1999).

Despite Linden Lab's stated desire to avoid gated communities as a policing strategy, attempts to foster community based on shared affinities, interests and values in SL have resulted in the creation of *de facto* gated communities wherein private islands can be purchased and governed according to the dictates of the landowner. Buying and subdividing private land thus create separate communities within SL, with each community generating its own internal norms, conventions and rights. For example, the island of Neufreistadt has citizenship, a constitution and democratic elections, complete with marshals who banish lawbreakers (Au 2006; Clark 2006). As a result, landownership becomes a central component in the control of deviance and is closely tied with economic factors. Residents are allowed to access SL for free but, in order to purchase land, they must purchase a 'premium' membership that costs $9.95 USD/month. Land itself, even though virtual, is not free. Private islands can be purchased at about $1,675 USD for 16 acres plus monthly 'maintenance' fees of $295 USD. Accordingly, even in virtual realms, security measures are increasingly restricted to those who can pay for them.

Private islands may be seen as the most viable solution to controlling deviance in SL, given the inability to incarcerate, reform or punish offenders in any way other than to ban them from areas of the social. When SL was smaller, civility was maintained by the subjects themselves, shunning lawbreakers and instructing new users in community mores. Yet with the growth of SL and the predominance of new users over more established ones, this small public community feel has disappeared and – just like in real life – public spaces are being abandoned in favour of an archipelago of secured spaces such as Neufreistadt. Our brief account of the rise of larger groups and greater anonymity in SL and how this creates difficulties for instructing people in community mores essentially reproduces the general sociological story of the rise of urbanism and its attendant anonymity. Security is managed in discrete spatio-ethical zones rather than being collectively maintained, as can be evidenced by SL being territorizalized into 'Mature' spaces and general spaces, even though all inhabitants are purportedly over 18 (Rose 2000). Another example can be found in Linden Lab's recent introduction of 'Estate Level Governance' where victims of violations that occur on private islands can report directly to the island owner rather than Linden Lab, and the owner can take direct action, such as banning the offender from the island, in order to resolve the issue (Linden 2007).

This fits with what Rose (1999) calls the 'securitization of habitat', wherein communities are urged to take personal responsibility for security. Rose describes this process as both collectivizing and individualizing. It is individualizing in that the state no longer provides security on behalf of all citizens (or in the case of SL, the state has *never* provided collective security), and collectivizing in that communities must take responsibility for preserving the security of their members. This form of community stresses responsibilization, self-governance and control over one's fate, and accordingly coincides with the individualized ethos of neoliberalism. Private islands become reverse ghettos engineered to keep threats out rather than to keep threats in (Davis 1990). But in neoliberalism community is not simply the territory within which deviance is to be controlled: 'it is itself a *means* of government; its ties, bonds, forces and affiliations are to be celebrated, encouraged, nurtured, shaped and instrumentalized in the hope of enhancing the security of each and all' (Rose 1999: 250). The social networks, friends and jointly created communities that inhabitants labouriously form function as a means of governance: these can all be lost if one misbehaves or even fails to protect oneself. Rose also describes an attendant change in how offenders are portrayed. Offenders are conceptualized as those who refuse to take on the duties and obligations attendant in belonging to the social sphere, and are accordingly prohibited access to certain realms of the social (e.g. shopping malls, recreational spaces and spaces of social interaction in both real life and SL). This exclusion is seen as resulting from conscious choices on the part of offenders. Offenders are unified as a group in that they 'refused the bonds of civility and self-responsibility, or they aspire to them but have not been given the skills, capacities and means'. In this way offenders are relocated in both imagination and strategy to marginalized spaces (Rose 1999: 259).

With such communities ostensibly becoming self-policing, the only behaviours that Linden Lab might then need to respond to are those that threaten the architecture of SL itself, such as hacker attacks that slow the operating platform or other actions that threaten the economic market. Policing individuals and their behaviour is not something that Linden Lab ever desires to undertake, as evidenced by a quotation from their Director of Marketing, Catherine Smith: 'Second Life is a service, a platform, much like the Internet ... As with the Internet, users are responsible for ensuring that their activities fall within the bounds of the law within their local jurisdiction.' She then emphasizes the 'terms of service' statement that SL residents must accept, which prohibits any action that violates a law or regulation (Turner 2007). Yet, despite the claim that Linden Lab is staying out of the policing and governance business, it responds quickly to 'grey goo' attacks that create self-replicating objects that overload the system's computers and thus slow down their ability to handle normal operations, and 'copy-bots' that copy objects and thus endanger their market value (CBC News 2006a 2006b; Holaan 2006; Turner 2007). Clearly there is a privileging of some forms of violation (e.g. against the economic system or against the world itself) as against others (e.g. against avatars).

Conclusion

It remains to be seen the extent to which these areas of inclusion and exclusion, along with the previous forms of governance we have discussed (designing out behaviours and promoting community standards and various methods of enforcing them), will ultimately answer the problems of governing deviance in SL, either for its corporate owners or its inhabitants. Others may argue that the fact that Linden Lab has granted intellectual property rights to SL inhabitants may eventually help compel the institutionalization of a more formal justice system. Virtual worlds have assumed the 'metaphor of property being a bundle of rights, the fundamental rights usually rendered as the rights to use, exclude, and transfer' (Lastowka and Hunter 2003: 38). And, as predicted by Lastowka and Hunter, when expectations of property rights are built into the system, there often follows the expectation of other constitutional rights as well. People become personally invested in objects they perceive as belonging to them, even though they may only be virtual property or bodies composed of pixels. This 'endowment effect' becomes even more pronounced when it comes to the subject of avatars, as identification of the avatar with the self is the norm (Taylor 2003b). Thus, desire for the entrenchment of other rights of avatars may eventually follow, accompanied by calls that are already being voiced for a more structured juridical process to protect these rights. Linden Lab's struggles with governance may have only just begun. Because governance processes develop so rapidly in such worlds, they may present a fertile site for researchers seeking to understand the evolution of governance in general.

Criminologists may 'hold games at arm's length from what matters, from where "real" things happen' (Malaby 2006: 97). Yet, as we have shown, virtual worlds like SL are increasingly important locations in social and economic life: '[P]eople live there, work there, consume there and accumulate wealth there, just as they do on Earth' (Castronova 2003). Such worlds also feature new kinds of behaviour deemed deviant, and new forms of governing them. We have mapped a number of different approaches to governing deviance that are established or nascent in SL.

This chapter shows both differences and key parallels between what goes on in the 'real world' and emerging patterns of deviance and governance in such worlds. In particular, we have demonstrated that, despite its novel property relations and its libertarian culture, in many ways, SL displays a familiar pattern in which its corporate owners largely control how deviance is governed. Yet Linden Lab also faces real constraints because of these unique property relations and that culture. We have illustrated further key inter-related tensions around identity and anonymity, and community and exclusion. 'Community' standards may be those enforced by Linden Lab, and community may be redefined in terms of who is included and excluded from particular enclaves.

We have begun to map what we believe will be an important new area of study. We hope this will continue to be explored by criminologists, as SL and other virtual worlds evolve in the days and years to come.

Notes

1 This statistic is slightly misleading as only 479,191 residents logged in within, for example, the seven days before 2 February 2008 and generally only about 45,000 residents are online at any one time.
2 Not only is studying virtual worlds time consuming but it may be difficult to convince research boards to award funding to studies that could be uncharitably characterized as 'hanging around and playing videogames all day'.
3 The exception to this rule is those who are under 18. They are barred from SL but have a teen version where they must prove their age – typically with an SMS-enabled phone – before being allowed entrance.

References

Akdeniz, Y. (2001) 'Controlling illegal and harmful content on the Internet', in D. Wall (ed.) *Crime and the Internet.* London: Routledge.

Au, W.J. (2006) 'Trademarking Utopia', *New World Notes*, 18 September (http://nwn.blogs.com/nwn/2006/09/trademarking_ut.html).

Au, W.J. (2007) 'That book by Nabokov', *New World Notes*, 12 June (http://nwn.blogs.com/nwn/2007/06/that_book_by_na.html).

Baudrillard, J. (1983) *Simulations.* New York, NY: Semiotext(e).

Bauman, Z. (2002) 'Violence in the age of uncertainty', in A. Crawford (ed.) *Crime and Insecurity: The Governance of Safety in Europe.* Cullompton: Willan Publishing.

Bauman, Z. and Vecchi, B. (2004) *Identity: Conversations with Benedetto Vecchi.* Cambridge: Polity Press.

Bell, L., Peters, T. and Pope, K. (2007) 'Get a (Second) Life!', *Computers in Libraries*, 27: 10–15.

Castells, M. (2000) *The Rise of the Network Society* (2nd edn). Oxford: Blackwell.

Castells, M. (2001) *The Internet Galaxy: Reflections on the Internet, Business, and Society.* Oxford: Oxford University Press.

Castronova, E. (2003) 'On virtual economies', *Game Studies*, 3: 2.

CBC News (2006a) 'Attack forces Second Life offline', 20 November (http://www.cbc.ca/news/story/2006/11/20/tech-secondlifeattack-061120.html).

CBC News (2006b) 'Copy program threatens Second Life's virtual economy', 15 November (http://www.cbc.ca/news/story/2006/11/15/second-life.html.

Chan, J. (2001) 'The technological game: how information technology is transforming police practice', *Criminal Justice*, 1: 139–59.

Clark, D. (2006) 'Virtual vandalism: mischief in an online realm can be almost as annoying as the real-world thing', *Wall Street Journal*, 27 November: R 6.

Cohen, S. (1985) *Visions of Social Control: Crime, Punishment, and Classification.* New York, NY: Polity Press.

Consalvo, M. (2007) *Cheating: Gaining Advantage in Videogames.* Cambridge, MA: MIT Press.

Davis, M. (1990) *City of Quartz: Excavating the Future in Los Angeles.* London: Verso.

Dibbell, J. (1998) *My Tiny Life: Crime and Passion in a Virtual World.* New York, NY: Holt.

Dibbell, J. (2003) 'The unreal estate boom', *Wired*, 11: 1.

Ducheneaut, N., Yee, N., Nickell, E. and Moore, R.J. (2006) 'Building an MMO with mass appeal: a look at gameplay in World of Warcraft', *Games and Culture* 1: 281–317.

Economist (2006) 'Living a Second Life', 30 September: 380.

Eustace, C. (2007) 'VPD: virtual police department', *Vancouver Sun*, 29 May.

Finch, E. (2002) 'What a tangled web we weave: identity theft and the Internet', in Y. Jewkes (ed.) *Dot.Cons: Crime, Deviance and Identity on the Internet.* Cullompton: Willan Publishing.

Fitzgerald, M. (2007) 'Does your business need a Second Life?', *Inc.*, 29. (http://www.inc.com/magazine/20070201/hidi-rosedale-sidebar-business.html)

Garland, D. (2001) *The Culture of Control.* Chicago, IL: University of Chicago Press.

Giddens, A. (1990) *The Consequences of Modernity.* Stanford, CA: Stanford University Press.

Goodman, M.D. (1997) 'Why the police don't care about computer crime', *Harvard Journal of Law and Technology*, 10: 465–94.

Grabosky, P.N. (2001) 'Virtual criminality: old wine in new bottles?', *Social and Legal Studies*, 10: 243–9.

Herman, A., Coombe, R.J. and Kaye, L. (2006) 'Your *Second Life*? Goodwill and the performativity of intellectual property in online digital gaming', *Cultural Studies*, 20: 184–210.

Hirschi, T. (1969) *Causes of Delinquency*. Los Angeles, CA: University of California Press.

Holaan, C. (2006) 'The dark side of Second Life', *Business Week Online*, 21 November.

Huey, L.J. (2002) 'Policing the abstract: some observations on policing cyberspace', *Canadian Journal of Criminology*, 44: 243–52.

Humphreys, S. (2007) ' "You're in our world now." TM: ownership and access in the proprietary community of an MMOG', in S. Van Der Graaf and Y. Washida (eds) *Information Communication Technologies and Emerging Business Strategies*. London: Idea Group Publishing.

Infoworld.com (2007) 'Second Life: the future of the OS', 29 January: 16.

Jewkes, Y. (2002) 'Policing the net: crime, regulation and surveillance in cyberspace', in Y. Jewkes (ed.) *Dot.Cons: Crime, Deviance and Identity on the Internet*. Cullompton: Willan Publishing.

Johnson, S.B. (1997) *Interface Culture: How New Technology Changes the Way we Create and Communicate*. New York, NY: HarperEdge.

Kirkpatrick, D. (2007) 'It's not a game', *Fortune* 155. (http://money.cnn.com/magazines/fortune/fortune_archive/2007/02/05/8399120/).

Lastowka, F.G. and Hunter, D. (2003) *The Laws of the Virtual Worlds*. Philadelphia, PA: University of Pennsylvania Law School.

Lazarus, D. (2006) 'Real fear in virtual world', *San Franscisco Chronicle*, 15 September: D1.

Leman-Langlois, S. (2006) 'Le crime comme moyen de contrôle du cyberespace commercial', *Criminologie, 39:* 63–81.

Levi, M. (2001) 'Between the risk and the reality falls the shadow: evidence and urban legends in computer fraud (with apologies to T.S. Eliot)', in D. Wall (ed.) *Crime and the Internet*. London and New York, NY: Routledge.

Levi, M. and Wall, D.S. (2004) 'Technologies, security, and privacy in the post-9/11 European information society', *Journal of Law and Society*, 31: 194–206.

Linden, C. (2007) 'Introducing: estate level governance', *Official Linden Blog*, 20 April (http://blog.secondlife.com/2007/04/20/introducing-estate-level-governance/).

Linden Lab (2007a) 'Community standards' (http://secondlife.com/app/help/rules/cs.php).

Linden Lab (2007b) 'Changes in abuse report resolution' (http://blog.secondlife.com/2007/04/18/changes-in-abuse-report-resolution/).

Linden Lab (2007c) 'Second Life grid FAQs' (http://secondlifegrid.net/programs/open_source/faq).

Ludlow, P. and Wallace, M. (2007) *The Second Life Herald: The Virtual Tabloid that Witnessed the Dawn of the Metaverse*. Cambridge, MA: MIT Press.

Malaby, T. (2006) 'Parlaying value: capital in and beyond virtual worlds', *Games and Culture*, 1: 141–62.

Marx, G.T. (2001) 'Identity and anonymity: some conceptual distinctions and issues for research', in J. Caplan and J.C. Torpey (eds) *Documenting*

Individual Identity: The Development of State Practices in the Modern World. Princeton, NJ: Princeton University Press.

Mortensen, T. (2002) 'Playing with players: potential methodologies for MUDs', *Game Studies*, 2. E-journal (http://gamestudies.org, an international peer-reviewed academic journal).

National White Collar Crime Center and Federal Bureau of Investigation (2005) *IC3 2004 Internet Fraud Crime Report, January 1 2004 – December 31 2004* (http://www.ic3.gov).

Poster, M. (2003) 'The good, the bad, and the virtual: ethics in the age of information', in G. Liestol *et al.* (eds) *Digital Media Revisited: Theoretical and Conceptual Innovation in Digital Domains.* Cambridge, MA: MIT Press.

Rose, N. (1996) 'Governing advanced liberal societies', in N. Rose (ed.) *Foucault and Political Reason.* London: UCL Press.

Rose, N. (1999) *Powers of Freedom: Reframing Political Thought.* Cambridge: Cambridge University Press.

Rose, N. (2000) 'Government and control', *British Journal of Criminology,* 40: 321–39.

Sandywell, B. (2006) 'Monsters in cyberspace: cyberphobia and cultural panic in the information age', *Information, Communication and Society*, 9: 39–61.

Sennett, R. (1971) *The Uses of Disorder.* New York, NY: Alfred A. Knopf.

Shields, R. (2003) *The Virtual.* London and New York, NY: Routledge.

Simon, B. (2006) 'Beyond cyberspatial flaneurie: on the analytic potential of digital games', *Games and Culture*, 1: 62–7.

Steins, C. (2007) 'A parallel universe: what the virtual can do for planning', *Planning*, 73: (1) 16–19.

Taylor, T.L. (1999) 'Life in virtual worlds: plural existence, multimodalities, and other online research challenges', *American Behavioral Scientist*, 43: 436–49.

Taylor, T.L. (2003a) 'Intentional bodies: virtual environments and the designers who shape them', *International Journal of Engineering Education*, 19: 25–34.

Taylor, T.L. (2003b) 'Living digitally: embodiment in virtual worlds', in R. Schroeder (ed.) *The Social Life of Avatars: Presence and Interaction in Shared Virtual Environments.* London: Springer-Verlag.

Taylor, T.L. and Kolko, B.E. (2003) 'Boundary spaces: majestic and the uncertain status of knowledge, community and self in a digital age', *Information, Communication and Society*, 6: 497–522.

Turkle, S. (1995) *Life on the Screen: Identity in the Age of the Internet.* New York, NY: Simon & Schuster.

Turner, J. (2007) 'A second income on Second Life', *Christian Science Monitor,* 99. E-journal (http://www.csmonitor.com/2007/0122/p14s02-stct.html).

Wall, D. (1997) 'Policing the virtual community: the Internet, cyberspace and cybercrime', in P. Francis *et al.* (eds) *Policing Futures.* New York, NY: St Martin's Press.

Wall, D. (2001) 'Maintaining order and law on the Internet', in D. Wall (ed.) *Crime and the Internet.* London and New York, NY: Routledge.

Wall, D. (2002) 'Insecurity and the policing of cyberspace', in A. Crawford (ed.) *Crime and Insecurity: The Governance of Safety in Europe.* Cullompton: Willan Publishing.

Wall, D. (2006) 'Surveillant Internet technologies and the growth in information capitalism: spams and public trust in the information society', in K. Haggerty and R. Ericson (eds) *New Politics of Surveillance and Visibility.* Toronto: University of Toronto Press.

Wall, D. and Williams, M. (2007) 'Policing diversity in the digital age: maintaining order in virtual communities', *Criminology and Criminal Justice*, 7: 391–415.

Whitson, J. and Haggerty, K.D. (2007) 'Stolen identities', *Criminal Justice Matters*, 68: 39–40.

Whitson, J. and Haggerty, K.D. (forthcoming) 'Identity theft and care of the virtual self', *Economy and Society.*

Williams, D. (2006) 'Why game studies now? Gamers don't bowl alone', *Games and Culture* 1: 13–16.

Williams, D., Ducheneaut, N., Xiong, L., Zhang, Y., Yee, N. and Nickell, E. (2006) 'From tree house to barracks: the social life of guilds in World of Warcraft', *Games and Culture*, 1: 338–61.

Williams, M. (2006) *Virtually Criminal: Crime, Deviance and Regulation Online.* New York, NY: Routledge.

Woolgar, S. (1991) 'Configuring the user: the case of usability trials', in J. Law (ed.) *A Sociology of Monsters: Essays on Power, Technology and Domination.* London: Routledge.

Yee, N. (2006) 'The labor of fun: how video games blur the boundaries of work and play', *Games and Culture*, 1: 68–71.

Yee, N., Bailenson, J.N., Urbanek, M., Chang, F. and Merget, D. (2007) 'The unbearable likeness of being digital: the persistence of nonverbal social norms in online virtual environments', *Journal of CyberPsychology and Behavior* 10: 115–21.

Chapter 7

Privacy as currency: crime, information and control in cyberspace

Stéphane Leman-Langlois

Introduction

Contemporary debates over the nature or extent of a 'right to privacy' are usually conducted at the level of politics, ethics and jurisprudence and have thus ignored a fundamental new development: the idea of privacy as a principle or *right* has been rendered moot by a number of new practical realities. The most important development is that privacy, or the information that constitutes it, has been transformed into an exchangeable currency. It is no longer a right in the classical sense of the word, where it served as a definition of the limits of the controlling power of the state; instead, it has become an adjustable quantity with different relative values for individuals, states and private enterprises. It may be exchanged for services, goods, personal safety, convenience or ease of use of existing services and goods. The citizen-consumer now has a quantity of 'disposable privacy' or 'privacy capital' that may be bartered for access to computer services, software or individual police protection; for the more rapid payment of welfare cheques or tax returns; to obtain new goods and services – air travel tickets, mortgage rates, motorcars, etc. – at lower prices; or for access to the virtual and physical premises where such services and goods can be obtained.

Further, in spite of the nearly exclusive focus on state action in contemporary literature about privacy, in reality privacy is no longer solely threatened by the state's ability to gather, store, analyse, disseminate and use information about its citizens. For instance, the dominant discourse on privacy focuses on the threat represented by closed-circuit television (CCTV) and, almost invariably, on *public* cameras – ignoring the thousands of privately owned cameras that surround the few installed by the police. In late-modern neoliberal times and the risk/information society, this 'Big Brother' understanding of threats to privacy has become obsolete. But, more importantly, this chapter suggests that the *meaning* of privacy has drifted away from a central concern with visibility and knowledge.

This chapter concentrates on cyberspace as a site for information exchange and, more specifically, on the open, industrial or commercial cyberspace where citizens, subjects or consumers converge in various types of activities, from banking to shopping to playing MMOGs (massively multi-player online games). Of course, many other forms of information collection and communication exist elsewhere – cyberspace itself is much, much broader than the limited set of activities most of us engage in online. Since it is the social meaning of privacy and personal information that is of interest here, I concentrate on areas where the individual is (relatively) aware of the nature of the information exchanged and of the entities involved.

Before we proceed, I should emphasize that privacy has always had many meanings, which tend to vary between authors, perspectives and contexts. Five different common conceptions of the term 'privacy' relevant to cyberspace behaviour are as follows:

- *Control over information*: assurance that personal information will be used according to contractual arrangements.
- *Secrecy of information*: ability to escape surveillance or to protect against unwanted prying; access to anonymity.
- *Desire to protect personal space*: psychological need to retreat to non-social space, to engage in individual activities.
- *Right to keep secrets*: rules defining institutional, social, political or administrative limits to collecting and sharing information.
- *Data security*: IT system safeguards against unauthorized access to protected information.

The first common use of the term 'privacy' is frequently found in end-user licence agreements (EULAs), where software vendors offer their clients varying degrees of assurance that any information provided to them will (within specified limits) serve only purposes agreed to by the parties. The same form of privacy is also offered by consumer loyalty programmes that collect data on consumer behaviour in exchange for special benefits ('air miles' or more prosaic 'points,' etc.). The second use relates to one's ability to keep secrets from various potentially interested parties, especially the state. This is closely related to our ability to remain anonymous, something made possible by modern urbanization – personal secrets were few and short-lived in smaller, close-knit communities. Paradoxically, this urban anonymity seems to have led to new desires to confess publicly even the most embarrassing secrets, whether on Internet forums or on 'reality' TV shows. (Although only a few are actually chosen to participate, great numbers of hopefuls invariably crowd early auditions.) The third common meaning of privacy is based on the purported existence of a fundamental human need to be alone, to retreat from constant social gaze or interaction. In fourth place is the normative, rule-based conception of privacy as a right, which gives rise to a set of regulations designed to protect it. This definition of privacy is usually presented as an element of a zero-sum game of power, where adding information on one side of the scale automatically lightens the other side. Finally, in the context of securing IT networks, privacy is conceived of as the implementation of effective technical barriers to illegitimate (ethics level), unapproved (administrative level) or unlawful (legal level) data access.

Some of these definitions rest on metaphysical absolutes; others imply undefined states of mind (desires, bio-psychological tendencies, calculations, etc.); and still others are insufficiently specified (measuring information secrecy requires evaluating the availability of all of one's personal information; since this cannot be done in practice, the level of secrecy can only be speculative).

For the specific purposes of this analysis, I define privacy as the total of all forms of personal information about an individual – whether or not such information is recognized as 'private' by its object/source or by its repository – that may be communicated (given, bought or otherwise transferred). This definition has the advantage of taking into account the many kinds of information that are not part of the traditional, and overly subjective, understanding of privacy as one's 'private affairs', as elements of knowledge that are held by their originator to be secret or to have limited distribution. Instead, it is a purely quantitative notion of privacy meant to circumvent the usual normative, technological or psychological pitfalls. My discussion of privacy covers a great deal of ground and includes habits, grocery lists, whereabouts, music preferences and all other forms of knowledge that can be formulated and compiled about a person. This comprehensiveness is important since, in the era of behavioural analysis and data mining, a surprisingly complete personal portrait can be produced from apparently insignificant titbits.

In late-modern society, this information – and other types we have yet to imagine – is disseminated over a dynamic web composed of a multitude of very different entities. The state and its various institutions are among these entities but, although still powerfully determinant through various forms of regulation and production, it no longer holds a monopoly in this matter. For the most part, information is collected, analysed, diffused and archived by non-state actors whose mission is to maximize the efficiency of many aspects of industrial production, distribution and consumption.

This chapter is organized into three main parts. First, I review the key social, demographic, economic and political factors that form the contingent context where our perception of privacy evolves. The second section analyses the most important modes of information exchange in cyberspace in order to reconstruct the main practical aspects of computerized privacy. The last section explores the function of personal information in the computer user's everyday experience of cyberspace. We see that shared private information does not accumulate in secrets vaults or give rise to totalitarian, clandestine police action (though it also does): rather, it structures our experience of cyberspace.

Late-modern society: consumers, risks, information and markets

Four dominant features of late-modern society interact to produce the social environment that transforms privacy, defined as personal information, into currency.

Consumers

The first feature is consumerism – the way we approach both the goods and services we desire and the means we use to obtain them. In a cash society, we fulfil our needs and desires through the use of legal currency: such currency has a limited, physically set value (but no intrinsic value, of course). It is owner neutral, immediately bearer usable and requires no interaction between the user and the issuer/guarantor (the state). In contemporary society, the use of this 'pure' exchange vector is on the decline. Most other forms of payment (cheques, but more importantly credit cards, debit cards and other like methods) are services that must be acquired by the user. They have stricter usage rules, necessitate a constant exchange of information between the issuer, the user and the vendor, and require financial compensation, etc. In non-physical cyberspace, these are the only accepted means of payment. (One has to be careful not to overstate the importance of e-commerce, since at present it is only a small proportion of total consumption.)

Consumer society, as Baudrillard noted (1970), is a culture founded on need rather than on promised abundance. Since goods and services are plentiful, few of us go hungry or have no roof over our heads, and most of us manage to fulfil quite a few of our decidedly superfluous desires. The consumer's subjective experience of reality is, however, of constant need, not of satisfaction – a continuing subjective impression of un-satisfaction that is fundamental to the production cycle. Any satisfaction must be fleeting, evaporating under the pressure of technological obsolescence and massive advertising, replaced by an insatiable desire for novelty and accumulation. This urge for the new applies not only to the goods and services we 'need' but also to the financial services we use to acquire them. Since the 1970s, credit cards have largely overtaken cash as the main form of payment. The seductive power of easily available credit services has created ever-increasing levels of debt and personal bankruptcy, as well as the lowest savings rate in history. (The other record low occurred during the great depression.) The Internet consumer is immersed in an intensive, continuous flow of information about desirable products and easy payment.

Risks

Ulrich Beck introduced a remarkably fertile concept in 1992 with his work on risk. While his primary focal points were the new risks produced by technology, specifically those associated with nuclear power and pollution, the idea of risk was quickly adapted to the study of multiple social phenomena, particularly crime and terrorism. Security experts define risk as a combination of likelihood and the potential severity of the effect, or 'criticality'. Whether a type of crime or terrorism is more 'risky' today than it was 30 years ago has become less important than the fact that such activities have now been reduced to their risk content – they now *are* risks. In Canada, one of the main post-9/11 changes in government was the creation of what is essentially a department of risk management, named 'Public Safety Canada' (PS). To PS, epidemics, destructive weather, industrial espionage, crime, terrorism and threats to computer security are all primarily risks and can all be managed centrally through a unified model (with different responses, of course).

In a risk society, criminal activity is not seen as evil, pathological or even illegal. Instead, it is one of many different risk factors that one should be informed about in order to take the proper steps to avoid or at least manage it (for instance, through insurance or by adopting safer behaviours). A risk-based understanding of crime is uninterested in matters of aetiology, rehabilitation or rights (whether the victims' or the offenders') but only in actuarial assessment and classification according to probability and criticality (Feeley and Simon 1992; O'Malley 1998, 2004).

One form of technology whose risks Beck paid far less attention to is IT, now at the forefront of media and government attention. We are constantly bombarded with information about formless, generalized IT risks: viruses, identity theft, paedophiles looking for our children on the Internet, black-hat hackers bent on turning our home computers into bots, terrorists destroying the power distribution infrastructure, etc. There are also periodic scares such as the infamous 'Y2K' bug (planes were predicted to fall from the sky), the 2000 warning from Richard Clarke (former White House National Security Council adviser) about an upcoming 'Digital Pearl Harbour' or the 2004 Microsoft 'JPEG' vulnerability/virus. As with risks linked to conventional criminality, we are asked to take action to manage our risks better: we are given information about risks, risk mitigation strategies are suggested (better password management, parental supervision, etc.) and we are drafted as civilian guardians of the net with such programs as 'CyberTip.ca', which encourage the reporting of the sexual exploitation of children on the Internet.

Information

Logically, risk assessment demands sufficient, timely, relevant information; the more information, the better the assessment. That the development of the risk society has coincided with increasing concern about the validity, quantity and flow of information is not fortuitous. Whether or not we take part in the 'information society', industries related to the production, treatment and transfer of information (entertainment, Internet, IT) are in a period of exponential growth. Since the 1990s and the invention (and subsequent disappearance) of the catch phrase 'information superhighway', governments have been increasingly concerned with the many aspects of the concepts of 'information society', 'information revolution' and 'knowledge economy', especially as they effect education, governance and industry. There are important social and political consequences to the use of these 'information society' concepts. For instance, they tend to increase important social and economic differences and grossly unequal access to information. They further obscure demographic, political and social areas where information is less abundant (see Mattelart 2001). They also legitimate the increasingly strict and powerful protection of 'information industries' and so-called 'intellectual property' (which, paradoxically, *disrupts* the flow of knowledge). Examples include the recording industry's all-out war against file sharers (Leman-Langlois 2003, 2006) or the motion picture industry's success at criminalizing the unauthorized recording of new releases in theatres and, of course, the creation of entirely new forms of 'crime', such as the 'attempted copyright infringement' in the US House Intellectual Property Bill 2007 (Ars Technica 2007). These very different phenomena point to one important development: information is, more than ever, a *product*, conceptually separate from other goods and services.

Just as with risk, this conclusion should not be taken as a claim that we are more or better informed than we were in the previous 'non-information' society, or that information makes us better or more productive individuals (Garnham 2000). Information can be false, erroneous, misleading, incomplete, contradictory or just plain confusing, and adding more of it does not necessarily solve these problems – it may actually exacerbate most of them. What is important is the new economic and political power generated by the production and exchange of information.

As well, as we see in a moment, information gives birth to new worlds where individuals can lead increasingly diverse and varied lives.

Markets

The changes discussed above are taking place in neoliberal times, where power structures are exploding away from the state and towards multiple other institutions: commercial, private, individual, communitarian, professional, corporate, supra-national, etc. Concurrent state disinvestment and deregulation have greatly enhanced the social power of most industrial markets. Though conventional policing remains, and is likely to remain a state function in the future (the growth of private policing remains essentially a North American phenomenon), cyberpolicing is overwhelmingly private. It is deeply enmeshed with the data surveillance inherent to any online activity. While some private actors are more than happy to call on 'the system' when it seems financially expedient (see Chapter 5, this volume), cyberspace is still 'lawless' space, in the sense that the public police remain nearly invisible – a state of affairs unlikely to change soon (see Chapter 6, this volume).

The state used to be the sole subject of any analysis of privacy, surveillance or the collection of personal files. Dystopian fictions (*1984*) and realities (the Stasi files) also put the state apparatus in the middle of all control structures. Recently, many authors note that the actual power of the state appears to be in relative decline in most contemporary societies (for instance, Wood 2004). This decline has been interpreted as an indication that Foucault's (1975) use of Bentham's 'panopticon' as a metaphor for surveillance, since it rests in part on the centralization of surveillance, no longer applies (Haggerty 2006; Dupont forthcoming). This seems only more so in cyberspace, where the state is far less visible and has no tradition of legitimacy. The idea that surveillance is antagonistic by nature is also outdated. On the other hand, the state's actual impact notwithstanding, evidence shows that behavioural change is still the main objective of surveillance, whether consensual or not, and the *object* of surveillance, the modern, 'rational' human capable of self-discipline, is also the same. The difference is that now conduct is changed not by the threat of punishment but by the promise of reward.

The industrial information exchange

Needless to say, immense amounts of information about citizens are being collected, analysed and acted upon in complete secrecy by the state, private enterprises and other citizens (Brodeur and Leman-Langlois 2006). In cyberspace, however, individuals also knowingly provide access to vast amounts of personal information. They also do it over the phone or in person, of course, but cyberspace seems many orders of magnitude ahead. Lyon (2006: 8) refers to this phenomenon as the 'panopticommodity', a world of surveillance in which the surveilled actively participate in revealing themselves and providing information about their physical characteristics, habits and preferences because doing so entitles them to various benefits. Whitaker's (1999) 'participatory panopticon' points out that globalized surveillance rests on what Foucault would deem 'positive power' – power derived through a reconstruction of consent. In this brave new world, the end of privacy is not the result of the actions of ill-intentioned or ill-advised entities: it occurs because we no longer value it.

Most authors see the disappearance or reduction of privacy as a modern social problem. Whitaker, for instance, warns of dire consequences, such as the destruction of social solidarity, the (further) disempowerment of the have-not classes and the exclusion of dissenters. As Mathiesen (1997) has already noted, the surveillance tools now available to the masses, rather than working to counter such problems, instead produce ever more frivolous, inconsequential gossip rather than useful information. Other analysts approach all technologies as intrinsically suspect and destined to augment the speed and intensity with which totalitarian practices are introduced (Mattelart 2001; Fischer 2006; Los 2006). Technologies that appear to invade a sacrosanct inner personal sphere in order to extract information are deserving of special scorn. The opposite extreme is to see technology as an answer to all modern political and social problems. Etzioni (1999: 2), for instance, presents a series of straw-man arguments ('to begin a new dialogue about privacy, I have asked ... if they would like to know whether the person entrusted with their child care is a convicted molester') that suggest that all privacy 'problems' can be solved with technology. Data mining and the automated computer analysis of information have also been presented as ways to protect privacy since no humans are used to pry into the personal affairs of the targets (Brodeur and Leman-Langlois 2006).

One extremely important aspect of information exchange is that a large proportion of the supposedly privacy-reducing technologies is being adopted not by governments or large corporations but by individual consumers who find them useful tools of social networking, communication, entertainment, etc. The argument that these users are unaware of the 'bad' side of the tools they use is becoming extremely thin and requires the assumption that a majority of the public is technologically ignorant. This ignorance hypothesis is essentially a normative argument based on the idea that important, significant or dangerous truths are being forgotten by citizens. It is true, of course, that the general public, and especially the so-called 'Internet generation', is far less techno-savvy than one might imagine. For instance, many university students are incapable of efficiently searching the Internet and are forced to use prepackaged, easy-access, mass-market information. However, the assumption that they are giving away privacy information because they do not see its 'true' value simply does not fit the facts. On the contrary, they have learnt that all information has a *market* value.

Cyberspace encompasses a broad range of activities involving information exchanges between individuals and various entities, and the nature, purpose and beneficiaries of the gathered data can differ widely. It is useful to break this vast range of activities into a few discrete, yet overlapping categories.

Virtual payment

As many have already pointed out, there are instances where we agree to provide information about ourselves in order to pay for goods, services and information that we want. The most common example is the use of credit cards (issued by banks or large retailers) or other forms of mediated payment, such as PayPal. These are not specific to cyberspace but cyberspace consumers, unlike 'meat space' consumers, cannot choose to pay in cash. Even bartering, on the Internet, leaves clear traces that have no equivalent in the physical world.

Users may not know exactly how much information is being recorded, how long it will be kept, to what extent sophisticated analysis techniques will add value to it (building consumer profiles, sharing credit histories with multiple other entities through Equifax, Experian and Transunion) or who may have access to it now or in the future. However, receiving a statement every month certainly indicates that one's purchases have been recorded. Various messages also hint that spending and reimbursement habits have been analysed, such as periodic rises in the allowed credit limit. (Conversely – or perhaps consequently – we may receive a message informing us that the normally required minimum payment has been suspended to 'help with unforeseen financial demands'. Interest costs continue to apply, of course.)

Unsurprisingly, in view of the enormous possible losses, the misuse of this type of personal information by third parties (such as so-called identity theft) is making the public increasingly wary and is one of the main problems limiting the growth of Internet commerce (Conference Board 2005). Consequently, the continuous analysis of spending habits has been introduced to identify 'abnormal' uses of credit cards, which are statistically associated with illegitimate use. Card holders who depart from their usual routines may get a phone call from the card issuer's offices to confirm that they have made the purchases being credited to the card.

Rewarding loyalty

Loyalty programmes are different in a key respect: the recording of one's purchases is not logically implied in their use. However, the literature included when someone joins, as well as information on corporate websites and in other publications, clearly states that information is collected, though it is often less clear about the intended uses of that information or who its beneficiaries are. Loyalty Group (2007) mentions that it collects information:

> to ensure the proper functioning of the AIR MILES® Reward Program; to meet the direct marketing, product development and research requirements of the AIR MILES® Reward Program and its participating Sponsors; and to improve the promotional offers and services of the AIR MILES® Reward Program and its participating Sponsors.

It is less explicit about the nature of the information being collected. For example, there is no mention of whether individual line items or only total purchases are recorded, whether the record is time stamped, whether mode of payment is noted, etc.

Third-party loyalty programmes, such as Air Miles, are most useful for conventional marketing, outside cyberspace, because they are actually subcontractors for the task of database management, which small and medium retailers might find onerous (leading them to revert to the classic cardboard fidelity card). By contrast, Internet retailers can create their own automated loyalty programmes easily and can start collecting visitor information right away, since their entire operation is already database dependent. Cyberconsumers are also often asked to create personal profiles where even more information about them is collected.

The user-friendly cyberspace

Amazon has one of the most sophisticated systems for collecting and using information about its customers, as well as visitors. In addition to defined personal data, it asks them to make recommendations and to identify the books they already own. The reward for this is, however, slightly different: participation creates a corner-bookstore, wave-to-the-owner feel for the colossal retail warehouse, making it a cosy, user-friendly space.

While it is true, in theory, that the Internet has given any individual user the capacity to 'publish' information and, conversely, to find millions of various sources of information, in reality this glut of data has created a need for simplification and streamlining. In fact, to a large extent the very creation of the World Wide Web was in part the application of a varnish of simplicity to the chaotic, infinite net of information (which has grown a thousand-fold since). Early on, Internet portals were introduced to provide further streamlining, offering a one-stop, pre-digested, standardized and easy-to-use library of selected sources of information (selected in part in terms of the portal owner's business ties to content providers).

Today, portals have grown to include just about any form of service in cyberspace. Microsoft's MSN is the most accomplished example of a multinational, multi-service portal where users can chat, read news (from MSNBC), manage their agendas, access videos, purchase music, books and airline tickets, find a date, consult an encyclopaedia (Microsoft's *Encarta*, of course) and much more. Portals from many other Internet service providers (ISPs) – for instance, Canada's Bell Sympatico's, the largest ISP in Canada – are in fact MSN clones. Microsoft has devised a uniform password system for all its member portals, sites and subsites called 'Windows Live ID' (originally, '.NET Passport') aimed at reducing the number of passwords users must remember to surf from one personalized service to the next. It also allows the creation of a centralized database of user behaviour.

Most major portals include a customization function where users can change the 'look and feel' of the interface and can select content categories according to their personal preferences, etc. (thus enabling 'My MSN', 'My AOL', 'My Yahoo' and so on). In most cases these preferences, as well as the user's behaviour within the portal, are recorded and analysed in order to tailor the content offered to the user's inferred 'tastes'. This also applies to advertisements placed on each new page consulted. Search engines such as Google, Yahoo or Ask Jeeves also try to make the Internet user's experience as personalized, and as simple, as possible by offering a variety of customization options. Amazon and other retailers with vast inventories have similar problems. Their interfaces often look like those of search engines and could leave users with nothing to help them find their way through thousands of choices. Amazon tries to counter this through book suggestions based on customer behaviour while browsing and purchasing items. (These suggestions also take into account the retailer's marketing strategy and current inventory.)

In all cases, most of these functions rely on cookies left on the user's computer, which serve to track behaviours and preferences and to link users to their profile on the site's database. Most commercial and government websites (except in the USA, where government websites are forbidden by law to use cookies or other types of tracking devices) install multiple cookies (27 per cent of all individual servers link to cookies; Security Space 2007). Cookies became the target of much scorn when consumer and privacy advocates learnt of their presence and function. To a large extent the concerns, and certainly the panic, were clearly exaggerated: in reality cookies are essentially harmless. Yet alternative browsers were quick to respond to the wave of concern and offered users the open management of cookies and the ability to refuse them in bulk or to choose among them. Eventually Microsoft's Internet Explorer, dominant in the market (82 per cent) because of its automatic presence in Microsoft's operating systems (since Windows 95), began to provide this service as well. However, most internet users remain entirely oblivious to cookies. What is more interesting, most (76 per cent) of those who are fully aware of their function choose to accept them in bulk anyway (Pew Internet 2000). While there are no recent numbers, this does not invalidate the point. The problem is, of course, that the selective management of cookies severely degrades one's experience of cyberspace, since multiple message boxes constantly appear on the screen to prompt users to exercise their freedom to accept or reject each cookie. Bulk refusal or deletion has an equivalent effect: any customization, automatic user recognition and preselected content vanish, and many websites will simply refuse to display any content at all (especially online merchants and financial institutions).

Finally, cyberspace is mediated by an array of applications that must be installed on individual computers. Most of these applications require information in order to work properly and may gather it any of three main ways. First, many software packages demand, or at least suggest, that the user 'register' their copy. This registration process usually involves communicating personal information. In most cases registration is elective but rewarded by special promotions, services or various gadgets. Secondly, it is not uncommon for programs to monitor the way they are used and to send that information back to their distributor. Popular music management packages routinely gather anonymous statistics (for instance, AOL's WinAmp, Real Networks' RealPlayer or Apple's leading iTunes/QuickTime). Users are informed of this in more or less explicit terms, sometimes deep into the scroll-down message box where they must click to agree to licence terms – Apple's iTunes/QuickTime EULA clearly states that computer state and usage information will be sent to Apple and its partners, but the agreement is a rebarbative 4,000 words long. Of course, some applications collect and report information without telling the user – using so-called 'spyware', which is beyond the scope of this chapter. Finally, software that has communication as its primary function obviously requires geographic or electronic identification co-ordinates in order to perform its function. Web browsers, at the minimum, give out Internet protocol addresses and various types of information about the computer's ability to reconstruct the pages requested by the user (browser type, operating system and so on). Other cyberspace communication tools, such as commercial Voip or Skype, AIM, ICQ or MSN, are also dependent on personal information. While tools that provide anonymity are available for simple web surfing, they would entirely defeat the purpose of the applications in this third category.

Showing oneself

The new catch phrase is 'Web 2.0.' Under this umbrella, analysts refer to any and all cyberspace applications that invite users to participate in their content, appearance or functionality. The aforementioned glut of information in cyberspace, the virtual infinity of its depth, means that individual websites are no longer efficient means of communication. There are exceptions, of course, but, by and large, independent personal websites are doomed to oblivion. Instead of building a personal website likely to become a molecule in an ocean of other such sites, Web 2.0 users actively participate in hugely popular sites. Wikis are built on this principle.

In Web 2.0, a sizeable proportion of netizens engage in behaviours with the *purpose* of letting third parties watch (some of the) activities they engage in, for either exhibitionist pleasure, personal pride or communication. All three motivations are apparent on social networking sites such as MySpace, FaceBook or the newer Widows LiveSpace, where technology is used to create friendship rings among individuals sharing like interests. In order for the concept to work, participants must list their interests, preferences, the place where they live, what they do for a living, their social status, etc. So far it seems to be a success: more than half of all teen netizens have created a personal profile on one or more social networking sites (Pew Internet 2007). The extent to which this creates an entirely new conceptualization of friendship and a new, more streamlined, efficiency- (robot-) driven social life will be debated for years to come. However, MySpace offers an interesting sociological 'site' where individual users can be observed managing their personal information and making choices between what is private and what is not. The most obvious observation is that the position, movability and porosity of the line between private and public are, literally, *infinitely variable* and, consequently, that no codification is possible.

Constructing the commercial cyberspace

Each of the aspects of information exchange listed above involves a specific conception of individual agency and purposes online. Cyberspace appears as a space of consumption, where individuals are eager to exchange various forms of payment for various goods, services and information. In that structure, personal information, including personal data (such as occupation, gender, credit card numbers, age, etc.) as well as accumulated facts about current behaviour, whereabouts, friends, etc., is property and has a variable exchange value. Privacy has therefore lost its old classical core; it is no longer conceivable in terms of a protected, secret, inner personal space filled with inherently 'private' information – information given an objective quality of intimacy. We have already briefly touched on the multiple rewards offered to those who share information about themselves. In the next section I explore further the matter of context and what we might call 'flexible space'.

Flexible space

Personal information modifies the structure, content and interactions possible in the cyberworld. This has little impact on those of us who read emails once a week or find phone numbers on Internet listings. However, there is a minority, and a growing one, of citizens who spend increasing amounts of their time on web-mediated activities of infinite forms. In these cases, we might categorize the reality-altering effects of the information exchange under two main headings.

Reflexive space

We might consider, for the moment, that the most advanced form of flexible space is what visitors will find at Linden Lab's Second Life (another is Makena Technology's There). Currently this is the most technologically advanced form of social networking, where users move through space as disincarnate floating points of view, presenting themselves to others as 'avatars' modified to their fancy. This form of cyberworld existence and interaction is quite familiar to those who have played computer or console third-person games. Yet two differences are immediately evident. First, the world is a continuous creation of other inhabitants – it is Web 2.0 at its current maximum. Secondly, the main object of the experience is communication and other forms of interaction with others – though, of course, few present themselves in Second Life as realistic facsimiles of their 'true self' (let us forget for a moment the sociological Gordian knot hidden behind this concept). Of course, online or local multiplayer games have had this type of social interaction feature for years, especially role-playing games. Many also allowed players to build their own 'maps' where capture-the-flag or 'deathmatch' games could take place. Yet Second Life, though derived from those concepts and technologies, is explicitly geared towards recreating a realistic, *ordinary* world where only some well circumscribed flights of fancy may take place. Deviance, crime, the misuse of software, the harassment of other citizens, etc. are punished and noted in the daily 'police blotter' on the main site (Second Life 2007; for more on crime in Second Life, see Chapter 6, this volume). Of course, one of the most important aspect of life in Second Life is continuous, microscopic surveillance and the collection of all and any information generated by actions taken by visitors.

One area where Second Life connects to physical space is money. The cyberworld's economy is booming, and the local currency ('Linden dollars') may be exchanged for any other currency – and all gains are tax free. The border between Second Life and 'real' life is clearly visible but effortlessly crossed. Continuing advances in technology will no doubt tend towards the greater integration of cyberspace with physical space. Neural activity sensors (see http://www.emotiv.com/2_0/2_1.htm) and semi-transparent eyeglasses will permit seamless integration and interaction with both the physically present and the 'avatars' (some of which will be machines) and other cyber-objects, in what is referred to as 'augmented reality'.

Augmented reality is not quite around the corner, and examples of flexible space that can be found today are less spectacular. However, they do offer a glimpse into the future, especially the evolution of such concepts as privacy and personal information. For the time being, paying sponsors can already update the way various objects look in game cyberworlds, whether the game is played on a remote server or on the user's own computer or game console. Limited at first to putting advertising hoardings in the environment, they can now remodel any cyberworld object: the phone one uses in the game, the car one drives, the medication one takes, the clothes characters wear, etc.

Though immersive 3D applications are obvious examples of flexible worlds, more prosaic examples abound. Common cyberspace individualization, from the consumer's point of view, appears as an individualized, private, personal relationship with the organization using the collected information.

Dynamic web-page structure allows a near-infinite variety in form and content, based on information collected from multiple sources. Examples include the following:

- Personalized advertisements in boxes and banners and inserts inside personal documents such as email (Hotmail, Acrobat Reader, Google toolbars, etc.) are placed by 'free' software packages. Portals offering 'free' email, such as Yahoo and Google, also put advertisements on their user interface, based on a content anaylsis of received and sent mail. The consumer accepts that the presence of such advertising is innocuous, since it does not represent a 'cost'. In some cases the advertisements divert allocated bandwidth or slow computer performance, but their cost is still seen as zero since no money is demanded.

- Advertisements disguised as 'suggestions' included in many media players, which automatically update links to Internet radio stations, news, entertainment or newly released products from the music/film industry. Users are encouraged to click on 'now playing' buttons and to explore commercial content.

- Icons and links to their and other commercial websites, placed on the user's desktop, in addition to Windows' 'start' menu items and browser 'favorites' or 'bookmarks' by almost all software packages.

- 'Personalized' services (My Yahoo, etc.) based on information given or collected during users' activities on the website (as well as on 'partner' sites).

- Banner ads, pop-up windows, interstitials (e.g. Unicast's Superstitial; Unicast 2007), 'gatekeeper' ads and multiple attempts to redirect users during normal web browsing, some with a fake user interface.

- 'Adware' – software especially designed to serve its distributor's clients' adverts on users' desktops. These include Aureate/Radiate, AdBreak, AdReady, Alexa, Comet Cursor, Cydoor, Doubleclick, DSSAgent, EverAd, eZula, Expedioware, Flyswat, HomePageWare,

SEBar, OfferCompanion, Hotbar, OnFlow, TimeSink, Web3000, Webhancer, Transponder, Wnad, ZapSpot, SurfPlus, AdvertBar, NetPal, CashBar, WurldMediaBHO, MessageMates, EWA, Ezsearchbar, CommonName, GoHip, DownloadWare, NetworkEssentials, ImiServerIEPlugin, TopMoxie, Lop.Com, BDE Projector, UCmore, OpenMe, JaypeeSysBHo, FlashTrack, NetRadar, NetZany, NetSource, NowBox, TrustToolBar, WinAd, Kontiki, 7faSSt Search and iWonCopilot.

First (and often still) thought of as nuisances, these various strategies of cyberspace customization are evolving into highly sophisticated, seamless and, more importantly, *useful* and *enjoyable* adjuncts to everyday computer use. Most computer users do not mind advertising – in fact, some of the most accessed content on YouTube consists of uploaded television commercials. Most people do not hesitate to give out personal information if privileges or other rewards are offered, or even if they are not (in the case of surveys, for instance).

Flexible space, in turn, enables behaviour modification and further data collection. The choices made by the user constantly refine the available information and allow continuous behavioural analysis. This also creates a world where users are consumers, where an ever-increasing proportion of possible behaviours are commercial relationships. Through the information exchange and flexible space, formerly neutral and/or unpredictable activities (click-throughs, adjusting page preferences, choosing news content and the like) can be transformed into revenue-generating behaviours. Status, identity and habits can become inter-corporation sellable *products;* as with mass media, the final product is not content but *audience* (or readership). Personal information is at the centre of this structure and therefore acquires a corresponding commercial value.

Secure space

One extremely important aspect of consumer-constructed flexible space is personal, familial and general security. Four levels of protection behaviours can be identified. At the basic level, individuals may feel various degrees of personal responsibility for their own security in cyberspace, such as using adequate passwords, not leaving passwords on a sticky note on one's monitor frame or in a non-encrypted text file (with the name, 'mypasswords.doc'), being aware of the identity of those asking for personal information, having working and up-to-date anti-virus, anti-spyware and firewall applications, securing personal, wireless local-area networks, etc.

At the second level, individuals may also recognize a collective responsibility as members of a variety of social groups: one's family, one's workgroup on a LAN or contacts on a mailing list, for example. This responsibility involves watching not only one's personal behaviour but also that of others. Family members may also need protection from web content or from ill-intentioned individuals. Many forms of techno-fixes exist to replace actual physical presence, such as filters blocking offensive or pornographic content (the extent to which such filters actually work is a separate matter). Protection of a workgroup's integrity may involve the control of members' activities on the intranet and/or internet. Logging software may be required, possibly accompanied by the automated analysis of logging practices (time of day, duration, frequency, etc.).

At the third level, most of us are part of a number of private networks where varying degrees of administrative, corporate or professional surveillance and control are applied (in most cases, work environments). We are asked at the same time to use provided IT resources within set limits and to report those who do not.

Finally, we are also part of a traditionally public security environment, where official, state institutions are deployed. We are officially forbidden from taking part in a (growing) number of activities online and, consequently (perhaps in return), we expect to be protected against crime. As the state is bound by traditional borders, its relevance in cyberspace is questionable. However, a number of sovereignty-affirming strategies have started to appear. Those dealing with heinous crimes are particularly well received by the public, who in general view state action as the only proper response to such deviance. New laws imposing data retention on ISPs and heightened interception capacity by intelligence agencies (the National Security Agency (NSA) has collected 2 *trillion* phone-connection records since 2002) are part of the new strategies. In Canada, the multiplication of interceptions by the Communications Security Establishment (CSE), NSA's counterpart, has raised extremely few eyebrows (CSE Commissioner 2006, 2007).

Individuals are warned of the risks of identity theft, of the misuse of valuable information, of the illegitimate use of their computer and of defamation. Very little can be done to prevent the last eventuality. The first three, however, have become the centre of a flourishing personal cybersecurity industry. Many manufacturers now offer plug-and-play USB biometric readers intended to replace all passwords. The average laptop has a built-in fingerprint reader. Anti-virus, firewall, and anti-spyware packages are also for sale or are pre-installed on new computers (some in the form of 'trial versions'). Most require a lifetime of subscriptions to the necessary updates. This security world functions much in the way traditional, meat-space private security does: it must first sell risk as a series of threats in order to sell risk management solutions. The presence of hackers, criminals, organized crime, foreign criminal organizations and other enemies is continuously used to convince 'law abiding' netizens to adopt more secure behaviours (for one example, see Symantec's 'Cybercrime stories' and 'Sandra's story' at Symantec 2007).

Of course, individuals are not only potential cyber victims but also cyber criminals. Anyone can violate copyright online by using copied software, images, information, music, video, etc., outside explicitly permitted limits. A growing number of these actions are officially labelled as crimes by western countries (Leman-Langlois 2005, 2006). Netizens are encouraged to police their own behaviour; they are targeted by 'education' campaigns devised by legal rights owners and their representatives – the Recording Industry Association of America (RIAA) in the USA, the Canadian Recording Industry Association (CRIA) in Canada, the British Phonograph Industry (BPI) in the UK and the Australian Recording Industry Association (ARIA) in Australia (e.g. BPI 2007; CRIA 2007). The ARIA (http://www.aria.com.au/) has a website devoted to 'Music industry piracy investigations': 'MIPI conducts investigative, preventative and educational activities in relation to music piracy in Australia' (http://www.mipi.com.au). Visitors are encouraged to take the 'Am I a pirate?' test, in order to make sure they are using music files appropriately – simply having paid for them being no guarantee (MIPI 2007). The CRIA warns that p2p users are not only victimizing music industry professionals but also putting themselves at risk of multiple forms of victimization: Trojan horses, malicious code, pornography distributed to their children and many other frightening possibilities (CRIA 2007).

If education fails, civil suits and criminal prosecution may ensue (as of August 2007, the RIAA had sued 18,000 individuals; see FoxNews 2007). Criminal prosecution is also increasingly likely, with stricter laws and demands for more proactive law enforcement practices (in the first half of 2007, the USA had criminalized 'attempts' at copyright infringements and Canada had done the same for the mere in-theatre recording of motion pictures).

The cyberspace behaviour of individuals who are responsible for others is further controlled through other forms of risk. For employees, there is the risk of data theft by hackers or spies; for parents, there are risks that their children could be exposed to child pornography or fall prey to Internet luring. Canada has a site devoted to cyberthreats against children at Cyberwise.ca. Cyberwise offers advice to parents, professionals, teachers, etc., as well as guides to increasing safety through 'true stories' of cyberhorror (one document is titled, 'Thousands of paedophiles on the net'; Cyberwise 2007). This is standard risk/neoliberal 'conduct of conduct' (Rose 2000: 325–7), where behaviour is controlled not through the threat of punishment but with mere 'information' about risks (O'Malley illustrates this point with control strategies aimed at drug users; 2004: 331).

Interestingly, Cyberwise is operated by Industry Canada through its Strategis portal 'Canada's business and consumer site'; see http://strategis.ic.gc.ca/, a remarkably apt illustration of the main points of this chapter – that control of behaviour in cyberspace is largely structured by the necessities of commerce.

Conclusion: information, surveillance and crime

We find ourselves at the juncture of a number of fascinating trends, some cultural, some geopolitical, some technological that, taken together, create a contingent context where privacy and personal information are being fundamentally redefined. It has become too late to argue for (or against) privacy in terms of secrecy of information, private life, anonymity – or in terms of the surveillants and the surveilled. These concepts assume that holders of information are reticent to share it, that surveillance is not consensual, that the targets, agents and beneficiaries of surveillance are always the same. More importantly, it will become progressively less useful to think of privacy as an intrinsic facet of one's inner sanctum. Projected outwards, personal information can be reflected back to the individual – as well as to others – as a customized, personalized world where life seems better. For now, this applies best to more exotic forms of virtuality, but current developments point towards the increasing integration of the cyber and the physical.

In this context, it is likely that forms of deviance involving the unauthorized use of personal information, if they do not interfere with commercial exchanges (as does the subversion of payment schemes), will gradually lose what little importance they have. Though valuable when part of an aggregate, the personal information of any individual is nearly worthless on its own. On the contrary, deviance from the rules set for the consumption of commercial content (such as copy and distribution rules) is bound to become a priority for criminalization.

As for the way we will treat the deviants, one aspect of the matter is fundamental. Beck's nuclear plants represented a risk because of the colossal power they harnessed. Cyberspace risks, on the contrary, are always presented as the work of ill-intentioned individuals or small organized groups. Cyberspace itself is never a threat; it is a neutral, cold, technological environment where boundless human desires can be satisfied. In short, cyberspace risks are not technological, they are criminal. Consequently, those most likely to be criminalized are individuals who misuse commercial information content. At the opposite end, those having the least to fear from the state's ability to criminalize are the corporate content producers and distributors – those who 'make' the commercial cyberspace.

So the state may be displaced from the centre, but it is never far. Furthermore, whether it is held by state agents or by others, most of the behaviour control power still radiates from the few towards the many. Though flexible space provides benefits to netizens, any transformation of reality within their power is strictly local, individual.

Under this new incarnation of 'privacy', can the old metaphor of the panopticon still be of use? Bentham's well-known design for the ideal prison was to be built as a circle of cells opening on a central surveillance tower. To provide an idea of constant surveillance despite the sensory limits of human wardens, the windows of the tower were to be darkened by curtains, hiding the occupants. Clearly, the central tower of surveillance, from which hidden guards watch a captive and atomized population, is no longer an entirely adequate representation of today's world of ubiquitous surveillance technology. Other aspects of the model, however, seem more durable.

First, the rediscovered problem of data concentration (now reborn in new laws being enacted by many countries that require data retention by communication service providers or that grant the police access to various private databases) shows that the state has not entirely given up its power to access and use information about citizens. It may, instead, simply be retiring from the business of database production and management. (In one interesting development, the US Federal Bureau of Investigation has offered to compensate ISPs for data retention costs; Washington Post 2007.)

Secondly, if panopticism can no longer be used to describe the structure of surveillance of entire societies, it remains a powerful model for local activity and analysis. For instance, in previous work (Leman-Langlois 2003) I have used a variation of the panopticon trope to account for the limited adoption of CCTV by police organizations in Canada. One common misunderstanding of the panopticon image stems from a confusion of the concept with reality, or the rationale with the results. When Foucault argued that society is *disciplinary*, he meant that modes of behaviour control have changed, not that individual subjects are actually more 'disciplined' – more respectful of rules, less adventurous, etc. Panopticism, in the same way, does not entail *actual* total surveillance and behavioural control through constant visibility. It simply means that controlling deviance is *understood as a problem of visibility* (including the 'visibility' of data traces). It is not surprising, therefore, that another idea of Bentham's was to involve every citizen in the surveillance of all behaviours, multiplying the eyes of the authorities (quite like the 'Bullywatch London' project; bullywatchlondon.org).

Thirdly, behaviour modification is still the ultimate goal of surveillance. The flexible space created as a reflection of personal information aims at creating proper, 'docile' cyberconsumers. The docile cyberconsumer refrains from deviant behaviours, helps the authorities find deviants, maximizes expenses online, responds positively to the customized advertising they experience, constantly gives more information about themselves in order to get more products, more advertising and so on.

Fourthly, one of the main arguments of this chapter has been that surveillance is becoming radically diffused. It is now accomplished by infinitely varied actors, for infinitely varied purposes; it is directed at infinitely varied targets, for infinitely diverse beneficiaries. While the state has been the traditional focus of attention, surveillance is now more continuous, dispersed through multiple spheres of life (home, work, leisure, but also simply walking one's dog). In physical reality, one's activities may be recorded by the state, of course, but also by one's condo association, one's neighbour, one's employer, entities located around the world, one's clients, one's service providers, etc. In cyberspace, the capabilities for surveillance and for the communication, analysis and use of knowledge are limitless. The panopticon's potential (realized or not) to see everything is still an important aspect of all forms of technosurveillance.

Of course, with the distribution of surveillance come two other phenomena: counter-surveillance and resistance. As Brin (Chapter 2, this volume) points out, surveilling those who surveil us may produce a checks-and-balances effect. However, one must take into account that organized surveillance is more constant, more structured and more powerful than what individuals can ever hope to achieve, even if they dedicated their entire working time to the task (Marx

2006), and even if their target was as easy to watch as they are. It seems illusory to expect individual, or even collective powers of surveillance – if they could in fact be harnessed, organized and targeted – to equate to that of specialized entities. Furthermore, the current reality is that individual surveillance is more concerned with individual targets: people love to spy on other people, for fun (YouTube), for security (NetNanny, webcams aimed at child or elderly care givers) and for profit (information sold to media organizations). Finally, counter-surveillance assumes that individuals actually feel a need for counter-surveillance; in reality, as we have seen above, the collection, analysis and use of personal information are becoming a voluntary, appreciated and beneficial activity in which they are happy to co-operate.

Resistance to surveillance is more interesting. Dupont (forthcoming) lists two main forms of resistance: information encryption and voluntary anonymity. Though relatively easy to acquire and to use, the tools necessary to resist surveillance in this way are, in fact, almost unheard of by the vast majority of netizens – in short, they do not 'exist', and the mere potential to resist is not, in itself, resistance. A great number of individual surfers do use fake names when registering on websites or give non-existing email addresses to defeat some of the annoyances of the web, particularly the tendency of many organizations to 'spam' their email lists. However, as we have already seen, this strategy is nonsensical in a growing number of areas where defeating the system voids any possible benefit that participation might have produced. In other cases, resistance or refusal to comply with data collection implies a series of real and/or perceived costs to the individual: penal cost for non-compliance with legal rules, risk increases for disregarding security protocols, financial costs for non-compliance with marketing schemes (loss of benefits, loss of access to lower prices, etc.), convenience and productivity costs for non-compliance with identification systems (for example, when turning off 'cookies' in one's browser).

This new world of privacy will have interesting implications for those who study technocrime. New possibilities for behaviour, criminalization, enforcement, private justice, market regulation, consumer discipline and many others, all occurring in an equally new, and constantly renewed, environment. The impact on theories based on opportunities, social capital, social learning etc., will have to be analysed. I suspect that the theoretical bases for criminology will need fundamental revision.

References

Alford, J. (2002) 'Defining the client in the public sector: a social-exchange perspective', *Public Administration Review*, 62: 337–46.

Ars Technica (2007) 'Attempted infringement appears in new House Intellectual Property Bill' (http://arstechnica.com/news.ars/post/20070730-attempted-infringmen-tappearsin-new-house-intellectual-property-bill.html).

Baudrillard, J.(1970) *La Société de consommation: ses mythes, ses structures*. Paris: Denoël.

Beck, U. (1992) *Risk Society: Towards a New Modernity*. London: Sage.

British Phonographic Industry (BPI) *Illegal Filesharing Fact Sheet* (http://www.bpi.co.uk/pdf/Illegal_Filesharing_Factsheet.pdf).

Brodeur, J.-P. and Stéphane Leman-Langlois, S. (2006) 'Surveillance-fiction: high and low policing revisited', in K. Haggerty and R. Ericson (eds) *The New Politics of Surveillance and Visibility*. Toronto: University of Toronto Press.

Canadian Recording Industry Association (CRIA) (2007) *Facts about File Sharing* (http://www.cria.ca/filesharing.php).

Communications Security Establishment Commissioner (2006) *Annual Report 2005–2006* (http://csec-ccst.gc.ca/ann-rpt/2005-2006/index_e.php).

Communications Security Establishment Commissioner (2007) *Annual Report 2006–2007* (http://csec-ccst.gc.ca/ann-rpt/2006-2007/index_e.php).

Conference Board (2005) *Identity Theft and Online Security Worries are Causing Changes in how People use the Internet* (http://www.conferenceboard.org/utilities/pressDetails.cfm?press_ID=2663).

Cyberwise (2007) *Des internautes pédophiles par milliers* (http://strategis.ic.gc.ca/epic/site/cybp-cybpa.nsf/vwapj/Article%2021%20-%20Des%20internautes%20pédophiles%20par%20millier.pdf/$FILE/Article %2021%20-%20Des%20internautes%20pédophiles%20par%20millier.pdf).

Dupont, B. (forthcoming) 'Hacking the panopticon: distributed online surveillance and resistance', in M. Deflem (ed.) *Sociology of Crime, Law and Deviance. Vol. 10. Surveillance and Governance*. Oxford: Elsevier.

Etzioni, E. (1999) *The Limits of Privacy*. New York, NY: Basic Books.

Feeley, M. and Simon, J. (1992) 'The new penology: notes on the emerging strategy of corrections and its implications', *Criminology*, 30: 449–74.

Fischer, H. (2006) *Digital Shock*. Montreal: McGill-Queen's University Press.

Foucault, M. (1975) *Surveiller et punir, naissance de la prison*. Paris: Gallimard.

FoxNews (2007) 'Record industry demands $3,000 from 50 Ohio university students' (http://www.foxnews.com/story/0,2933,258041,00.html).

Garland, D. (2001) *The Culture of Control*. Chicago, IL: University of Chicago Press.

Garnham, N. (2000) ' "Information society" as theory or ideology: a critical perspective in technology, education and employment in the information age', *Information, Communication and Society*, 3: 139–52.

Haggerty, K. (2006) 'Tear down the walls: on demolishing the panopticon', in D. Lyon (ed.) *Theorizing Surveillance: The Panopticon and Beyond.* Cullompton: Willan Publishing.

Leman-Langlois, S. (2003) 'The myopic panopticon: the social consequences of policing through the lens', *Policing and Society*, 13: 43–58 (reprinted in Kappeler, V. (ed.) (2006) *The Police and Society: Touchstone Readings* (3rd edn). Long Grove, IL: Waveland Press.

Leman-Langlois, S. (2005) 'Theft in the information age : music, technology, crime and claims-making', *Knowledge, Technology and Policy*, 17: 140–63.

Leman-Langlois, S. (2006), 'Le crime comme moyen de contrôle du cyberespace commercial', *Criminologie*, 39: 63–81.

Leman-Langlois, S. and J.-P. Brodeur (2005), 'Les technologies de l'identification,' *Revue internationale de criminologie et de police technique et scientifique*, 58: 69–82.

Lessig, L. (2002) 'Privacy as property', *Social Research*, 69: 247–69.

Los, M. (2006) 'Looking into the future: surveillance, globalization and the totalitarian potential', in D. Lyon (ed.) *Theorizing Surveillance: The Panopticon and Beyond.* Cullompton: Willan Publishing.

Loyalty Group (2007) 'Full privacy comment' (https://www.airmiles.ca/arrow/login/FullPrivacyCommitment).

Lyon, D. (2006) 'The search for surveillance theories', in D. Lyon (ed.) *Theorizing Surveillance: The Panopticon and Beyond.* Cullompton: Willan Publishing.

Mathiesen, T. (1997) ' The viewer society : Michel Foucault's "panopticon" revisited', *Theoretical Criminology*, 1: 215–34.

Mattelart, A. (2001) *Histoire de la société de l'information.* Paris: La Découverte.

Marx, G. (2006) 'Mots et mondes de surveillance, contrôle et contre-contrôle à l'ère informatique', *Criminologie*, 39: 43–62.

Music Industry Piracy Investigations (MIPI) (2007) *Am I a Pirate? Some Common Questions and Answers* (http://www.mipi.com.au/amiapirate.htm).

O'Malley, P. (ed.) (1998) *Crime and the Risk Society.* Aldershot: Ashgate.

O'Malley, P. (2004) 'The uncertain promise of risk', *Australian and New Zealand Journal of Criminology*, 37: 323–43.

Pew Internet (2000) *Trust and Privacy Online: Why Americans Want to Rewrite the Rules* (http://www.pewinternet.org/PPF/r/19/report_display.asp).

Pew Internet (2007) *Social Networking Websites and Teens: An Overview* (http://www.pewinternet.org/PPF/r/198/report_display.asp).

Register (2007) 'MySpace erases 29,000 sex offenders' (http://www.theregister.co.uk/2007/07/25/myspace_erases_offenders/).

Rose, N. (2000) 'Government and control', *British Journal of Criminology*, 40: 321–39.

Second Life (2007) 'Police blotter' (http://secure-web11.secondlife.com/community/blotter.php).

SecuritySpace (2007) *Internet Cookie Report* (http://www.securityspace.com/ s_survey/data/man.200707/cookieReport.html).

Symantec (2007) *Cybercrime Stories,* (http://www.symantec.com/avcenter/ cybercrime/index_page4.html).

Unicast (2007) *Unicast Online Ad Display Systems* (http://www.unicast.com/ how-we-do-it/unicast-ad-display-systems.shtml).

Washington Post (2007) 'FBI seeks to pay telecoms for data,' (http://www. washingtonpost.com/wp-dyn/content/article/2007/07/24/ AR2007072402479_pf.html).

Whitaker, R. (1999) *The End of Privacy: How Total Surveillance is Becoming a Reality.* New York, NY: New Press.

Wood, J. (2004) 'Cultural change in the governance of security', *Policing and Society,* 14: 31–48.

Chapter 8

Information technology and criminal intelligence: a comparative perspective

Frédéric Lemieux

Introduction

During the past 30 years, law enforcement agencies have acquired a vast array of information technologies designed to help them perform their mission to prevent crime. This growing use of sophisticated analytical and investigative technologies points to an important trend, particularly visible in USA since the 1980s. In the USA and elsewhere, the increase in the exploitation of available technologies is, to a large extent, the result of heavy support from federal government initiatives. According to a report published by the RAND Corporation (Schwabe *et al.* 2001), the US federal government has invested billions of dollars to promote the use of IT by police forces. Consequently, a number of agencies specializing in the research and development of technology for law enforcement and corrections were created. These initiatives were launched to circumvent three problems faced by US local and regional law-enforcement services: 1) poor needs assessment capabilities; 2) poor in-house technology development capabilities; and 3) a lack of resources for the procurement of new technologies (Schwabe *et al.* 2001: 116–17).

The 1990s were a decisive decade for the development and deployment of IT across the US criminal justice system, especially in the law enforcement sector. For example, the war on drugs contributed to the establishment of the Counter-drug Technology Assessment Center (CTAC), created to develop new systems for federal, state and local police forces. Further, this period was also marked by a significant phenomenon that Haggerty and Ericson (2001) described as a transfer of technologies from the military sphere to the police apparatus. The so-called 'Military techno-structures of policing' were sponsored by the National Justice Institute (NIJ) and the Department of Defense and their Joint Program Steering Group, which was created to adapt military technologies for use in law enforcement (including surveillance technologies, information systems, etc.; see US Government 1994). During the same period, Congress added more funds for the Office of Community Oriented Policing Service's 'Making officers redeployment effective' programme to encourage the introduction of crime-mapping systems and information management technologies into law enforcement practices (USDoJ 2006).

Just before 9/11, the NIJ and US Department of Justice appropriated 130 million US dollars for the Crime Identification Technology Act 1998 to assist police agencies in the enhancement of their information systems and forensic science capabilities.[1] The Crime Identification Technology Act authorized 250 million US dollars per year for assistance to states over a period of five years for a broad range of crime technology activities. The Act provided support for system integration in criminal justice processes to help states develop and upgrade their anti-crime technology from the patchwork of existing programmes, to integrate law enforcement and public safety records and communications, and to facilitate the interface of national criminal information and public safety databases.

Despite these massive investments in the development of IT for law enforcement agencies, statistics on the actual use of crime data for either analytical purposes or commandment review remain few. In fact, as Mamalian and LaVigne (1999) suggested in their 1997–8 study, only 13 per cent of police departments made use of computerized crime mapping. According to a RAND survey 23 per cent of local departments use some crime mapping and analysis for command review and operational planning. The report also shows that the formalization (and, presumably, computerization) of command review and operational planning increases with the size of the population served by the department (Schwabe et al. 2001). Furthermore, although the calculation of basic crime statistics is an important part of these analyses, their application to operational police work remains relatively limited.

After the 2001 terrorist attacks, investments in IT shifted drastically, as more funds were appropriated to the improvement of the computer systems of many federal agencies, to the development of intelligent pattern-recognition systems and to the recruitment of analysts and translators. According to a report published by the

Governmental Accounting Office (2004), data mining is increasingly seen as a useful tool to help detect terrorist threats as it enhances the collection processes and the analysis of public and private sector data. The report suggests that agencies may use such data not only for investigations of known terrorists but also to perform large-scale data analysis and pattern discovery in order to detect potential terrorist activity by unknown individuals.[2]

One example of a large-scale development effort launched after the terrorist attacks is the Multi-state Anti-terrorism Information Exchange System, known as MATRIX. This system, used by five states, had the capability to store, analyse and exchange sensitive terrorism-related and other criminal intelligence data among agencies within a state, between states, and between state and federal agencies (see Markle Foundation 2003). The MATRIX programme was shut down in June 2005 after federal funding was cut in the wake of public concerns over privacy and state surveillance. The programme was similar to the Total Information Awareness (later renamed as Terrorism Information Awareness – TIA) programme, a federally funded initiative at the Defense Advanced Research Projects Agency (DARPA), which was also terminated following public concern (Brodeur and Leman-Langlois 2006). Driven by advances in computing and data storage capabilities, by the growth of the volume and the availability of information collected by the public and private sectors, data mining enables government agencies to analyse extremely large quantities of data.

The federal government is deeply involved in the development of IT for law enforcement agencies. However, according to a study published by Garicano and Heaton (2006), even though IT adoption has had significant effects on a wide range of police organizational practices, its anti-crime impact is negligible. This finding is in accord with Manning's (2003) work about the effectiveness of crime-mapping technologies in reducing crime. Despite these results, police agencies continue to purchase and implement expensive computer and information network systems. This chapter attempts to explain this paradox. It begins with a summary of key police organizational doctrines and new trends in policing in the last 10–15 years. It then explores the actual implementation and integration of technology in various criminal intelligence outfits worldwide. This discussion is divided into the 'hard' technologies of databases and communications networks and the 'soft' technologies that support data analysis. Finally, I consider the possibility that the rising police management doctrine – intelligence-led policing (ILP) – encourages the use of technologies because of its intrinsic logic, which sees crime as crime patterns and which defines crime fighting as a matter of discovering those crime patterns through information processing.

Police management doctrine and IT

Over the past decades, police agencies have invested heavily in information and data-mining technologies in order to increase operational effectiveness. This technological arsenal has given the police the potential to access and analyse information from social and criminal environments. The claims made for IT and its use by law enforcement agencies could be subsumed under two types of rationality. Under the first one, requests and justifications for funding computer and communication technologies were based on efficiency principles. Police agencies argued that their response rate to citizens' emergency calls, their ability to allocate resources according to adequate prioritization and their crime reduction results would all be improved by the exploitation of IT (Larson 1989; Manning 1992). The second type of rationality is a response to cultural and political pressures. Faced with criticism, many police agencies have developed a doctrine of aggressive proaction, where police work was to be enhanced by the effective co-ordination of crime-fighting operations and the more efficient allocation of resources (Crawford 1997).

Proactive policing models have surfaced during the past decades and have changed how the police control crime and organize their operations by relying on analytical technologies. Both the 'community-oriented policing' (COP) and the 'problem-oriented policing' (POP) models are fundamentally oriented towards information gathering inside communities, including crime pattern analysis (crime mapping) and smarter strategies for resource deployment (Goldstein 1990; Scott 2000; Braga 2002). The two models were meant to enhance police decision-making when designing crime prevention programmes and operational strategies. However, the impacts on crime reduction are far from obvious and have become the subject of scholarly debates (Manning 2003; Garicano and Heaton 2006).

More recently, several law enforcement agencies have adopted ILP – a British police model based on a doctrine heavily influenced by a corporate and commercial vision in which police organizations adopt a 'client-centred approach' by targeting serious crimes and repeat offenders. ILP implementation therefore requires another weapon in the police arsenal: crime-targeting analysis. The adoption of this model therefore increases the use of analytical and investigative technologies that process and organize police information in order to 1) support decisions and resource deployment; 2) co-ordinate police action across various areas of jurisdiction; and 3) ensure continuous learning via feedback on operational results (John and Maguire 2003).

The intelligence production process used by police organizations is essentially based on that employed in the military and security intelligence community (Morehouse 2000). Although the works of Godfrey and Harris (1971) and Harris (1976) introduced police departments to the fundamentals of the cyclical intelligence-production process, for a long time it remained closer to rhetoric than actual application (Maguire 2000: 316; Norris and Dunnigan 2000; Ratcliffe 2002: 51; Tilley 2003: 334). In the 1990s, criminal intelligence activities spread to English-speaking and various European countries, and several police organizations started to integrate the key terminology and concepts related to this process (Gottlieb *et al.* 1994). However, dissemination of the ILP model did not proceed in an integrated or systematic fashion. Although the reasons invoked for change – mostly related to the efficiency of police activities – were the same for the vast majority of police departments, the actual application of the model was essentially piecemeal and heavy adaptations were imposed. The diversity of legal constraints, jurisdictional parameters, organizational cultures and criminal problems resulted in a wide array of different standards and practices.

Under this model, police intelligence work focuses on information about criminal phenomena and law-breaking individuals or groups. This information is stored in databases and is used in investigations, profiling analysis, threat analysis, operation planning, crime trends and crime mapping (Ouimet 1995). Knowledge generated by these analytical techniques makes it possible to envision the actuarial management of crime. Just as the penal system in the 1990s developed the analytical capability to predict repeat offending and crime risks (Marx 1988; Ericson and Haggerty 1997), police departments are now able to produce prospective analyses on emerging criminal trends. Threat and risk assessments have now become part of the vocabulary and activities of the police through their criminal intelligence units (Maguire 2000). This has drastically modified the role of the police, with analysts and rank officers now required to be more knowledgeable about crime patterns, crime distribution and effective crime-reduction operations (see Ericson and Haggerty 1997; Brodeur and Dupont 2006 for the concept of 'knowledge workers').

Although the crossover of information gathered by public and private agencies continues to be governed by a legislative framework dictated by privacy protection requirements (Klosek 2000), normative frameworks have significantly expanded in recent years (Brodeur *et al.* 2003). Mining government and private databases containing nominal information creates a range of privacy concerns. These include concerns about the quality and accuracy of the mined data; the use of the data for purposes other than for why the data were originally collected, without the individual's consent; the protection of the data against unauthorized access, modification or disclosure; and individuals' right to know about the collection of personal information, how to access that information and how to request a correction of inaccurate information (Taipale 2003).

The following section describes the deployment and use of IT by some law enforcement agencies around the world. These findings are a part of an international comparative analysis conducted in 2004–5 (Lemieux 2006). The sampling used in this research was based on the organizations' reputations and their extensive criminal intelligence experience. Selection was based on various criteria, such as the age and size of the organization, its resources, its jurisdiction (local, regional, national and supranational) and the type of criminal activity targeted. The sample was further diversified by including organizations located in non-western countries (Asia and Latin America).

Criminal intelligence services and IT: a cross-cultural comparison

For the purpose of this research, the following 12 police organizations were visited: 1) the British National Criminal Intelligence Service[3] (NCIS-UK); 2) the Australian Crime Commission (ACC); 3) the Federal Police in Belgium; 4) the Royal Canadian Mounted Police (RCMP); 5) Europol; 6) Interpol; 7) the Singapore Police Force; 8) the Cantonal Police of Geneva (Switzerland); 9) the Cantonal Police of Vaud (Switzerland); 10) the Police and Customs Co-operation Centre (Switzerland–France); 11) the Columbian Departemento Administrativo de Securidad (DAS); and 12) the National Police of Columbia. The data are based on 76 semi-structured interviews with analysts and managers from those criminal intelligence services. This section focuses on two aspects of the criminal intelligence process: criminal data warehousing and mining, and analytical methods and technologies.

UK

The National Criminal Intelligence Service (NCIS) was set up as a separate body in April 1992 in order to centralize the gathering and distribution of intelligence on serious and organized crime. The NCIS provided intelligence backup to other agencies such as the National Crime Squad and prioritized matters related to drug and firearms trafficking, financial crime, illegal immigration and organized crime. Internationally, the NCIS liaised with Interpol and Europol and other international law-enforcement networks. The NCIS was also in charge of the flagging system and of the development of the NCIS Alert database, along with several other national police databases, including the Elementary Information System. This system holds the national data collection on serious and organized criminals and their activities. The Elementary database provides automatic link generation, which builds complex relationships across documents and police records while simultaneously organizing, grading and qualifying information to help prevent duplication problems in analysis.

The NCIS also developed a database (Diamond) containing information on drug seizures and itineraries (both at the national and international levels). To sustain this database, the NCIS obtains seizure-related details from police organizations on a regular basis. One of its intelligence products is a series of estimates of the availability of drugs on the domestic market. This type of assessment, however, is unreliable, for three reasons. First, many seizures are simply not recorded by police agencies. Secondly, more sophisticated techniques, such as purity analysis, chemical properties analysis and sale prices, are rarely used because of their high cost. Furthermore, under the British legal system the prosecution need only provide evidence regarding the true nature of the substances seized (cocaine, heroin, etc.). This makes more sophisticated analyses unnecessary from a judicial point of view, which reduces the amount of drug-related information available to police analysts. Finally, since the NCIS has no power to enforce the law, it has some difficulty monitoring and evaluating the impact of police operations on the availability of drugs on the domestic market. In the autumn of 2004, the Home Office completed a study of the relevance of including information on the purity, chemical properties and sale prices of drugs in the intelligence process and assessments (forensic intelligence analysis). In cases where information is available, the results suggest that police agencies often do not include it in their investigations because it is not always allowed in court.

In past years, NCIS developed several flagging methods to identify suspicious activity in police databases, including financial disclosure reports. These blank reports are available on the Internet and are accompanied by an information sheet containing several indicators for use by financial institutions to identify 'suspicious activities' for which disclosures have to be filed. Once financial institutions have been accredited by the NCIS, they can complete the form directly on the Internet, via a secure portal called money.web. In order to gain more knowledge on money-laundering schemes in the UK, the NCIS developed an automated system (ELMER) that can process a large volume of disclosure reports (over 100,000 during the financial year 2003). The system is meant to conduct profile analyses for given geographic areas, suspicious individuals and high-risk financial institutions (e.g. bureaux de change).

However, three major problems hinder the effectiveness of the NCIS and disclosure reports analysis. First, a large number of financial institutions developed a 'hyper-vigilance syndrome' after the Proceeds of Crime Act was passed in 2002. This resulted in a mountain of disclosure reports with no real foundation, thus clogging up the processing of information.[4] Secondly, several banking institutions were concerned about the security of online forms and opted to mail in hard-copy reports instead. This caused delays in the transmission of information and incurred additional resources for handling the paperwork. Thirdly, although they are provided with a disclosure guide and a list of indicators, financial institutions sometimes make mistakes in recognizing suspicious activities (laundering, the financing of terrorism, etc.), resulting in either the entry of erroneous data or the need for NCIS employees to corroborate reports with banking institutions. This system is currently under review, and recommendations were made by the British government to improve the underperforming IT system, to enhance the training and guidance provided by the Financial Intelligence Unit of SOCA and to increase dialogue between the participants of the 'Suspicious activity reports' scheme.

A Home Office white paper published in April 2007 outlined plans to increase significantly the use of data-mining techniques by police organizations. Provisions in the Serious Crime Bill 2006–7, currently under review by Parliament, will formalize the data-matching practices for fraud detection. It seems reasonable to predict that, in the near future, law enforcement agencies in the UK will be able to mine data far more speculatively, using a wider range of databases (including tax records, private company databases and almost all public or private information sources, except health records).

Australia

The Australian Crime Commission (ACC) began its operations in 2003. Its mission was to improve Australia's ability to meet the threats posed by serious and organized criminal activity. Unlike the NCIS, the ACC has extensive investigative powers (in special circumstances) and can conduct intelligence operations without having to rely on information shared by other police agencies. However, the relative youth of this service and its lack of staff suggest that part of its work consists of networking and of negotiating access to outside information sources. Also in contrast to the NCIS, the ACC does not share staff with other national or regional police services and thus cannot benefit from their information collection capacity.

To optimize the production of criminal intelligence, the ACC created several databases and communication networks.

The Australian Law Enforcement Intelligence Net (ALEIN) is an 'extranet' used by law enforcement and government agencies in Australia and New Zealand. This network makes it possible to disseminate criminal intelligence over a large area (national and international) and constitutes an important exchange medium by making police information available in 'real time'. In 2003–4, over 12,000 users entered almost 23,000 documents into ALEIN for the recording of 78,000 information queries.

The informational capacity of the ACC is dependent on the Australian Criminal Intelligence Database (ACID), which provides access to most police and government agencies involved in crime fighting. ACID is a central database used both as a police information storage system and as an intelligence/factual information dissemination system. However, although ACID was meant to be a central database, few police departments use it as their main information management system – in fact, only police agencies in Queensland and Southern Australia. Preferring to retain the bulk of their data for their in-house systems, most police agencies have instead opted to create automated links with the central system. In 2003–4, there were over 8,000 registered users, who sent more than 125,000 intelligence reports containing the identification of 539,000 criminal entities and generating over 600,000 links. During the same period, users made approximately 736,000 queries in ACID.

In January 2004, the Australian authorities set up the Australian Identity Protection Register (AIPR) to compile information held by law enforcement agencies on authors and victims of identity theft. Within this program, the ACC gathered the information needed to detect and curb the proliferation of false identities. Since June 2004, AIPR has recorded over 4,000 fraudulent identities in Australia.

Lastly, the ACC was involved in developing the Australian Law Enforcement Reference and Targeting (ALERT) system, structured to visualize data contained in information systems in order to identify emerging trends more quickly. This program will also be hooked up to ALEIN and ACID. Feasibility studies are underway to finalize these technological platforms.

Belgium

The Federal Police information management system is the responsibility of the Operational Support Directorate – more specifically, the National Databank Branch. This structure was tasked initially with the research and development of databases and with the provision of support to police departments regarding the use of information systems – with respect to the application of data entry legislation and regulations. The structure has responsibility for managing information for the police community as a whole, including local police agencies. The National Databank Branch also works in co-operation with the Telematics Branch to develop automated systems, methodologies and automation programs aimed at optimizing information processing. It also produces police statistics regarding legal matters, law and order and other activities.

The centralized national general databank (BNG) is a 'global' database that local police departments and branches of the federal police (patrol police and judiciary police) contribute to. It includes several modules that deal with all the information produced by police organizations. The central module contains information on facts and is linked to records concerning offenders, victims, modus operandi, licence plates, bank accounts, phone numbers, etc. The BNG also includes a flagging system used to establish the connections between the entities being investigated by the different police departments. In the short term, the BNG plans to add information concerning corporate bodies (legal businesses) and criminal organizations.

Other modules contain photos of offenders, digitized fingerprints and police controls (linked with the Schengen Information System – SIS). The BNG also provides access to the National Registry, in which all Belgian citizens and residents are registered. The databank, however, does not contain criminal records or any information on convictions. Therefore, despite the vast wealth of data available in the BNG, investigators prefer to use the ViCLAS[5] form to complete their data collection for serial assaults and murders.

It should also be noted that the BNG includes both concrete and non-concrete information – i.e. information related to offences reported to police (statements) and information related to specific research techniques (information reports). To obtain such information, three coding levels are available in the system:

- Level 1: information related to facts.
- Level 2: all the information contained in a statement.
- Level 3: more specific information, such as the type of drug or the route or network associated with the trafficking operation.

The benefit of centralization and the broad coding of information is the standardization of data entry and access to all Belgian police officers. Encoding has made it possible to overcome the language barrier since codes are unique and are translated in a trilingual user manual. However, there are still several problems regarding the quality of codes, especially at the time of entry. Since the 2001 Belgian police reforms, contact with local police departments has not yet been completely restored, which means that information is still not systematically entered into the BNG by all police departments.

Canada

The Royal Canadian Mounted Police (RCMP) has several technological infrastructures for the collection and analysis of data. The RCMP uses the Canadian Police Information Centre (CPIC), an integrated, automated system containing tactical information on crimes and criminals. This system makes it possible to obtain information on specific subjects quickly in order to conduct investigations or to carry out intelligence operations. Many other government enforcement agencies have access to this system, including the Canada Border Services Agency which, for instance, can check if an arrest warrant has been issued for a Canadian citizen crossing the border. The RCMP also systematically uses the National Criminal Data Bank (NCDB). The NCDB contains criminal information provided by investigators. This bank can be used by specialized units to compile or retrieve information in the course of various investigations. All in all, this is a centralized databank managed by the RCMP and used by other police departments.

Like all other members of the Criminal Intelligence Service Canada (CISC), the RCMP also contributes information to the Automated Criminal Intelligence Information System (ACIIS). ACIIS is the CISC-managed national repository of information and intelligence on organized and major crime. All member agencies co-operate with each other in the collection, collation, evaluation, analysis and dissemination of criminal intelligence through the ACIIS network (see http://www. cisc.gc.ca/aciis/aciis_e.htm). Information is collated in the form of summaries and is accessible to member organizations of the CISC.

The RCMP has replaced its Integrated Police Information Reporting System (IPIRS) with the Police Reporting and Occurrence System (PROS). PROS allows users to query detailed information on events and makes it easier to document, manage, query and exchange information contained in police records. The system is adaptive, which allows for the easy integration of new technology in order to keep pace with the needs of police departments. The first version of PROS was implemented in 2004, and the system has been operational since March 2006. According to the RCMP, PROS is a key component of the Integrated Justice Information (IJI) initiative, whose objectives are to improve the exchange of information and the integration of the IT infrastructure of the justice system. It is also an important element of the Canada Public Safety Information Network (CPSIN), a national network of partners developed to improve access to electronic information compiled by the criminal justice system and law enforcement agencies.

Finally, in 2005–8, the RCMP planned to implement gradually real-time identification (RTI) capacity into the fingerprinting and criminal recording system. Due to the electronic transmission and standardization of information, RTI offers state-of-the-art technology that provides quicker turnaround times for identification requests and for criminal record updates. This project will also make it possible to interface with foreign information systems, such as the Federal Bureau of Investigation's (FBI) Integrated Automated Fingerprint Identification System (IAFIS) and Interpol's information system. Unlike the Belgian federal police, the RCMP (also a federal agency) does not have full control of data entry in criminal databases. The RCMP depends on voluntary information exchange by local and provincial police agencies to develop compatible network platforms. This contrast illustrates the trends towards centralization in Belgium and decentralization (Canada).

Singapore

Given the specific organizational culture of the Singapore Police

Force (SPF), criminal intelligence is considered one of the three main pillars of the force, alongside investigation and gendarmerie activities. Following a modest beginning in the 1970s and 1980s, criminal intelligence developed significantly in the 1990s. It was then that the SPF set out to develop a more substantial intelligence programme by creating a department whose mission included centralizing police information and producing strategic analyses. In 1999, the Criminal Intelligence Department implemented an information system that, today, underlies the entire organization. In 2003, the SPF information system was evaluated and several adjustments were made to increase its performance. At present, the SPF information system represents to a certain extent the key element of the organization's learning capacity, thus ensuring its position as a vital function in the organization. The free flow of information between the Criminal Intelligence Department and the various operational units of the SPF is ensured by an extensive network of liaison officers and analysts.

The C-CRIS (Computerized Criminal Intelligence System) is the SPF's primary automated information management system. This system makes it possible to centralize a large volume of data concerning offenders and criminal events. The system is also used to connect other databases, such as the Criminal Investigations Management System (CRIMES) and the Criminal Records Office System. The C-CRIS was developed on the basis of an HP/UNIX (secure WIN 2000) operating system using the ORACLE database. It is connected to a local area network and wide area network and is protected by a virtual private network that allows for the encryption of sensitive information.

In concrete terms, the C-CRIS contains a diverse range of information: persons, objects, places, organizations (legitimate and unlawful), telephone numbers, intelligence reports, road vehicles, ships and aircraft. To process all these data, the system is connected to a series of modules, making it possible to analyse geographic distribution (GIS ArcView), to identify connections between information (WATSON) and to locate quickly the entities being sought (complex search system with free text – FTS and STQ). It should also be noted that the C-CRIS has a tracking and flagging system. Police officers can identify the entities they wish to investigate and are kept updated on the matter via emails.

The C-CRIS is currently being used by four of the eight departments in the Ministry of Home Affairs: the Central Drug Office, the Department of Prisons, the Immigration and Border Surveillance

Department and the SPF. It is used as a technological platform that allows these departments to exchange – in real time and in a secure fashion – the information necessary to the carrying out of their respective missions. Use of the C-CRIS is strictly regulated by a data security system and by standards of user accountability in order to ensure secure information processing and exchange. The SPF has also created audit committees tasked with monitoring the integrity of the system and its procedures.

Although this system aims at information centralization, several existing databases cannot be integrated to the C-CRIS due to incompatibility problems. What is more, there are significant problems related to the system's stability, especially because of the overwhelming amount of encoded information. Finally, the implementation of many interfaces with other agencies of the Ministry for Home Affairs has significantly increased C-CRIS maintenance problems. These multiple difficulties have brought discredit to the system's reliability and mistrust has spread among users. To overcome these major inconveniences, the Criminal Intelligence Department plans to invest several millions of dollars into upgrading its system.

IT in international intelligence services: Europol and Interpol

Europol provides support to member states by facilitating the exchange of information via the liaison officers seconded to the European Police Office, in accordance with the legislative provisions of individual member states. It produces strategic reports and operational analyses to guide police activities in member states. Europol also provides support to joint investigative teams via national Europol units and supports the operational liaison structure linking European police services in order to ensure the efficient exchange of experiences and 'best practices' in the fight against cross-border crime. Lastly, Europol makes available its expertise and technical assistance in the course of investigations and police operations, under the control and legal liability of the states involved.

Europol's international mission and functions are governed by a number of statutes, regulations and internal directives. First and foremost, the Europol Convention, as part of the Treaty of the European Union (Section K.3), sets out the operating rules for the European Police Office and specifies its areas of activity, means of action and structure. It also outlines a framework for the processing and exchanging of information between member states, including rules governing the use of nominal data. There is also a set of legal texts, approved by the Council of Europe, which regulates co-operation agreements and the sharing of personal information between Europol and 'third' states or organizations. Finally, there are directives concerning the use of analysis records, the rights and obligations of Europol liaison officers, confidentiality rules regarding information shared with Europol (namely, the identification of levels of security), financing rules, budgetary control mechanisms and the rights of the public concerning access to Europol-produced documents.

The Europol Convention calls for the installation and management of an automated information system to enter, access and analyse data. The Europol Computer System (TECS) connects all member states and consists of three key modules. The first is the Europol information system, which contains personal data on individuals suspected of having committed or being currently involved in 'serious' offences (i.e. organized crime). National Europol units make this file directly accessible for consultation by Europol liaison officers and by national police departments. The initial version had been in place since 2002 but, in December 2004, the management committee announced the implementation of a new version, available to all member states who contribute directly to the database. The second one is the analysis records system, which is used to study specific criminal phenomena or groups. It contains data on offenders, witnesses and victims. At present, only analysts have access to this file. Finally, TECS includes an index system that allows Europol liaison officers and non-participating states to consult the inventory of data contained in the analysis file for eventual association.

Because the information contribution or need is not equivalent between every member state, Europol has developed two mechanisms to facilitate direct interorganizational interaction. Liaison officers are designated by national police departments in order to provide a credible, personalized link between Europol and member states. In the case of large-scale operations, Europol provides a special analyst who can structure and encode the information necessary to the investigation. Some of the data are then entered into TECS, in accordance with the Europol Convention and the legislation of member states. This is eventually made available as an analysis work file, thus taking its place in the cyclical analysis process.

The International Criminal Police Organization (ICPO – Interpol) was created in 1956 with the mandate to support organizations devoted to fighting crime. To do so, it offers analytical products designed to give perspective to global crime trends and to discover particularities in regional crime problems. Interpol acts only in response to explicit requests by statutory organizations or members states – over 182 countries, each represented by a delegate who sits on the Interpol General Assembly.

Given Interpol's mission, the intelligence process remains rather straightforward. To collect information, analysts use four major sources: open sources (newspapers, scientific journals, etc.), Interpol databases, questionnaires addressed to police organizations in member states with specific questions on specific forms of crime, and direct contact with police officers and analysts in member states targeted by the intelligence operation. Based on this information, analysts establish a general overview of the situation and identify possible trends or the emergence of new phenomena. Analysts also prepare reports for member countries that may be affected by the phenomena.

This system has several drawbacks. First, it is sometimes difficult to exploit some sources of information since Interpol members are not required to contribute to Interpol databases, which leaves some files with little information. Secondly, the ones that do contain information are often less than totally reliable. The main information management system used by Interpol is a relational database containing an offence codification system.[6] This system makes it possible to search for police information using an array of criteria based on member states, parts of the world, types of offenders, types of crime, time periods, etc. As a rule, however, Interpol considers that the information contained in this system has already been validated by member states, and it has no rigorous or systematic method for evaluating the data. One can safely assume that the quality of the police information provided to Interpol varies greatly from one member state to another. Thirdly, the questionnaire filled out by police organizations is plagued by several sources of bias, including a low response rate and a marked difference in the quality of the information collected. Lastly, the ability to establish direct contact between Interpol analysts and police organizations depends on the status of those involved, and it is not uncommon for civilian analysts to face resistance from police officers, whose mistrust hinders the exchange of information.

Interpol has set up a new electronic communications network to improve co-operation among police organizations. Established to facilitate the fight against transnational crime, the I-24/7 allows national officers to query Interpol databases directly and to exchange photographs, videos or genetic data. The system is currently in the implementation phase and is a key technological innovation in the area of international police co-operation. More specifically, this communications network is based on Internet technology but uses high-tech protection systems. The I-24/7 system is protected by a virtual private network and high-level encryption, and it is available on the Internet through a series of firewalls. Once information reaches national central bureaus, it is decoded by a virtual private network box. This box isolates workstations and facilitates regular updates of the safety mechanism. Besides allowing for the consultation of databases, this system makes it possible for the Criminal Analysis Section to disseminate the results of its work.

As is the case with Europol, Interpol activities in the area of police co-operation and the exchange of information are governed by a series of legislative provisions. The organization's constitution sets out internal rules that govern Interpol's operations, its structure, its decision-making mechanisms and the way it processes information. With respect to the last, Interpol's activities are limited to specific aims[7] related to the prevention and repression of ordinary criminal offences. Of course, because of extreme differences in the social and political context of member states, the religious, political, military and ethnic aspects of the data being processed have undermined the ability and willingness of member states to exchange information through Interpol.

One critical difference between Interpol and Europol lies in the capacity of the latter to conduct operational and strategic analyses and to be involved in ongoing international investigations (Gerspacher and Lemieux 2005). This operational advantage allows Europol direct access to first-hand information and promotes the enhanced control of data entry (information validation, reliability, entry delays, etc.). For the same reason, some members of the EU have begun to question Europol's power and legitimacy. Among other things, it is accused of having expansionist ambitions that come at the expense of state sovereignty. Europol has countered that its operational involvement in the fight against international organized crime necessarily involves actions that may go against the sacrosanct principle of the sovereignty of nations.

As can be seen with the cases presented in this chapter, the legal status of organizations tasked with intelligence activities can affect their ability to expand their information-gathering capacity, to implement updated technologies or to develop an extended network of contacts. Criminal intelligence organizations have either of two statuses: organizations with executive or law enforcement powers (i.e. police departments) or organizations that have no such powers (i.e. criminal intelligence organizations). This distinction is crucial since it directly affects the informational capability of organizations, as well as the quality of the criminal analyses they produce. Police departments have executive powers to perform operational duties that generate a large number of sources of information, that have a strong ability to detect offences and that foster the diversification of expertise in several criminal areas. Their direct access to investigative files, internal police databases and police informants, the presence of a pool of analysts with a diversity of skills and, above all, the possibility to initiate new intelligence operations have a direct impact on access to first-hand information and crime databases. On the other hand, intelligence agencies have no executive power. Without the authority to conduct field operations, most criminal intelligence services find themselves in an 'information distributor' role, limited to facilitating communications between police departments. Of course, their mandate usually also includes producing strategic criminal analyses and participating in the development of crime-fighting policies. However, they remain dependent on organizations vested with executive powers, especially when trying to gain access to police data.

The special powers given to the ACC (e.g. examination power) are meant to overcome most of these obstacles and to allow the ACC to conduct its own intelligence operations, as well as special investigations (with the approval of the executive committee). Still, criminal intelligence services have no legal means to 'compel' police organizations to co-operate in the exchange of information. This co-operation is based essentially on the willingness of police departments and the extent of informal networks developed by the individual employees of the intelligence outfits. Most of these problems were noted in the UK NCIS and in Europol and Interpol.

Once gathered, information must still be compiled in automated information management systems in order for it to be used effectively. Although technology has accelerated information processing and retrieval, many limitations remain. There are, for example, interoperability issues between the systems used by police departments, sometimes even within organizations themselves. Some police units compile the information in their possession in parallel databases, which are never integrated into the main system. Automated systems are also affected by the level of confidentiality assigned to information. The normative framework that governs the security of information sometimes leads to over-cautiousness when determining the levels of confidentiality, sometimes unduly limiting access to relevant data in intelligence operations. Together, these restrictions promote 'linkage blindness' in intelligence activities.

Analytical technologies

The previous sections offered a glimpse of the hardware structure behind typical intelligence gathering, processing and communication. The critical analysis stage, where data become intelligence, involves the intensive use of 'soft', or process, technologies. Our interviews with analysts made it possible to identify a wide array of methods used in police organizations and intelligence services. The vast majority of those methods are based on descriptive qualitative analysis and tend to be rather unsophisticated. Table 8.1 is a list of the methods most frequently mentioned during our interviews (the rank order is in function of their frequency of utilization).

Strategy and risk

Generally, criminal intelligence services perform two types of analyses: 'strategic' and 'tactical' or 'operational' (Gill 2000; Maguire 2003; Cope 2004). The first one provides long-term overviews of criminal phenomena, more detailed analysis of the causes of crime patterns and proposed strategic solutions to prevent or reduce crime (in Table 8.1, this corresponds to an analysis of the results, an analysis of crime patterns, market profile, risk analysis, prospective analysis, threat analysis and situation report). Tactical analysis focuses on the identification of specific, individual crime problems and it uses nominative and specific information about criminal entities (persons, groups) and related elements (objects, bank accounts, phone numbers, specific sites or locations, etc.). This can lead to direct operational responses (in Table 8.1, this corresponds to crime mapping, comparative case analysis, specific profile analysis and network or link analysis). These analyses rely heavily on technologies to run complex information processes and graphical visualization.

Usually, these two levels of analysis are performed to support police officers. Investigators and police managers need them to establish target priorities, to plan police operations and to design or enhance police strategies in reducing crime. Many criminal intelligence services also produce threat or risk analyses to identify and prioritize criminal problems. The simple fact is that most of these analyses are based on

Table 8.1 The most often used analytical methods, in decreasing order of frequency

Method	Description
Situation report	Description of crime trends
Comparative case analysis	Comparison of information from different incidents in order to establish connections based on the attributes of the offender, an item, the modus operandi or situational elements
Analysis of crime patterns	Incorporates various types of analyses, such as the analysis of trends, hotspots and profiles. This makes it possible to identify specific or serial crimes
Threat analysis	Analyses and evaluates the nature, scope and long-term impact of a criminal phenomenon or group
Analysis of networks	Analysis focusing on ties between individuals or organizations within a criminal network. This type of analysis aims to identify the nature of the said ties, the role of each individual and the strong/weak points of the criminal organization
Specific profile analysis	Produces a behavioural profile of an offender based on the characteristics of an incident or by using other contextual information
Risk analysis	Evaluation of various levels of risk presented by individuals or criminal organizations towards potential victims – either the general public or law enforcement agencies
Analysis of results	Evaluation of the effectiveness of law enforcement activities, such as patrol strategies, crime reduction initiatives or specific investigative techniques. This type of analysis makes it possible to identify best practices or make improvements
Prospective analysis	Forecast which consists in identifying the predictable lines of the evolution of a given situation and reviewing action likely to change this evolution in a deliberate fashion

partial or incomplete information, and they are tainted by a lack of expertise about criminogenic effects and their consequences on crime patterns. This is especially detrimental to strategic analysis. The following paragraphs discuss two examples of priority identification processes based on a threat or risk analysis approach.

The first is the National Police Security Image (IPNS), produced by the Belgian federal police, which is used to rank security problems by order of importance. Strategic priorities are determined based on four dimensions: scope, potential impact or consequences, perception by the population and possible future evolution. Each of these dimensions is measured using quantitative or qualitative indicators (nominal or by category) entered into computer software that can model decisions based on multiple criteria (Decision Lab 2000). The software uses the PROMETHEE and GAIA methods developed by the University of Brussels and marketed in Canada. It was designed for use in resolving various multi-criteria decision problems, including the determination of priority tasks. This method breaks down the previously mentioned dimensions into arrays of indicators and prioritizes them according to their average weight (average sensitivity ratio), which makes it possible to classify priority security problems.

This has several limitations. First, there is a problem regarding many of the criteria used, as well as with their estimated value. For instance, it is difficult to determine the real costs of drug trafficking or the monetary impact of human trafficking. Secondly, there are limitations because it is impossible to compare and rank dimensions, indicators or criteria measured in different units. For instance, the impact of road accidents is measured in the number of deaths and injuries, while the impact of fraud, money-laundering or thefts is gauged in terms of monetary losses. The model offers no help in resolving the matter of whether the objective 'weight' of 2,000 deaths on the road is greater or lesser than the financial fallout of money-laundering activities (even if estimates for the latter were actually reliable).

Furthermore, the model does not calculate the statistical interaction effects between the different criteria associated with each of the security problems. For instance, the interaction effect between such criteria as 'growth of the problem', 'cost' and 'number of known criminals' can cause the sensitivity ratio to fluctuate considerably from one problem to another. In fact, the model will only be effective and rigorous when it manages to group together security problems of a similar nature, when it identifies better the criteria used and the estimates, and when it sorts out the interaction effects between these criteria.

Another example is the threat assessment model developed by the RCMP, known as SLEIPNIR. This model is based on a set of attributes narrowly focused on describing criminal organizations. Each of these attributes is given a rating by an analyst assigned to a specific criminal group. There is a choice of five values – unknown, nil, low, medium and high – each of which corresponds to a number calculated beforehand using algorithms. In order to standardize the choice of ratings, analysts use a guide containing definitions. Ideally, a police organization aims to study all the criminalized groups in its territory. This model allows analysts to measure and compare the means used by criminal organizations, the extent of their activities and their modus operandi (especially the use of violence). It makes it possible to determine comparative levels of dangerousness. The SLEIPNIR model is used by the RCMP to set priorities in its fight against organized crime. At present, the threat assessment model includes 19 attributes, mostly informed by the ACIIS.

Like other such systems, SLEIPNIR presents several problems on conceptual, terminological and methodological levels. First, it seems that the attributes used in the model do not apply to all forms of organized crime. Indeed, the attributes describe mostly criminal organizations that are established and powerful and that correspond to a very conventional image of organized crime. Consequently, when the model is applied to different criminal structures, such as 'street gangs', analysts find themselves unable accurately to estimate the level of dangerousness of these groups. More specifically, several studies have shown that street gangs are far less hierarchical, that their ethnic makeup is far less important (ethnic diversification, alliances, etc.), that their area of activity varies with opportunities, that they use violence far more spontaneously, that they are easily able to adapt to new environments and that they often operate at the local or regional level. Hence, if the SLEIPNIR model is applied at the provincial, regional or local level, street gangs known for the viciousness of their activities will be given a lower dangerousness rating than traditional criminal organizations. This tool therefore generates a conceptual asymmetry of organized crime that is not in line with the concerns of the different jurisdictional levels. Secondly, the definitions of the attributes and of the rating criteria seem to be ambiguous. Analysts might understand and interpret these definitions differently, thus influencing the priority ranking of criminal organizations. It is important to note that, at the time of our fieldwork, other police and intelligence services were in the process of implementing a threat assessment approach based on the SLEIPNIR model (e.g. the ACC and the SPF).

Tactics

Tactical, or operational, analysis is often useful for investigative purposes or for the deployment of patrols in urban areas. At the tactical level, analysts use several types of software for crime mapping and diagrams to establish links between criminal organizations, individuals and illicit activities (e.g. Analyst Notebook, Elementary and Watson software). These tools allow analysts to produce documents destined for investigators. They also provide visual analysis tools for operational intelligence and advanced querying functions that maximize the power of the data. Investigators are able to import, track and use data from a wide range of sources. Using technologies developed by private corporations (I2 inc., Memex, Xanalys, etc.), these software packages can identify links between contacts and can reveal associations between activities not immediately apparent to the naked eye.

During our visits to intelligence services, operational analysts were happy to show us how they use analytical technologies. One of the most interesting was found in Switzerland, in the Canton de Vaud. The cantonal police use software to map and link serial property crime over the canton and abroad by looking at forensic trace evidence, such as footprints, fingerprints, tool traces, images and video from surveillance cameras (see also Ribaux *et al.* 2003). Given the particularities of the country, serial criminal phenomena are usually analysed according to their narrow incidence in the cantonal territory. Because the cantons work in different legal frameworks, the Judicial Co-ordination Service tends to treat crimes as strictly local, oblivious to the possibility of trans-cantonal organized crime because of its partial picture of the activities and the perpetrators. Specialized brigades, such as that of the Cantonal Police of Vaud and those of the federal police, aim to remedy this situation.

Yet another innovative means to exploit criminal information is pre-crime data-mining analysis. This method is used by the DAS in Colombia, particularly to establish behavioural profiles linked to drug trafficking at airports, train stations and other points of exit. This technique allows the police to identify suspicious behaviours or patterns, and border officers can then use these profiles to conduct specific searches on travellers or any goods crossing the border. The same technique is employed for monitoring terrorism in many airports around the world, where preventive data mining is used to create random behavioural or identity profiles related to potential terrorism threats. The technique comes from the business world, where corporations create consumer profiles with credit card data and other types of information about consumer behaviour (Ména 2004). These analyses rely on a huge amount of police information, which must be made available on time. Obviously, the accuracy and timeliness of police data are critical to the production of realistic, 'actionable' statistical profiles for use by border officers. Because police data are frequently unreliable or late, the DAS must produce more profiles and randomize those already existing in order to circumvent the criminal groups' counter-intelligence capacity.

These results show that strategic analytical methods are still embryonic. In fact, the use of sophisticated software packages (for instance, by the Belgian federal police), remains the exception. Indeed, it seems that critical problems tend to emerge right at the beginning, at the conceptualization and operationalization phases of crime analysis. This situation leads to flawed assessments of crime patterns or criminal organizations, which could considerably affect the comparative analyses used to establish policing priorities.

Tactical analysis seems more readily permeable to IT, generally because investigators and analysts deal with critical, priority information flows, the complexity of criminal cases and many real-time information requirements. IT has quickly established itself as a requirement in this environment and is used heavily to structure information for analytical processes (visualization) and for quick records retrieval from large databases. One critical point is that police managers have promoted the use of software to structure and aggregate data to keep track of current and/or short-term trends. Sometimes, IT is exploited to produce predictive analyses and to inform proactive strategies aimed at reducing crime rates (as in the case of the DAS). IT is then seen as a crucial tool for complex investigations and as resource management rather than a 'sophisticated' solution to fight crime.

Conclusions

Factors favouring the adoption of technologies

The findings presented in this chapter suggest that intelligence services use IT in criminal intelligence gathering and in analytical work in widely varied ways. Yet, in general, the exploitation of technological tools for gathering and/or mining data and analysing information is limited and does not necessitate sophisticated processes: the investigative tools and analytical technologies are rarely employed to their full potential. Most often, IT in criminal intelligence is used simply to record and, later, to retrieve information related to crimes. Using different software packages and computer programs, police officers and analysts surf in police data warehouses, looking for information in past criminal incidents or in current investigations. However, when a criminal investigation becomes complex and requires more resources, the use of specialized software to assist investigators is quite common.

Obstacles to technology

However, several obstacles remain relating to adoption, introduction and adequate exploitation of IT in criminal intelligence services. First, as Sheptycki (2004) pointed out, police organizations, like any other institution, suffer from organizational pathologies that undermine the exploitation of technologies in police intelligence systems. According to his findings and those in this chapter, several problems are linked to cultural biases about methods of analysis, resulting in faulty interpretation, information overload and data isolation, especially in complex investigations or in highly politicized environments (such as those of Europol and Interpol).

In addition, criminal intelligence services are especially vulnerable to information system incompatibility. This lack of interoperability between police information systems undermines the efforts deployed by intelligence services to provide an accurate criminal analysis or 'crime picture'. This situation can be illustrated by a well-known example related to police system incompatibility in Canada. A few years ago, several Canadian law-enforcement agencies adopted the ACIIS as their main information system about serious and organized crime. Unfortunately, not all police organizations acquired the system at the same time and, consequently, they operate different, incompatible versions of the ACIIS. It is therefore possible that, in the same province, the major city, provincial and federal police find it difficult to share information due to version disparities. Of course, this situation can be explained in part by the simple fact that information systems are constantly updated and become obsolete rapidly. However, a market dynamic is also at work. On one hand, the corporations who produce and market the software packages are trying to sell new products rather than old systems, in part because they need to absorb the cost of research and development. On the other hand, high-ranking police managers are also looking for the 'best' and newest technology available on the market.

Further, the way data are entered into police information systems represents a critical limitation to the efficient use of police IT. Indeed, a large portion of the information recorded by the police is unstructured, such as free text, pictures and video and audio recordings. Running contents searches inside banks of such types of information is difficult and requires powerful and highly sophisticated computer hardware and software. Such software packages need artificial intelligence capabilities in order to recognize and 'learn' patterns and their evolution, to refine searches in databases and to update predefined queries for information changes or system modifications. This technology is already available on the market and is currently used by well funded security intelligence services, who are facing the same data analysis problems. However, police agencies and criminal intelligence services generally do not have at their disposal the financial and technical means required to acquire the software, to integrate it into their systems and to train their employees to exploit it efficiently.

Finally, the spread of IT in policing is currently limited by some scepticism on the part of analysts and investigators, who are doubtful of its practical, everyday usefulness. In fact, many sceptics have argued that the exploitation of IT to reduce crime is wishful thinking, encouraged by high-level administrators who want to develop and expand the model of intelligence-led policing into the organization. They do not consider themselves to be 'number crunchers'. It is interesting to note that most analysts and investigators view IT not so much as a crime reduction tool but as one that can enhance their investigative capacity. They see it as a powerful tool for organizing the information they need to solve current criminal cases, to map the path of the investigation and to identify potential gaps in the evidence. These findings contradict other studies that claimed that law enforcement agencies tended enthusiastically to trust the technology and to use it in a sophisticated manner to attack crime and criminals.

In sum, our findings show that, in reality, criminal intelligence outfits rarely use IT directly to fulfil their institutional mission to prevent or reduce crime. However, they do make use of the technology to gain access to organized and structured information to assist the operational and strategic decision-making process. IT serves management performance objectives linked to information gathering, sharing, processing and structuring rather than serving directly operational activities. Obviously there is a critical difference, in criminal intelligence, between IT applied to management and IT used for crime analysis. This chapter shows that practical problems, such as systems compatibility, agency networks and regulations undermine IT applications for management. Similarly, it shows that the use of IT applications for crime analysis is limited by the fact that technology tools do not represent an answer to common conceptualizations of criminal problems and are not a substitute for cognitive work in crime analysis. It must be concluded, therefore, that the adoption of IT in criminal intelligence outfits is driven by dominant police models and management styles (namely, ILP) rather than by the actual performance of concrete benefits.

Notes

1 See the Appropriations Act 2001 for the Justice Department and other federal agencies (Public Law 105–553).
2 The Defence Intelligence Agency's Verity K2 Enterprise mines data from the intelligence community and Internet sources to identify foreign terrorists or US citizens connected to foreign terrorism activities.
3 Shortly after our field research, the NCIS was integrated into Serious Organized Crime Agency (SOCA), along with the National Crime Squad, the National Investigation Service of the former HM Revenue and Customs, the Organized Trafficking Investigation Section of HM Immigration Service and the Organized Crime Section of MI5.
4 Although the Proceeds of Crime Act 2002 requires that financial institutions report all transactions of more than 15,000 euros, they often do so for lesser amounts when the grounds for the transaction, recipients or geographic areas (the Caribbean, Spain, etc.) seem suspicious. According to the 2002–03 NCIS annual report, the number of disclosures jumped by 60 per cent compared with 2001–02.
5 ViCLAS is the Violent Crime Linkage Analysis System – a Canadian national database for tracking violent offenders.
6 There are also other specialized databases connected to the central system and containing information for forensic data analysis (e.g. DNA), 'autonomous files' that contain sensitive data related to ongoing police co-operation projects.

7 Interpol's activities include 1) the search for individuals who are to be arrested; 2) the obtaining of information on a person who has committed or participated in, or who is likely to commit or participate in, directly or indirectly, an ordinary criminal offence; 3) obtaining preventive information from police authorities regarding a person's criminal activities; 4) the search for missing persons; 5) the search for witnesses or victims; 6) the identification of a person or body; 7) the search for or identification of objects; and 8) the description or identification of modus operandi, of offences committed by unknown individuals, of the features of forgeries or counterfeits, or the seizure of objects with respect to trafficking activities.

References

Braga, A. (2002) *Problem-oriented Policing and Crime Prevention*. New York, NY: Criminal Justice Press.

Brodeur, J.-P. and Dupont, B. (2006) 'Knowledge workers or "knowledge workers?" ', *Policing and Society*, 16: 7–26.

Brodeur J.-P., Gill, P. and Tölborg, D. (2003) *Democracy, Law, and Security: Internal Security Services in Contemporary Europe*. Burlington, NY: Ashgate.

Brodeur, J.-P. and Leman-Langlois, S. (2006) 'Surveillance-fiction: high and low policing revisited', in K. Haggerty and R. Ericson (eds) *The New Politics of Surveillance and Visibility*. Toronto: University of Toronto Press.

Crawford, A. (1997) *The Local Governance of Crime: Appeals to Community and Partnerships*. London: Oxford University Press.

Ericson, R.V. and Haggerty, K.D. (1997) *Policing the Risk Society*. Oxford: Clarendon Press.

Garicano, L. and Heaton, P.S. (2006) *Computing Crime: Information Technology, Police Effectiveness and the Organization of Policing CEPR Discussion Paper* 5837 (http://ssrn.com/abstract=944874).

Gill, P. (2000) *Rounding up the Usual Suspects?* Aldershot: Ashgate.

Godfrey, E.D. and Harris, D.R. (1971) *The Basic Elements of Intelligence*. Washington, DC: Law Enforcement Assistance Administration.

Goldstein, H. (1990) *Problem-oriented Policing*. New York, NY: McGraw-Hill.

Gottlieb, S., Arenberg, S. and Singh, R. (1994) *Crime Analysis: From First Report to Final Arrest*. Montclair, CA: Alpha Publishing.

Governmental Accounting Office (2004) *Data Mining: Federal Efforts Cover a Wide Range of Uses* (GAO-04-548). Washington, DC: Governmental Accounting Office.

Haggerty, K.D. and Ericson, R.V. (2001) 'The military technostructures of policing', in P. Kraska (ed.) *Militarizing the American Criminal Justice System: The Changing Roles of the Armed Forces and the Police*. Boston, MA: Northeastern University Press.

Harris, D.R. (1976) *Basic Elements of Intelligence – Revised*. Washington, DC: Law Enforcement Assistance Administration.

John, T. and Maguire, M. (2003) 'Rolling out the National Intelligence Model: key challenges', in K. Bullock *et al.* (eds) *Crime Reduction and Problem-oriented Policing*. Cullompton: Willan Publishing.

Klosek, J. (2000) *Data Privacy in the Information Age*. New York, NY: Quorum Books.

Larson, R.C. (1989) 'The new crime stoppers', *Technology Review*, November–December: 26–31.

Lemieux, F. (2006) *Normes et pratiques en matière de renseignement criminel: Une comparaison internationale*. Ste Foy: PUL.

Maguire, M. (2000) 'Policing by risks and targets: some dimensions and implications of intelligence control', *Policing and Society*, 9: 315–36.

Maguire, M. (2003) 'Criminal investigation and crime control', in T. Newburn (ed.) *Handbook of Policing*. Cullompton: Willan Publishing.

Mamalian, C. and Lavigne, N. (1999) *The Use of Computerized Crime Mapping by Law Enforcement. Research Preview Series*. Washington, DC: National Institute of Justice, US Department of Justice.

Manning, P.K. (1992) 'Information technologies and the police', *Crime and Justice*, 15: 349–98.

Manning, P.K. (2003) *Policing Contingencies*. Chicago, IL: University of Chicago Press.

Markle Foundation (2003) *Creating a Trusted Information Network for Homeland Security*. New York, NY: Markle Foundation.

Marx, G.T. (1988) *Undercover: Police Surveillance in America*. Berkley, CA: University of California Press.

Ména, J. (2004) *Homeland Security: Techniques and Technologies*. Hingham, MA: Charles River Media.

Morehouse, R. (2000) 'The role of criminal intelligence in law enforcement', in M.B. Peterson *et al.* (eds) *Intelligence 2000: Revising the Basic Elements*. Sacramento, CA: Law Enforcement Intelligence Unit.

Norris, C. and Dunnigan, C. (2000) 'Subterranean blues: conflict as an unintended consequence of police use of informers', *Policing and Society*, 9: 385–412.

Ouimet, M. (1995) 'Vers une police informée', *Revue internationale de criminologie et de police technique*, 1: 87–94.

Ratcliffe, J.H. (2002) 'Intelligence-led policing and the problems of turning rhetoric into practice', *Policing and Society*, 12: 53–66.

Schwabe, W., Davis, L.M. and Jackson, B.A. (2001) *Challenges and Choices for Crime-Fighting Technology: Federal Support of State and Local Law Enforcement* (MR-1349-OSTP/NIJ). Washington, DC: RAND Corporation.

Scott, M.S. (2000) *Problem Oriented Policing: Reflections on the First 20 Years*. Washington, DC: US Department of Justice, Office of Community Oriented Policing Services.

Taipale, K.A. (2003) 'Data mining and domestic security: connecting the dots to make sense of data', *Columbia Science and Technology Law Review*, 5.

Tilley, N. (2003) 'Community policing, problem-oriented policing and intelligence-led policing', in T. Newburn (ed.) *Handbook of Policing*. Portland, OR: Willan Publishing.

US Department of Justice (USDoJ) (2006) *Making Officer Redeployment Effective (MORE): Using Technology to Keep America's Communities Safe*. Washington, DC: Office of Community Oriented Policing Services.

US Government (1994) *Memorandum of Understanding between Department of Defense and Department of Justice on Operations other than War and Law Enforcement*. Washington, DC: Department of Justice and Department of Defense.

Chapter 9

Scientific policing and criminal investigation[1]

Jean-Paul Brodeur

Introduction

According to a report written under the auspices of the US National Research Council, the topics that were the least researched in the field of police studies were human rights, riot control, police discretion, the use of firearms and deadly force, and, lastly, criminal investigation (National Research Council 2003: ch. 1). The researchers identified 22 research topics and sifted through 17 sources of data from 1967 to 2002 (two journals of abstracts, and twelve criminal justice and three professional journals) to determine which of these topics were quoted with the most (or the least) frequency. Crime, drugs, women (as victims), police and community relations, performance evaluation and police effectiveness, and police organization were the most frequently cited topics. I referred above to the bottom-listed topics. The researchers took other measurements of researched topics in their sources of data, but criminal investigation was always listed among the six least researched topics, often coming in last place.

This rating is comparative, as all ratings are. Although criminal investigation is at the bottom of the list, this does not mean there is no body of research on criminal investigation: there is an early body of research on which the significant work of Kuykendall (1982, 1986) and Klockars (1985) rests. However, the total body of work on criminal investigation is in no way comparable with the impressive production on uniformed patrol. This dearth of research could not be in greater contrast with police fiction: almost all police fiction focuses on police investigation, most particularly on homicide investigation.

There is now an emerging trend in police fiction that reflects the spirit of our times with its emphasis on science and technology. On television, *Crime Scene Investigation* (*CSI*), a series based on the scientific analysis of pieces of circumstantial evidence collected at a crime scene, met with so much success in the USA that it gave rise to two 'spinoffs' based on new cities where the action takes place (*CSI New York*, and *CSI Miami*). There is also a classic board game and a computer game patterned on the series. There is a parallel development in written crime fiction. Writers such as Patricia Cornwell (*The Book of the Dead*) and Kathy Reichs (*Déjà Dead*) have created a new type of sleuth, the forensics expert. Both writers have a background in forensics. Patricia Cornwell was a technical writer and computer analyst for six years at the Office of the Chief Medical Examiner in the US State of Virginia; Kathy Reichs holds a graduate degree in forensics anthropology. This emphasis on forensics actually built on the increasing part scientific policing took in the training of crime investigators. There are a growing number of manuals and monographs that introduce potential detectives to the use of specialized techniques of investigation based on the application of scientific technology, such as testing suspects with a polygraph (National Research Council 2003). Some of these procedures date far back in time, such as police interrogation (Inbau and Reid 1967; Deeley 1971; Ben-Shakhar and Furedy 1990; Eisen *et al.* 2002); other techniques that are presented in the literature are older than is generally believed, such as audio electronic surveillance (Greenman 1938; Dash *et al.* 1959). We are now witnessing a multiplication of publications on investigative tools that have a high profile in the media, such as DNA fingerprinting (Levy 1996; Krude 2004) and the various forms of profiling (e.g. geographical profiling – Rossmo 2003; psychological profiling – Ainsworth 2001; Turvey 2002). Although it is highly controversial in respect of race and ethnicity and its efficiency is still untested, profiling is developing into a speciality of its own. The general impression given by crime fiction, the media and by police training manuals is that criminal investigation has become a quasi-scientific process that increasingly relies on the application of various kinds of technologies (forensics, identification, surveillance and so forth).

I examine in this chapter whether this impression of the pervasiveness of scientific investigative technology is supported by real criminal investigation as it is actually performed by detectives. The chapter is divided in two parts. First, I present the findings of empirical research that I undertook for several years on criminal investigation, more specifically on homicide case clearance. Secondly, I discuss the significance of these findings for articulating a theory of criminal investigation, drawing a contrast between two kinds of theories of investigation. A first kind of theory, which I call 'epistemic', conceives police investigation as a knowledge-based process that relies to a significant extent on scientific technology; a second kind of theory, which I call 'pragmatic', views criminal investigation as an opportunistic process aimed at securing court convictions, sometimes at the expense of truth. I try to assess which kind of theory is the most adequate to account for criminal investigation. These two parts of the chapter are followed by concluding remarks.

Empirical findings

From 1999 to 2004, I conducted empirical research on criminal investigation (Brodeur 2005). I first developed a research project and submitted it to a large urban police force in the Province of Quebec. After protracted negotiations, I was finally authorized to have access to the police investigation files for the period extending from 1990 to 2001 and to conduct interviews with the investigators.

I wanted to answer two questions in my research. The first was empirical: what were the determinants in the *resolution* of a case, defined as the identification and arrest of the perpetrator(s) of a crime? The second question was theoretical: what part were played by knowledge – understood as *true* information – and the technological means of collecting it in policing? At first blush, criminal investigation qualified as the best testing ground for the hypotheses that policing is knowledge work (Ericson and Haggerty 1997). Following the seminal work of Ericson and Haggerty, the assertion that crime investigation is information processing became dominant in the research literature (Innes 2003: 27 and ch. 5). Consequently, I examined with particular care the role of such knowledge factors as forensics, data banks, criminal intelligence and surveillance technology in the clearing up of criminal cases.

With regard to method, I followed a two-pronged approach. First, I undertook a content analysis of a random selection of investigation files on *resolved cases* from 1990 to 2001. There also were a number of unresolved cases in my sample, which I compared with the resolved cases. I initially selected 25 resolved cases for each of the following offences: homicide (including attempted homicides and conspiracies), sexual assault, robbery, fraud and narcotic offences. The 125 cases were selected according to a random procedure that avoided sample biases with regard to year and territorial district. As I began my analysis, I realized that only the homicide cases produced sufficiently detailed files for my purposes. For the other offences, a 'file' usually consisted of a few pages recording a complaint or, in a minority of cases, describing the swift arrest of the perpetrator by uniformed patrol or by a civilian. For instance, in one of the cases involving rape, the rapist was identified by the victim and located by her mother, who walked the neighbourhood streets with her daughter in order to find him. Nearly all narcotic files consisted of a short narrative of a sting operation targeting a street drug peddler, this sting operation often being conducted by patrol officers wearing plain clothes rather than by investigators. On an examination of the police files, most of the non-homicides cases vindicated Ericson's (1981: 136) initial perspective that 'the detectives' work was to deal with suspects delivered to them or otherwise identified through the work of others'. Knowledge production viewed as a process that extended in time and that was underpinned by scientific methods played almost no role in these inquiries.

Because of the dearth of material in the non-homicide files, which reflected police priorities, I decided to focus on resolved murder investigations. The number of files recounting a typical murder investigation filled at least one storage box in the archives. Approximately half the cases generated enough files to fill several boxes. In the end, I collected a maximum sample of 153 homicide cases involving 193 suspects (depending on how I processed my data, the greater figure of 153 cases was occasionally a bit lower). I broke down these cases into 163 variables that were computerized. Most of the variables referred to the investigative process, but several represent features of the case itself (e.g. information on the victims and perpetrators). This work in police files was combined with lengthy interviews with key informants from the homicide squad (supervisors and best practitioners). The work proceeded in three stages. I first completed a draft of the documentary analysis and submitted my findings to the investigators I interviewed. I then fine tuned my analysis in the light of their comments. This three-step procedure was the result of past experience in police research. I am convinced that it is of no value to interview criminal investigators (and intelligence officers) without being thoroughly acquainted with their work and without being in a position to question, albeit in a non-confrontational way, the claims they make in the course of an interview. This procedure of discussing their own files with the investigators proved to be rewarding for both parties.

The following are some of the empirical findings of my research. These findings were selected on the basis of their relevance for assessing the part played by knowledge and scientific technology in homicide inquiries.

Clearance time

I first determined how much time it took the police to identify the perpetrator(s) of a homicide and related offences (attempted murder and conspiracy, representing less than 10 per cent of the sample). I make a distinction between 'identification' and 'location' inquiries because they rest on different investigative techniques. The number of identification inquiries (131 cases) and location inquiries (153 cases) is not the same. When there are multiple perpetrators in a single case, the identification inquiry generally succeeds in finding their respective identities within the same timeframe, whereas locating the various suspects may vary in time. Notwithstanding the fact that they spring from the same case, I made a separate count of the investigations undertaken to locate the various suspects implicated in one case.

I compared my findings with one of the few research projects on homicide investigations that also attempted to estimate the clearance time and to single out the most influential factors in reaching a resolution (Wellford and Cronin 1999). Wellford and Cronin collected a sample of 798 murder cases in four US cities for the period 1994–5 (589 of these cases were solved and 209 had remained unsolved). They then coded 215 factors related to the characteristics of the case and its investigation as found in the police files. Their research was limited to the police files, and they did not conduct interviews with investigators or make field observations. Wellford and Cronin compared two cities with high clearance rates with two cities with low rates (the numerical significance of high and low clearance rates is not specified, although they refer respectively to 94 per cent and 67 per cent as high and low rates). The municipal police force I selected had an average clearance rate of 70 per cent of its cases between 1990 and 2001 – a little below the aggregated Canadian average of 77 per cent. It is reasonable to believe that the average clearance rate of the four cities selected by Wellford and Cronin would not be very different from 70 per cent, although a little higher. Consequently, the performance of the Canadian force can be compared with the police departments selected by Wellford and Cronin. Table 9.1 compares my sample with the police departments selected by Wellford and Cronin.

Table 9.1 Time needed to solve a case (Brodeur, and Welford and Cronin, 1999)

Time elapsed	Brodeur		Welford and Cronin
	Identification (n = 131)	Localization** (n = 153)	Clearance = arrest (n = 589)
None*	62 cases		
1 hour or less	10	51 cases	
5 hours or less	13	8	
24 hours or less	8	16	69 cases
Total % (no time to 24 hours or less)	71%	49%	28.7%
2–3 days or less	8		
4–7 days or less	4	19 (12.4%)	125 (21.2%)
More than a week	5	18	99 (16.8%)
More than a month	2	11	154 (26.2%)
More than a year	7	15	23 (3.9%)
Total % (1 day + to 1 year+)	20%	41%	68%
Missing values	12 (9%)	15 (10%)	19 (3.3%)

Notes
* The identification and localization of the main suspect(s) coincide immediately or nearly immediately with the arrival of the patrol.
** When there is more than one suspect, the number of localization inquiries may be higher than the number of identification inquiries. Many suspects may be identified at the same time through one identification inquiry only. It may, however, take several localization inquiries to track them down.

These findings lead to two conclusions. First, the overwhelming fact stemming from these findings is the very short time it takes to identify the suspect(s) who will be arrested and prosecuted. In my own Canadian sample, 71 per cent of suspects were identified in 24 hours or less (discounting the missing values, this percentage increases to 78 per cent). This percentage dropped to 49 per cent when I took into account the added time needed to locate and arrest the suspect(s). Still, we can conclude that half the cases were cleared in 24 hours or less, using the stronger criterion of location/arrest. These high figures drove me to double-check all my time calculations for the entire sample, and they stood up to the test. The criterion of arrest was also used by Wellford and Cronin (1999) to classify a case as resolved, with the following result: 28.7 per cent of the cases in their sample were solved in 24 hours or less, which is significantly lower than what I found but still impressive, as almost one third of Wellford and Cronin's cases were solved within 24 hours. The difference between the two samples decreases as we move to longer periods of time: some 50 per cent (294) of Wellford and Cronin's sampled cases were resolved in one week or less as compared with 61 per cent of my own. To conclude, resolving a murder case is accomplished quickly in a significant proportion of cases: adding all the cases for the five police forces under consideration, 52.2 per cent of the 742 (153 + 589) cases are cleared by an arrest in less than a week. With respect to my own sample, we see the 55 per cent of the identification inquiries are resolved almost immediately, and that one third of the perpetrators are also immediately put under arrest.

The second conclusion allows of a weak and a strong formulation. The weak formulation is that clearing up cases is only part of what investigators do, and that a complete theory of criminal investigation must take into consideration what else they are doing. The strong formulation would be to claim that developing models for case-solving and articulating a theory of criminal investigation are different endeavours, the first one being an exercise in pragmatics and the second an exercise in knowledge. I briefly explore the weaker formulation. I wanted to interview the best investigator of the homicide unit, according to its supervisors. They – and all members of the unit I interviewed – quickly agreed on a name. This investigator did not owe his reputation to his ability to crack difficult cases (which he also had) but to his skills as a courtroom manager of homicide cases. His biggest score was to have avoided a mistrial in a very high-profile case where the perpetrator – a mass murderer who had finally been overwhelmed by people he had taken as hostages – acted as his own attorney and nearly succeeded in bringing chaos to the court proceeding. In this case, the challenge was not to clear the case, which was a self-solver, but to overcome the obstacles that the accused multiplied throughout the court proceeding by his spirited defence. In the follow-up to this interview, I asked the detectives whom I interviewed whether they were mostly case solvers or courtroom evidence managers, and they all chose the second alternative.

Identification factors

I estimated which factors were decisive in identifying the perpetrator(s) of a criminal offence. I selected 15 different factors, whereas Wellford and Cronin (1999) listed 8. Table 9.2 presents in terms of percentages the importance of each factor. The percentages were calculated on the basis of the number of suspects. The first number of 144 suspects was computed by adding all the suspects in single-suspect incidents to the first suspect in several-suspects incidents. The second number of 24 suspects refers to all the second suspects in cases with two or more suspects. Finally, the third number of 11 suspects refers to all other suspects in cases with more than two suspects.

These 15 variables can be compressed into three sets: first, the external human sources variables (factors 1–8, except factor 4 (patrol) and the last factor); secondly, the police-centred factors (patrol, routine inquiry, criminal intelligence, surveillance and instigation); and, thirdly, technical sources (line-ups and photographic identification, scientific policing, (including forensics) and 'other' (e.g. computer checks). The findings show some consistency. With respect to identifying the first (or only) suspect, external human sources are the determining factor in 73 per cent of the cases; police-centred factors were decisive in 16 per cent of cases and technical sources in fewer than 3 per cent. All other suspects (columns 2 and 3) were identified through external human sources. The increasing importance of police informants for the identification of second and third-column suspects reflects the fact that the first suspect arrested often turns in the others. These results are consistent with Wellford and Cronin's (1999: Table 9, p. 27). In close to two thirds of their sample (64 per cent), the offender was identified by witnesses at the crime scene or by some other external source. The role of physical evidence collected at the scene is negligible (the determinant in 1.9 of the cases).

Table 9.2 Determining factors in the identification of suspects (per cent)

Determining factors	Identification: suspect 1 (n = 144)	Identification: suspect 2 (n = 24)	Identification: additional suspects (n = 11)
Eyewitness	22.5	25.0	–
Spontaneous confession	20.5	3.7	–
Police informant	12.5	27.0	33
Patrol	10.6	–	–
Victim/co-victim	10.6	12.0	16
Denunciation (relative)	2.6	–	–
Denunciation (spouse)	0.7	–	–
Routine inquiry	2.0	–	–
Electronic and/or physical surveillance	1.3	–	–
Instigation	1.3	–	–
Suspect photograph	0.7	–	–
Criminal intelligence	0.7	–	–
Scientific policing	0.7	–	–
External assistance	0.7	–	–
Other	1.3	8.2	27
Missing values	8.0	8.0	8

Location factors

The findings in Table 9.3 are also presented in three columns that correspond to the number of suspects in a case, computed in the same way as Table 9.2. Since my research focuses on the work of criminal investigators, I make a distinction between the location of a suspect and the arrest of this person. Locating a suspect is an investigative task, whereas the physical arrest may not be – it was actually effected by a SWAT team in 6 per cent of the cases (this is not reflected in Table 9.3).

The findings regarding clearance time are confirmed by Table 9.3. In half the cases, the offender is either immediately arrested by the patrol or a witness or surrenders to the police. Nevertheless, these findings show that the successful outcome of a location inquiry is determined by factors other than those prominent with respect to identification. Routine inquiry and physical surveillance play a bigger part, and so does electronic surveillance. Electronic surveillance was increasingly a key determinant in locating second and third suspects. The explanation for this was given to me in the course of my interviews: electronic surveillance is more effective when there is more than one suspect. The investigators can use the tactic of feeding back to the various suspects whom they interrogate parts of intercepted conversations in order to destabilize them.

Three negative findings ought to be stressed. First, computer searches play a very marginal role in locating a fleeing suspect. Secondly, surveillance technology also plays a very minor role in locating a suspect – the most efficient means are the traditional ones, such as tailing subjects. Finally, private security played no role in solving the murder cases of our sample, either in relation to the identification or the location of perpetrators. Although it was originally meant to include the private sector, the variable 'external assistance' refers only to assistance provided to the police by other criminal justice agencies (e.g. corrections). Private investigators, it should be emphasized, played no part whatsoever in the homicide cases we analysed.

Scientific policing

The previous tables show that scientific policing and forensics played no immediate role in identifying and locating suspects. I also inquired about the role played by each of the techniques listed in Table 9.4 in solving a case (important, average, no role, expertise not performed). Even when estimated important, the role of expertise was essentially ancillary: except in one case, it was never a key determinant.

Table 9.3 Determining factors in the localization of suspects (per cent)

Determining factors	Localization: suspect 1 (n = 144)	Localization: suspect 2 (n = 24)	Localization: additional suspects (n = 11)
Patrol (*flagrante delicto*)	23.5	14	–
Suspect surrenders	20.0	–	–
Routine investigation and physical surveillance	16.3	48	60
External assistance	5.5	–	–
Suspect overpowered by witness	3.3	–	–
Police informant	2.6	–	–
Caught solving another case	2.6	–	–
Electronic surveillance	2.6	10	20
Denunciation (relative or friend)	2.6	–	–
Information from correction	2.0	–	–
Wanted person ad	2.0	–	–
Wounded by victim	1.3	–	–
Instigation	1.3	–	–
Criminal intelligence	0.7	–	–
Computer searches	0.7	–	–
Other	3.3	28	20
Missing	9.7	–	–

Table 9.4 The role of scientific expertise

Type of expertise	Number of cases (n = 144; 179 suspects)	Percentage
Autopsy	3	1.6
Crime scene	0	–
Blood samples	4	2.2
Chemical analyses	5	2.8
Ballistics	3	1.6
Fingerprints	3	1.6
DNA analyses*	4	2.2
Lie detectors*	11	6.1
Hypnoses	0	–
Data banks	7	3.9
Sum total	40 (40 – 15 = 25)	22.3% (40) and 13.9% (25)

Note
*The lie detectors and the DNA analyses played no part in identifying suspects. Their role was strictly exculpatory (15 suspects).

Table 9.4 lists the number and percentage of cases where scientific expertise played an important — but still ancillary — part. It shows that scientific policing played an auxiliary role in the identification or location of some 22 per cent of all suspects, the contribution of each technique being respectively important in less than 3 per cent of the cases. Kuykendall (1986: 193) also concluded that scientific policing was of marginal value in identifying suspects. Actually, two of the most useful techniques – the polygraph and DNA fingerprinting – exclusively played an exculpatory role (excluding a suspect). Polygraph evidence is not admissible in Canadian courts. The investigators only use it as a last resort before classifying a case as inactive. For the period we investigated, DNA fingerprinting was infrequent, and the police had to wait several months to obtain the laboratory results. No DNA analysis was conclusive in identifying a suspect. Subtracting the 15 cases where the polygraph and DNA analyses played an important part, we are left with 25 cases (13.9 per cent of the suspects investigated). The most useful technique was the querying of criminal intelligence data banks, which played a significant role in 7 cases (3.9 per cent). I included crime scene investigation and hypnosis, although they played no part, because they have a large role in crime fiction (particularly crime scene investigation). I also could have included such staples of crime fiction as 'crime profiling', which also played no part. I discussed extensively the role of expertise and scientific policing in the course of my interviews. Their role was generally perceived to be important in setting the stage in murder court proceedings. However, their contribution to solving homicide cases was said to be modest.

Theories of criminal investigation

Criminal investigation is a quest for information that can be used as court evidence to secure the conviction of one or several suspects. The claim that to investigate is to process information is less of a finding – the end result of a process of inquiry – than of an assumption that was the starting point of most research on criminal investigation. This assumption is not only consistent with commonsense but is also rooted in the very meaning of the words 'inquiry' and 'investigation', both of which are derived from the Latin. 'To inquire' comes from a word – (in-quaerere) meaning to 'search for' and 'to interrogate'. It had already taken the meaning of looking for the perpetrator of a serious crime by the thirteenth century, where it was linked with the expression 'blood inquiry'. 'Investigation' derives from 'investigatio', which originally meant the process of tracking down (literally, to look for a vestige) a prey. Thus the claim that criminal investigation 'is fundamentally a form of information work' (Innes 2003: 113) is grounded in the semantics of the word 'investigation'. It is to this extent almost a tautology, which must nevertheless be taken into account if we are to do research on criminal investigation. This starting point is, however, very broad and allows for contrasting research perspectives that do not stress the same aspects of the investigative process. I briefly review two different theoretical approaches.

The epistemic approach

The adjective 'epistemic' is generally applied to things relating to knowledge or to the degrees of its validation. In this chapter, the epistemic approach is understood as stressing that the collection and processing of information through the application of forensic technology and various non-technological procedures – for instance, the interrogation of suspects – are the key feature of criminal investigation, most particularly of homicide investigation. The most articulate example of this approach to criminal investigation, albeit not the only one, is provided by Martin Innes' book on the investigation of murder (2003). In his theory of crime investigation, Innes makes a distinction between various kinds of messages according to the degree of their validation. *Information* is relevant data as opposed to 'noise'; *knowledge* is information believed to have factual status;[2] *intelligence* opens new fields of police action to generate further knowledge; and, lastly, *evidence* is knowledge formatted according to legal standards of proof (Innes 2003: 113–14). Criminal investigation is essentially viewed as the production of 'information', understood as a generic referring to the four variants presented above. In respect of my own empirical findings, this epistemic approach has several distinct features.

First, this approach is centred on the activity of detectives – plain-clothes criminal investigators belonging to special units. Even when all police are broadly viewed as knowledge workers *à la* Ericson and Haggerty (1997), the epistemic approach according to which detectives are conceived almost exclusively as information collators would not fit all police activity. As I suggested above, a theory of crime-solving is distinct from a theory of what criminal investigators actually do, as a great deal of crime is cleared up by patrol officers rushing to a crime scene independently of the action of detectives and catching the perpetrator red-handed. This kind of intervention does not require any knowledge work. The practical consequence of this observation is that recommendations to increase the clearance rate should not be directed exclusively at detectives but should aim to increase their co-ordination with uniformed police officers.

Secondly, the epistemic approach focuses on major crimes, such as murder, drug trafficking and organized crime. If one wants to develop a theory of criminal investigation, understood in the narrow sense of what criminal investigators do to solve a crime, one has to see them at work. As Richard Ericson showed in his classic study of two general investigation detectives' offices, the detectives' task was 'to process readily available suspects delivered to them or otherwise identified through the work of others' (1981: 136; also see Greenwood *et al.* 1977: 225; Hobbs 1988: 186). Such a task offers no grip for an epistemic theory of criminal investigation. Even if more than half the homicides in our sample were immediately solved without any detective work, murder investigations are still a fertile ground for observing detectives performing investigative work. Because of the high profile of murder, detectives have no discretion in selecting the promising cases for a speedy clearance while discarding the unpromising cases for a clearance pay-off. Every case must be investigated. This obligation generates a paradox for the epistemic theory. It cannot be questioned that, once an investigation has started, it is an information-gathering process that is expanding as long as the case remains unsolved. It has been established that the probability of solving a case drastically decreases according to the time devoted to solving it. On the one hand, the longer the investigation, the more it is information work. On the other hand, the lengthier is the opportunity for information work and the less chance there is of solving the case. The paradoxical consequence of this reasoning is that the epistemic theory of criminal investigation becomes more accurate as an investigation is failing. The technological paraphernalia is used as a last resort, usually to small avail, when all else is failing.

This consequence points to a third feature of the epistemic theory: it does not take into the consideration the judicial outcome of an investigation – that is, the conviction of the accused. To all research purposes, it stops at the point where a suspect is identified (arrested and charged), leaving outside its scope the conviction process. However, my own findings show that detectives are primarily courtroom evidence managers and that much of their time is spent securing a conviction. Taking post-case court processing into account reveals another crucial feature of the epistemic approach. The epistemic approach is deductive: it works from theory to context, applying abstract conceptual definitions of its key concepts to the actual business of criminal investigation as performed by detectives. For instance, it credits police detectives with a knack for intelligence, whereas police organizations have been criticized for their ineptitude at producing intelligence (United States Congress *et al.* 2002; Suskind 2006). More crucially, courtroom evidence is defined as grounded *knowledge* formatted according to the canons of legal discourse (Innes 2003: 114). Although the epistemic theory does admit that the police may exclude part of their knowledge from being produced as legal evidence for strategic reasons reflecting the politics of adversarial justice (Innes 2003: 114–15), it does not really consider the darker underside of police information work. When it reaches the courtroom stage where securing a conviction is of paramount importance, due-process requirements are superseded by the imperative to get results, the emphasis on means giving way to a focus on results (Klockars 1985). Police evidence presented in court often results from coercion and deception, and it may also stem from lies and perjury that are incompatible with the meaning of knowledge (and, needless to say, justice). The epistemic theory suffers in this regard from a memory lapse as it forgets that detectives were first described as 'secretive rogues' (Kuykendall 1986: 179). Defining the court evidence presented by detectives as *knowledge* is, at best, ingenuous. Research on the growing number of publicly acknowledged false convictions has shown that the police have produced as court evidence information that they explicitly knew not to be factual.

We saw previously that technological investigative means were used as a last resort, generally to little avail, when all else had failed. In the course of my research, I compared resolved murder cases with unresolved ones. My main finding was unexpected: the massive recourse to investigative technology – for instance, electronic surveillance, computer searches and DNA testing – is a distinctive feature of unresolved cases rather than a characteristic of cleared cases. One of the consequences of the extensive use of investigative technology is the dramatic increase of investigative costs. There are two famous cases of unresolved – or partially resolved – homicide cases in Canada. The first is the terrorist bombing of an Air India flight that left from a Canadian airport in June 1985 and exploded over the Atlantic, killing all 329 people onboard. Two people were finally accused of the bombing in 2003, and they were acquitted by the presiding judge in 2005 after a lengthy trial. The acquittal stirred such a furore in Canada that, in 2006, the government appointed a public commission of inquiry to review the failed police investigation. This investigation lasted for 20 years and its costs were over 120 million CAD. If we add to the cost of the investigation the money spent on the trial and for the budget for the commission of inquiry, the total sum spent in relation to this unsolved crime is in excess of 150 million CAD. The probability that the case will ever be solved is very slim.

The other notorious Canadian case is even stranger. Female prostitutes began to disappear in Vancouver in 1991. Giving in to public pressure, the Royal Canadian Mounted Police and the Vancouver Police formed, in 2001, the joint Missing Women Task

Force. In 2007, one suspect – Robert Pickton – was finally accused of the murder of 26 women (the total number of missing women is estimated to be between 65 and 69). To avoid confusing the jury, the judge decided to prosecute first six of the murder cases for which the evidence was apparently stronger (no complete body has ever been found on the grounds of Pickton's farm – where the murders are alleged to have been committed – only parts of different corpses, which were the object of DNA tests that succeeded in identifying 31 victims). Pickton was finally found guilty of these six murders but, astonishingly enough, the jury returned a verdict of *unpremeditated* murder. This must be one of the very few instances where a serial killer was convicted of several unpremeditated murders, if not the only one. This unreasonable verdict is believed to have been a compromise crafted to avoid a hung jury, a possible result of the weakness of the evidence. Yet the criminal investigation of this case – which is not yet finished – will end up costing even more than the Air India terrorist inquiry. It has already cost some 130 million CAD, and Pickton is still scheduled to stand trial for another 20 victims, although it is acknowledged that the evidence against him is even weaker in these cases. All the investigative technology that could be marshalled failed to resolve the Air India affair and could not produce evidence strong enough to convince a jury that a serial killer had premeditated his killings.

The pragmatic approach

According to Klockars (1985: 85–6; also see Kuykendall 1986: 191), detectives can be divided into those who are concerned primarily with either means or ends. This distinction may also apply to analysts of criminal investigation. The epistemic theory obviously focuses on means, and especially on the collection and processing of information, which offers no guarantee in respect of the result of the investigation. The pragmatic approach is result oriented and mainly accounts for the consequences of an investigative process. A consequentialist theory of criminal investigation has several features.

First, it focuses on the external outcomes. Outcomes obviously comprise clearance rates in their various definitions, but they are not exclusively defined by statistical measurements. For instance, the conviction of a high-profile crime boss may produce a destabilizing ripple effect throughout his organization. Pragmatists are also more sensitive to the different nature of the means used by detectives to produce results. Maguire *et al.* (1993) were commissioned by the UK

Home Office to perform a study of the assessment of investigative performance. While to fulfil their commission they had to address at length the issue of clear-up rates, they also endorsed the detectives' characterization of their investigative work as 'a mosaic of little tasks' (Maguire *et al.* 1993: 3). Consequentialist research, such as Greenwood *et al.* (1977), also tended to see in the diversity of detective work its defining feature. As I found in my own research, some of these tasks have a thin relationship to information work, as when detectives establish a stake-out or use decoys to catch a suspect in the act and to proceed to an arrest.

Secondly, a theory focusing on external outcomes cannot avoid looking into the post-case processing. Although the clearance rate is generally defined by the arrest of a suspect, such an arrest is not the definitive closure of a case: if the arrested suspect is eventually cleared by the court, the investigative case has, in theory at least, to be reopened (although this is not always so). Consequently, the second feature of the pragmatist approach is that it includes the post-case (post-arrest) segment of the investigation. Indeed, I found in my own research that this was the stage of the inquiry that required the most detective time, investigators endorsing my description of what they mostly did as the presentation and management of court evidence (also see Lévy 1987; McConville *et al.* 1991; Sanders and Young 2002). This work also consists of 'a mosaic of little tasks', such as making sure that the witnesses appear in court, summarizing their testimony for the prosecutor and affording protection for witnesses whose lives are in danger.

The post-clearance work takes on a special significance for assessing whether investigative work is information work. I cannot review all the courtroom tactics used by the police and the prosecution. I can, however, comment on some of them to the extent that they help us to decide between an epistemic and a pragmatic theory of criminal investigation. First, the material support of a piece of information (e.g. an audiotape) is as important for the purposes of evidence as is the information that is recorded on it. For instance, if the police cannot establish – through a complex 'chain of possession' process linking audiotapes to the intercepted communications of suspects – that recorded conversations presented in court are authentic and were not tampered with, they cannot be admitted as evidence. Secondly, a witness's credibility plays as big a part as what this person has to say. As we have seen, forensics and what is referred to as scientific policing play almost no part in solving crime. However, they play an important part in the courts because judges and juries are favourably impressed by expert opinion and scientific procedures and technology. Scientific expertise and evidentiary technology are used at the trial level as instruments for recasting the meanderings of the actual investigation in the form of a consistent knowledge-based process. Experts belong to forensics laboratories operated by the state and regularly appear in court, and their scientific competence comes to be taken for granted over the years. However, special experts recruited by the prosecution or the defence are subject at times to a ferocious cross-examination that tries to undermine their credibility. It is also well known that victims of sexual assault have their reputation targeted by the defence, although these destructive cross-examinations have been banned in many jurisdictions. The general point of the preceding observations is that, in court, the vehicle of information – be it an object or a person – is subject to as much scrutiny as the information itself.

As for all consequentialist practices, result-oriented investigations are vulnerable to the belief that the ends justify the means. The effects of such a belief on criminal investigation can only be detected through an *inductive approach* that is the third core feature of a pragmatic theory of criminal investigation. This particular form of induction proceeds from grounded field research to a theoretical elaboration that does not preclude from the outset contentious findings. This type of approach should be called critical induction in order to put it in contrast with naïve empiricism. For all its theoretical sophistication, the epistemic approach to criminal investigation shares with hard-boiled positivism a tendency to be blind to the mistakes of the knowledge workers and, more generally, to police deviance.

Knowledge workers and experts make honest mistakes, as anyone in the knowledge business does. Also, they may not be as conscientious as they should, given the fact that their testimony often leads to a court conviction and a penal sanction. In November 2007, Charles Smith, a Canadian pathologist who performed more than 1,000 autopsies, publicly apologized for the harm that was caused by the testimonies he had given in court over the last 20 years. Smith is the subject of a public inquiry in Ontario because of the great number of errors that he made in the course of his practice as a forensic pathologist.

Police investigators generally assess the credibility of their special witnesses and informants before they testify for the prosecution. However, there are situations where the investigators neglect to test their sources of information either intentionally or unintentionally. They may even entice a paid informant to lie on the witness stand to get a conviction. This is but one of the means that are used in the context of a general practice of 'framing the guilty', which was described to me by Egon Bittner during an interview he granted me in 1999:

> See, the police very often are convinced that they have the goods on somebody, but those goods don't work in the courtroom … And they engage in the practice for which they have a very peculiar term, as I heard it. It's called 'framing the guilty'. Well, the idea of framing is of course framing the innocent, but they frame the guilty. What they mean by that is that they catch somebody, they know that he did what they think he did, but they don't have the evidence. So they lie. Now, the fact that police lie on the witness stand is a well-known fact, everybody knows that, including the judges, I might say … I spoke to a man I befriended … he resigned from the New York Police Department with the rank of Lieutenant – and in our conversation he turned out to be one of the strongest critics of American policing … When I brought up this business of framing the guilty, he says he finds this to be the least objectionable part of policing. He says, in this struggle against crime, circumventing what is a bizarre and baroque system of restraint in the courtroom is not such a terribly great transgression (Bittner cited in Brodeur 2007: 122–3).

In the course of my own research, I was in a position to verify the assertions made by Bittner. In June 1995, a Quebec superior judge cleared members of a notorious Montreal criminal gang of all charges against them that related to their importing into Canada 16.5 tonnes of hashish when it became obvious that the police had fabricated evidence against them. This spectacular dismissal of a criminal trial because of the police tampering with the evidence caused a great shock, and so the Quebec government established two commissions of inquiry into the investigating practices of the police force involved in the case (I participated in one of the inquiries as director of research). It came out very clearly that this was indeed a case of framing the guilty, as later police investigations independently showed that this criminal gang was involved in massive operations of importing drugs, which resulted in several convictions. I also learnt that lies and false evidence were current police practices and were well known by judges. What made this case so different was that the judge dared to dismiss the trial in the face of fabricated evidence by the police.

However we may assess the practice of framing the guilty (known career criminals), it should not hide the fact that there are also cases where people without any past criminal histories were wrongly convicted of very serious offences and thrown in jail on the basis of flimsy evidence. DNA tests have been hailed as a most significant tool in the police arsenal. It may be an even more significant tool for the exoneration of the wrongfully convicted. From 1993 to April 2007, some 200 people wrongfully convicted in the USA of offences punished by very long terms in jail – mostly murder and rape – were exonerated by DNA tests and freed, often after having served part of their lives in prison (see http://www.law.northwestern.edu/wrongfulconvictions). When means other than DNA analysis are taken into account, the number of people exonerated from wrongful convictions is significantly higher. In Canada, three high-profile cases of wrongful convictions for murder – the Don Marshall case in Nova Scotia, the Guy-Paul Morin case in Ontario and the David Milgaard case in Saskatchewan – have generated public government inquiries (Nova Scotia 1989; Ontario 1998; the Commission of Inquiry into the Wrongful Conviction of David Milgaard was created in Saskarchewan in 2004 and has not yet published its report). The cost of these inquiries is extremely high, running into millions of Canadian dollars. After Milgaard's exoneration in 1999, the real culprit was found and convicted. Milgaard was awarded 10 million CAD in compensation for his ordeal. The police may, however, also err on the opposite side when they fail to investigate thoroughly an obvious suspect. The Stephen Lawrence Inquiry in the UK was appointed to investigate such a case (Macpherson 1999).

Conclusion

The above observations are not intended to resolve the issue of whether an epistemic or a pragmatic approach should be applied to criminal investigation. Although I recognize that the epistemic approach is more focused than the pragmatic one, I also believe that it is too narrow and overly simplified. First of all, solving cases is a much broader notion than detective work in the sense that it involves many other people than detectives. The people immediately involved in solving a case – neighbours identifying the perpetrator, citizens performing an arrest, a police patrol, officers and other participants – are not all performing information work. Secondly, solving a case is, in a great number of instances, a brief process bearing little resemblance to the painstaking gathering of clues and their clever interpretation as depicted in detective fiction. However, detective work extends in time beyond the simple business of crime-solving, which is generally achieved quickly. The longer it takes to solve a case, the more the awaited resolution is solely dependent on the work of investigators. However, the more clearing a case depends on the extended work of investigators, the fewer are the chances the case will be cleared. Paradoxically, detectives come into their own as knowledge workers when they are failing to solve a case. Thirdly, a theory of criminal investigation that leaves out the post-arrest processing that leads, in most tried cases, to a court conviction misses an essential dimension of criminal inquiries. Finally, a theory of criminal investigation that does not address the issue of investigative fallibility is woefully incomplete. Theories of policing as information or knowledge work are relatively insensitive to the perversions of knowledge. Egon Bittner aptly captured what separates criminal investigation work from the true pursuit of knowledge:

> [the detectives'] reliance on informants about criminal affairs creates an information movement, [in] an information-structuring sense. It is not the kind of information gathering that is characteristic of science, where the scientist keeps his eyes open and, perhaps informed by a theoretical perspective, takes in whatever he or she sees without any preconceived notion of relevance. Truth is the thing that is relevant, and if things turn out to be the opposite of what a theory led him to expect, well, then that's what he finds. And I think it's not that way in information-gathering in the police. That is, the police are interested in hearing only particular kinds of things, and if they don't hear what they would like to hear, they will reformulate what they do hear to fit their expectations (Bittner, cited in Brodeur 2007: 122).

In respect of what was said above, things have taken a turn for the worst in post-911 times. For various historical reasons, one of the most important being the mind and body divide found in almost all civilizations, the idea of physical violence and the idea of intellectual knowledge belong to different, if not antithetical, categories. Both surveillance technology and human intelligence, as it was collected and processed by the security services, utterly failed to prevent the terrorist attacks perpetrated on US territory on 11 September 2001 and elsewhere (for example, in Spain, Indonesia and the UK). To remedy this failure, the recourse to physical violence against arrested opponents is once again viewed as a legitimate way of extracting information. On 8 March 2008, President George W. Bush used his veto to shut down a congressional effort to limit the Central Intelligence Agency's latitude to subject terrorism suspects to harsh interrogation techniques, such as waterboarding, a technique in which restrained prisoners are threatened with drowning (Myers 2008: 1). Although such techniques are prohibited by the military and law enforcement agencies, recent history has shown that this prohibition may be circumvented by rendering suspects to be interrogated to the one agency allowed to use torture, or to countries known to practise it. This regression to the application of 'pain-inducing technologies' is not only contrary to a worldwide United Nations' ban on the use of torture, of which the USA is a signatory, but it is also unreliable as a means to produce self-incriminating information and predictive knowledge about future terrorist attempts: a person under torture will confess to anything to stop the ordeal to which he or she is being subjected. Bacon's maxim is not reversible. Knowledge is power, but power is not knowledge, however hard it tries to break people and bend facts to its designs. The renewed amalgamation of violence and confession should give pause to our endeavours to fit all policing into a well intentioned quest for meaning and truth.

Notes

1 This chapter draws in part on a forthcoming book: *A Treatise on Policing*. I was awarded a Killam Scholarship in 2002 to undertake the research for this book. I wish to thank the Canadian Council of Arts for financial assistance that led to the writing of this chapter and the forthcoming book.

2 This characterization of knowledge, which is borrowed from Mead (1932), is highly questionable. Conceiving knowledge as a type of *belief* undermines the basic contrast between faith and knowledge, which is a cornerstone of the western philosophical tradition. In using the defining pattern applied by Mead and Innes in the case of knowledge to frame a definition of faith, we would have to characterize faith as *information believed to have no factual status*. This is nonsensical and also outrageous for believers.

References

Ainsworth, P.B. (2001) *Offender Profiling and Crime Analysis*. Cullompton: Willan.

Ben-Shakhar, G. and Furedy, J.J. (1990) *Theories and Applications in the Detection of Deception: A Psychological and International Perspective*. New York, NY: Springer-Verlag.

Brodeur, J.-P. (2005) 'L'enquête policière', in *Criminologie*. Montréal: Les Presses de l'Université de Montréal.

Brodeur, J.-P. (2007) 'An encounter with Egon Bittner', *Crime, Law and Social Change*, 48: 105–32.

Dash, S., Schwartz, R.F. and Knowlton, R.E. (1959) *The Eavesdroppers*. New Brunswick, NJ: Rutgers University Press.

Deeley, P. (1971) *Beyond the Breaking Point*. London: Arthur Baker.

Eisen, M.L., Quas, J.A. and Goodman, G.S. (eds) (2002) (eds) *Memory and Suggestibility in the Forensic Interview*. Mahwah, NJ: Lawrence Erlbaum Associates.

Ericson, R.V. (1981) *Making Crime: A Study of Detective Work*. Toronto: Butterworths.

Ericson, R.V. and Haggerty, K. (1997) *Policing the Risk Society*. Toronto: University of Toronto Press.

Greenman, F.F. (1938) *Wire-tapping: Its Relation to Civil Liberties*. Stamford, CT: Overbrook Press.

Greenwood, P.W., Chaiken, J.M. and Petersilia, J. (1977) *The Criminal Investigation Process*. Lexington, MA: D.C. Heath.

Hobbs, D. (1988) *Doing the Business*. Oxford: Oxford University Press.

Inbau, F.E. and Reid, J.E. (eds) (1967) *Criminal Interrogations and Confessions* (2nd edn). Baltimore, MD: Williams & Wilkins.

Innes, M. (2003) *Investigating Murder: Detective Work and the Police Response to Criminal Homicide*. Oxford: Oxford University Press.

Klockars, C.B. (1985) *The Idea of Police. Law and Criminal Justice Series*. Vol. 3. Beverly Hills, CA: Sage.

Krude, T. (ed.) (2004) *DNA: Changing Science and Society*. Cambridge: Cambridge University Press.

Kuykendall, J. (1982) 'The criminal investigation process: toward a conceptual framework', *Journal of Criminal Justice*, 10: 131–45.

Kuykendall, J. (1986) 'The municipal police detective: an historical analysis', *Criminology*, 24: 175–202.

Levy, H. (1996) *And the Blood Cried Out: A Prosecutor's Spellbinding Account of the Power of DNA*. New York: NY Basic Books.

Lévy, R. (1987) *Du suspect au coupable: le travail de police judiciaire*. Genève: Éditions Médecine et Hygiène.

Macpherson, Sir W. (1999) *The Stephen Lawrence Inquiry: Report of an Inquiry by Sir William Macpherson of Cluny advised by Tom Cook, the Right Reverend Dr John Sentamu, Dr Richard Stone*. London, HMSO: The Stationery Office.

Maguire, M.L., Noaks, L., Hoobs, R. and Brearly, N. (1993) *Assessing Investigative Performance: A Study Commissioned by the Home Office*. Cardiff: School of Social and Administrative Studies, University of Wales, College of Cardiff.

McConville, M,, Sanders, A. and Leng, R. (1991) *The Case for the Prosecution*. New York, NY: Routledge.

Mead, G.H. (1932) *The Philosophy of the Present*. Chicago: University of Chicago Press.

Myers, S.L. (2008) 'Bush vetoes bill on C.I.A. tactics, affirming legacy', *The New York Times*, 9 March: 1.

National Research Council (2003) *Fairness and Effectiveness in Policing: the Evidence*, Committee to Review Research of Police Policy and Practices, Westly Skogan and Kathleen Frydl, eds. Committee on Law and Justice, Division of Behavioral and Social Sciences and Education, Washington, DC: The National Academies Press.

Nova Scotia (1989), *Report of the Royal Commission on the Donald Marshall Jr. Prosecution*. Halifax: Royal Commission on the Donald Marshall Jr. Prosecution.

Ontario (1998) *The Commission on Proceedings Involving Guy Paul Morin: Report (the Honourable Fred Kaufman, Chairman)*. Toronto: Ontario Ministry of the Attorney General, Queen's Printer for Ontario.

Rossmo, K.D. (2003) *Geographic Profiling*. New York, NY: CRC Press.

Sanders, A. and Young, R. (2002) 'From suspect to trial', in M. Maguire *et al*. (eds) *The Oxford Handbook of Criminology* (3rd edn). Oxford: Clarendon Press.

Suskind, R. (2006) *The One Percent Doctrine: Deep inside America's Pursuit of its Enemies since 9/11*. New York, NY: Simon & Schuster.

Turvey, B.E. (ed.) (2002) *Criminal Profiling: An Introduction to Behavioral Evidence Analysis*. New York, NY: Academic Press.

United States Congress, Senate and Select Committee on Intelligence (2002) *Additional Views of Senator Richard C. Shelby, Vice Chairman, Senate Select Committee on Intelligence: September 11 and the Imperative of Reform in the U.S. Intelligence Community*. Washington, DC: US Congress.

Wellford, C. and Cronin, J. (1999) *An Analysis of Variables Affecting the Clearance of Homicides: A Multistate Study*. Washington, DC: Justice Research and Statistics Association.

Chapter 10

Sorting systems: identification by database

David Lyon

Introduction

National identification systems, which first appeared in the twentieth century, are rapidly becoming universal. While always a possible means of state interference in everyday life, this aspect of national identification systems is often downplayed in the light of plausible rationales for their introduction. The information technologies on which they now depend, however, are becoming increasingly more sophisticated and powerful, which may mean gains in efficiency but which also accentuate questions about civil liberties and human rights. The reason for this is that administrative identification now involves automated systems for social sorting. Although long a contentious issue, what makes new ID card systems different is their reliance on searchable databases and networked communications. Such networked databases enhance the surveillance capacities of ID card systems, bringing them in line not only with other administrative systems but also offering a means of overall communication and co-ordination. Identification systems, and especially 'national ID card' systems, therefore represent an important dimension of surveillance societies, and thus raise urgent questions.

While technological determinism may claim that new technologies inevitably have 'impacts', the purpose of this chapter is to show that policies concerning such areas as immigration, anti-terrorism or identity theft that permit the use of the networked, searchable databases take such systems to a higher level of surveillance (Stalder and Lyon 2003). When used in conjunction with other, frequently adopted ID technologies, such as radio frequency IDCRFID and biometrics, searchable remote databases enable extensive and intensive forms of citizen monitoring hitherto unimagined.

New ID card systems are best thought of as a form of surveillance, especially the kind of surveillance that has been growing rapidly since the later part of the twentieth century. Such surveillance typically depends on data from the human body (van der Ploeg 2005), is automated, is connected with control – especially access control (Galloway 2004) – and aims to achieve universal coverage (Staples 2000; Lyon 2007). In ID systems, biometrics offers the body as a means of authentication: the database–card relationship is electronic (often using RFID scanning to facilitate automatic functioning) and both travel and transactions are accessed and controlled. Further, national ID card systems aim to encompass the entire adult population of a specific country.

ID cards associated with databases are therefore systems of social sorting, permitting extensive discrimination between different populations through classification categories that often include ethnicity and religion. Thus the challenge is to establish systems that avoid exclusionary bias and in which accountability for handling personal data is of paramount importance. To explore this issue further, the first step is to consider the relationship between 'eligibility' and 'legibility'.

Citizenship: eligibility and legibility

The reasons why new ID card systems are different from older ones are rooted in the relationship between eligibility and legibility. A citizen's eligibility for various rights and services may be proved through an identification system that indicates who exactly are *bona fide* citizens. The device for proving eligibility is, however, a means whereby the state achieves greater legibility: citizens may be brought more directly under the government's gaze through unique identification systems, what Scott (1998) refers to as government administration 'seeing like a state'.

Although often taken for granted, citizenship is a contested issue, especially for refugees and asylum seekers or for nationals whose children are born abroad. To distinguish between genuine citizens and imposters, governments require a reliable means of verifying identity. Most modern states name, count and classify their citizens, which they do through documentary evidence, such as birth certificates, or by conducting censuses. The twentieth century, however, saw the increasing use of ID cards and passports as a means of checking who really is a citizen of a particular state (Torpey 2000; Salter 2003).

As nation-states evolved, citizenship became associated with rights, privileges and responsibilities (Abercrombie *et al.* 1983; Giddens 1987). Being a member of a certain family, clan or class came to mean less for citizenship than proving one was a resident of a particular state, born of specifiable parents in a particular place. The details of one's birth, marriage and death took on an administrative rather than a religious significance in the burgeoning bureaucracies of government. The state thus sought to distinguish between genuine and false citizens so that the rights of citizens were extended only to those who were genuinely eligible.

The means of keeping track of these personal details – the 'surveillance' that makes life legible – is thus very ambiguous. On the one hand, tremendous benefits accrue to citizens through being able to vote, to be educated or to hold health insurance. On the other hand, the state can also use those records to limit the activities or movements of citizens or, worse, to deem certain citizens as second class and to consign them to inferior or even brutal treatment. In the 1930s, Nazi Germany used early IBM machines to analyse census data, registrations and ancestral records to sort undesirable Jewish citizens from desirable ('Aryan') ones, and in Rwanda in the 1990s, the Belgian colonial ID card system was used to single out Tutsi targets for Hutu slaughter. In both cases, horrendous genocide was the outcome (Black 2001; Longman 2001).

Today, every nation-state from Mexico, to Morocco, to Mongolia has complex and sophisticated ways of keeping tabs on individual citizens, the records of which are stored in large-scale departments, such as employment, education, health and taxation. Since the later part of the twentieth century, most of these records have been computerized. This improves efficiency because, in theory at least, of the hugely increased storage and transmission capacity and, importantly, because of the state's ability to search those databases remotely. The ambiguities of such state surveillance have, however, never gone away. If anything, they have become more marked. Identification systems, for example, may simplify our interactions with government departments, granting ready access to information or benefits but, equally, they can be used to make dubious and sometimes dangerous distinctions between classes of citizens, advantaging some at the expense of others.

Why social sorting is central

The early twenty-first century saw the development of several new national identification systems. Indeed, some systems, such as those in Malaysia ('Mykad') and Japan ('Juki-Net'), have their roots in administrative and commercial ventures of the later twentieth century, but others, such as those in Italy and the UK (approved in the UK Parliament in March 2006), are in part responses to 9/11 and the 'war on terror'. The USA has yet to develop a national ID system but the current attempt to rationalize and integrate federally the driving licence system (which previously was run on a state-by-state basis) into the Real ID may turn out to be a de facto national ID system. In Canada also, while there is as yet no clear plan to develop a national ID system, the logic of both administrative and security arrangements points in this direction (Clement *et al.* 2008).

ID cards of various kinds have been used for centuries and, in modern times, especially in association with colonialism, crime control and war (Cole 2002). The purpose behind these older cards was that the holder could produce, on demand, a document to prove his or her identity. New national ID card systems, however, are based on a national registry – a database (or databases in some cases, such as the UK) containing personal information that can be searched and checked independently of any need to see the citizen's card. The unique identifier contained in the card is also the key to unlock the database(s) and is thus itself a source of considerable power (Clarke 2006a). To understand the significance of this we must consider the context in which new, often multi-purpose, national ID systems are being developed.

The information revolution that began in the 1970s as a result of developments in microelectronics revolutionized the storage, retrieval, processing and transmission of data. This revolution was as much about the communication of data as about data storage and processing. Personal data could be passed with ease from one department to another such that what once required official permission or even legal warrant became a routine procedure. From the bureaucratic point of view, computers that communicated with each other appeared to enhance organizational efficiency by offering data matching between, say, customs and employment or education and police departments, but citizens now had less say in what happened to their personal records.

The computerization of government administration ushered in the era of what Clarke (1988) calls 'dataveillance'. Clarke defines dataveillance as the 'use of personal data systems in the investigation or monitoring of the actions or communications of one or more persons', and he observes that this facilitates 'mass surveillance' as opposed to the more familiar 'personal surveillance'. The latter might be used, for example, to track suspected criminals whereas the former may be a means of identifying individuals as members of a category of interest to the surveillance organization. The information intensiveness of computing and communication power that expanded rapidly from the 1970s onwards allowed for more fine-grained decision-making that contributed further to a 'data imperative' in which more and more data were sought in the name of maximizing knowledge and efficiency.

As Clarke argued two decades ago, reliable identification methods are essential in the quest for what he described as a 'dossier society'. With a range of data systems in place – gathering data for various purposes – alongside some means of connecting them via telecommunication networks, only consistent identification is required for a cost-effective system of dataveillance to develop, without the need for a central or national data bank. Such a system permits data matching (sometimes called record linkage) that offers new and possibly illuminating combinations of data which may help to enhance physical security or to detect or prevent error, abuse or fraud, thus improving tax or welfare schemes in the public sector or financial and insurance services in the private sector. Suspicion may arise about such systems, however, where previously no grounds for suspicion existed, just because of an apparent data match. And I say 'apparent' because many matching schemes have been exposed as erroneous. At roughly the same time as Clarke discussed dataveillance (in the mid-1980s), Marx and Reichman (1984) showed that half the matches in a New York State program were spurious.

By the 1990s, however, software had been developed that made searching through a database much easier. As Lessig (1999: 151) points out, early systems of monitoring involved noting differences only and they did not collect searchable records. Today's machines notice any and every transaction that, together, become searchable records. This makes profiling possible and enables what Gandy (1993) calls the 'panoptic sort'. This sort discriminates between different classes of people — say, Internet users on the basis of the sites they visit or frequent flyers, who may receive better services in return for their 'loyalty' to the airline. Such a sort may be manipulatory or, over time, it may become normalizing: the categories themselves help make possible certain kinds of actions and also have consequences for how we conceive of ourselves or others (Hacking 1993, 2002).

Searchable databases enable discriminatory judgements to be built into systems, and such judgements may as easily work against individuals as for them (Lessig 1999). Although data protection and privacy laws (such as the UK Data Protection Act 1998) have been passed to limit such activities, it is difficult to keep pace with technical change or with the ingenuity of those who try to sidestep the legislation. In the case of ID card systems, the unique personal identifier makes it possible to obtain access to several kinds of database; and the more multi-purpose the system, the more databases are likely to be involved. If the UK ID card system would, as is claimed, guard against 'identity theft', then this suggests that commercial data relating to banks and credit cards would be accessible as well as data relating to government departments, such as immigration or health.

The combination of computing and communications capacities in surveillance – and this is clearly true for ID systems – has a further implication that, though indirect, is nevertheless singularly significant. It promotes a reliance on those who provide expertise, both technological and commercial. In an era of outsourced services, the role of technologists and business people in organizational bureaucracies has become increasingly significant, such that it is inappropriate to understand the surveillance of personal data without considering the technological (usually software) and business practice (information management) priorities that now inform the handling of personal data. This trend was made possible, of course, by the economic restructuring that accompanied the technological revolution, and it helped to produce what we now call globalization and also stimulated such innovations as outsourcing, which is now applied to many aspects of ID systems.

This interplay of technological and business practices with organizational control occurs in the development of ID card systems. In any computerized system, the key to records retrieval is to have consistent and, if possible, unique identifiers – in this case, for individual citizens. What may appear as efficiency to some may appear to others as potential social control or, more precisely, subtle forms of governance (for a critical view from a computer scientist, see Clarke 2006b). But where does this governance originate? In part, national ID systems may be seen as a means of increased state control, but they are also the products of technical and business expertise. So-called smart cards have been in use for some time in commercial settings, but it is only recently that they have been employed by governmental administration (Stalder and Lyon 2003). Moreover, these systems, along with related biometric passports, rely on techniques of identity management developed in the online Internet world. Modes of regulating who may or may not have virtual access to websites and other electronic domains are thus now applied to the offline world of borders and citizenship classification.

The growth of biometrics as a means of verification (checking that the individual is who he or she claims to be) and identification (checking that the individual's record matches that in the relevant database) should also be noted. All new ID systems use some kind of biometric, based on a feature of the human body. Fingerprints, iris scans, facial topography and hand scans can all be used as biometrics, and these enhance many modern passports and ID card systems. Biometrics are employed to increase accuracy and to reduce the possibilities of fraud. While PINs and passwords may be forgotten or lost, the body is always available and provides a direct link between the record and the person. As noted below, however, there remain some problems with the use of biometrics in surveillance.

Through both biometrics and networked ID systems, governmental administration now operates in a world fraught with subtle nuances – identities and identifications. In this world, those with access to resources (international businesspeople, tourists and so on) are highly mobile, and their identification systems (from credit cards to frequent flyer cards) tend to accelerate their ease of movement. For others – working (or, worse, unemployed) migrants, refugees, asylum seekers and those with distinctive 'Muslim' or 'Arab' names – these systems tend to militate *against* movement, both within and between countries. While older, twentieth-century understandings of citizenship stressed the *inclusion* of all eligible people in systems of health, welfare and legal protection, newer citizenship practices, including ID systems, seem to stress the *exclusion* of undesirable elements (Bigo 2004).

As the economic and political disparities between the global south and north have grown, resistance to the rich north has taken new and, for some, unexpected forms. In particular, the deep-seated humiliations of the Arab world at the hands of western colonial and economic powers have helped to spawn what is now regarded as a key international problem – a sort of permanent crisis: global terrorism. Certain key events, starting symbolically (though not historically) with 9/11, have instigated the rapid growth of new surveillance and identification systems once more geared to establishing unambiguously who is a bona fide citizen of which country (Ball and Webster 2003; Lyon 2003). The difficulty is that many people are on the move, for many reasons, and ID systems are now sought that can classify these people according not only to citizenship but also to status – temporary, permanent, national and so on. As we have seen, searchable databases already facilitate social classification and categorization. In this context, they appear to be a godsend.

New ID systems not only raise questions about the reality of the very citizenship rights that identification was once supposed to guarantee – freedom of movement, freedom from want, equality before the law and so on – but they are also themselves subject to globalizing forces. Governments now seek ways of 'harmonizing' their identification procedures for both border crossing and for internal policing and controls. Once again, this is facilitated by the new technologies. The International Civil Aviation Organization is a prominent player in this process. It has set standards for biometric passports and, by implication, for new national smart ID programs, such as that in the UK. International conventions are held to develop 'globally interoperable systems' for identification in the field of 'MRTDs' (machine-readable travel documents) (ICAO 2008). A recent example of this is the Federal Bureau of Investigation's request for biometric ID data on criminals and terrorists to be shared between several countries that are already signatories to message interception systems – Australia, Canada, New Zealand and the UK. This 'Server in the Sky' would ratchet current police and intelligence data-sharing practices up to a new and unprecedented level of integration, if approved (*Guardian* 2008).

This globalizing of surveillance (Mattelart 2007), through the regulation of mobility and transactions and through 'interoperable' agreements on technology standards, appears to be contributing to what Gandy (2006) calls the 'cumulative disadvantage' associated with social sorting systems that use searchable databases. Although he discusses this in the context of discriminatory practices in the insurance industry (which frequently have the effect of exacerbating racial disadvantage), the same kinds of sorting mechanisms produce disadvantage at an international level, affecting immigrants, asylum seekers, refugees and the like in disproportionate ways.

Sorting, therefore, is central to new ID systems. It permits what might be called remote control, especially 'policing at a distance'. It contributes to what Haggerty and Ericson (2000) call the 'surveillant assemblage' – the only partially co-ordinated 'coming together' of many and varied contemporary practices and processes that record, monitor, locate, track, observe and identify individuals so that they can be profiled and their personal data mined for further analysis. Indeed, identification processes are central to this assemblage. This is apparent in post-9/11 international policing and anti-terrorism activities (Lewis 2005) and also in more mundane matters, such as international financial transactions. It is often argued that improved identification practices, and especially the development of national ID systems, could increase the effectiveness of many components of information-based social interactions or, in other words, the surveillant assemblage.

Critical commentary and future directions

Identification and citizenship belong together in the modern world. Citizenship has increasingly come to be viewed as an individual matter for which a system of personal records is required. While this now appears in the broad swath of 'dataveillance' that exists across a range of government departments, the common denominator is the need for identifiers that will distinguish one individual from another. Increasingly, however, such identifiers are used across different domains.

As Rule (1973) pointed out more than 30 years ago, the US driving licence is often used as a universal ID in that country. Today, the pressure is on to find IDs that work for several purposes – border crossings, fraud control, access to government information and perhaps commercial (video rental) and semi-commercial (libraries) purposes as well. This is shaping the field in fresh ways: as we have seen, the same criteria for identification are now sought across national boundaries.

The key developments in this story could be read as technological progress but, whatever one's judgement, it is the (let us assume) unintended consequences that count. However much one acknowledges, rightly, the ambiguity of surveillance as seen in such areas as ID card systems, the key problem is that, once established, systems can easily acquire an apparent life of their own, which is much easier to initiate than to halt or redirect. When such agendas as the 'war on terror', curbing the migration of undesirable groups and even the quest for solutions for credit card fraud shape the development of ID systems, the 'impersonal' demands of a classic bureaucracy do seem to be somewhat undermined.

ID card systems offer unique identifiers and are thus critically significant for all government activity. This activity can range from anti-terrorism to access to government information. But the chief difficulty always lies in the powers granted to the state (now in alliance with corporate and technical bodies), which has control over the means of identification. In the UK case, the lack of clarity about the primary purpose of the ID system is a key issue for those attempting to evaluate the progress of its development (Select Committee on Science and Technology 2006).

There are other serious difficulties. One is the reliability of ID systems and of the biometric tests on which they rely (Zureik and Hindle 2004). The twin problems of 'failure to enroll' (FTE) (the biometric is unrecognizable) and 'false non-match' (the subsequent reading does not match the properly enrolled individual biometric) remain, yet it appears that decisions have been made about biometrics before full trials have been conducted. As many as one in six people may not be able to use their cards readily to obtain healthcare or pensions because of FTE problems, even though they may in principle have 'entitlement' (Grayling 2005). At their moment of vulnerability, they will actually be handicapped further.

Beyond this, ID systems may subtly classify populations according to opaque criteria. Major FTEs occur, for example, with non-white – black, Asian, Hispanic – people, which may produce a bias towards whiteness (Pugliese 2005). It is this ability to engage in social sorting that may, in the long term, be even more insidious than the fears about reduced mobility in countries where the police may demand ID documents at any time (Lyon 2004). Such systems will have the capacity to sort between those who are eligible for services or access and those who are ineligible, but less than visible mechanisms will also operate that will skew the system against those already likely to be disadvantaged. Such social sorting tends to produce a second-class citizenship rather than supporting solidaristic and egalitarian practice.

Beyond this, increasing global integration and harmonization remove decisions from the local, human scale and introduce other actors (technology experts, entrepreneurs) into the drama. Now that cultural and national identities have become such a contested dimension of life in the contemporary world – carrying a heavy freight of life chances and choices, memories and hopes – it is ironic that parallel efforts are being made to reduce them to machine-readable formulae and algorithms for ease of bureaucratic, policing and corporate administration. However human beings are identified by others – and especially by impersonal machine systems – it is not surprising that countervailing tendencies appear, challenging and offering alternatives to those identifications.

Conclusion: challenges to the regulators

How can new ID systems, whose use is so consequential for those citizens identified and classified by them, be made accountable to others beyond political constituents and corporate shareholders? Is there a larger framework than combatting fraud or regulating immigration or even national security within which the administration of citizenship via ID systems may be understood? Put another way, can ID systems be made compatible with the desires of ordinary citizens, not merely for national security but also for human security, which is both more global and more personal?

At present, the British case of a multi-purpose national ID system does not offer much promise in this regard. It is far from clear that even national security will necessarily be enhanced by the emerging system. Many have suggested that national security would be better served by improving border security and conventional intelligence gathering – an idea that was underscored by the August 2006 alleged Atlantic flight terrorist plot involving more than 20 Britons. Although the US administration claimed that the operation showed the need for more advanced passenger data (*New York Times* 2006), it is clear that the alleged plot was foiled by the use of informers, undercover agents and tip-offs.

Many ordinary citizens object to the various ID systems that have appeared over the past few years. Municipalities and states in Japan and the USA have objected to the new uses of personal data by refusing to co-operate, and in the UK numerous vocal protests accompanied the passage of the Identity Cards Bill through Parliament. Objections to the Australian 'Access Card'– a proposed multi-purpose identifier that appeared to its opponents as a backdoor national ID card – almost led to its defeat under the John Howard coalition government and to its subsequent abandonment by the new Kevin Rudd Labour government that came to power in November 2007 (see www.privacy.org.au/Campaigns/ID_cards/index.html). Such objections should be considered by the regulators, from the case against ID systems altogether (that they are superfluous and their objectives can be met by other means) to arguments about testing and improving the technologies *before* they are adopted and bringing in measures in line with at least EU data protection requirements (there is disagreement, however, as to who is responsible for ID card developments within the EU; see www.statewatch.org/news/2006/jul/09eu-id-cards.html/).

Assuming, pragmatically, that it is now too late to turn back the ID system tide in the UK, the challenge for the regulators is to take every opportunity to install rigorous safeguards and transparency and accountability of use. The eventual system need not be as negative as its critics fear. Other countries that have yet to adopt or even to debate ID systems would do well to heed the whole debate as it has unfolded in the UK. Even though the Home Affairs Committee of the UK Parliament concluded that the ID proposals were ineffective, costly and a violation of civil liberties, the proposal has been pushed forward.

Former Prime Minister, Tony Blair, assured the British public, against the evidence, that the civil liberties objections no longer carried weight, and this seems to be linked to the often-heard argument of despair that cards are already carried for other purposes anyway. Why not one more? The reason why not is that other cards, such as driving licences, credit cards and passports, are held voluntarily. The non-obligatory nature of the initial ID system should fool no one. Once it is needed for a range of service access, it will become de facto compulsory. Moreover, the voluntary cards have a single purpose, such as for drivers, consumers or tourists, whereas the ID card system gives the government powers – and this is the regulatory challenge – to monitor activities across a range of roles that include the three aforementioned as well as those more conventionally associated with governmental administration.

The challenges to would-be regulators of ID systems are thus manifold and urgent. If hard-won civil liberties are not to be stripped away in the name of a 'war on terror' or because of dubious claims about greater administrative efficiency in service delivery, then ID systems need to be scrutinized very closely. The best possible ID system must address such civil liberties risks. The oversight of technical and legal provisions should be made more transparent and workable, and public concerns should be heeded much more diligently. It is difficult to escape the conclusion that, at present, the political need to be seen to be doing something and persistent pressures from high-technology companies are dominating the issue.

The best framework for considering such matters is the notion of human security. Although not in competition with 'national security,' human security begins at a local community level and with the real, everyday concerns of individuals and families. Combatting terrorism is not usually high on such priority lists, although freedom from fear and want are likely to be. According to Kaldor (2005), such human security concerns may be locally rooted but they are simultaneously based in rights, multilateralism and legitimate government and have a regional focus.

One could object, of course, that, without evidence of socially or politically negative consequences – actual cases, that is – resulting from the implementation of new national ID card systems, the citizens of countries that are adopting such schemes can sleep easy. However, it must be observed that these are early days for ID systems with central databases and biometrics, and little evidence is likely to have appeared because no country has, as yet, fully implemented such a scheme. It is clear, however, that the new technologies underlying ID systems have to be refined to the point where they can be said to have proved their reliability. Of more serious concern, it is also clear that the rationale for most systems includes particular attention to marginalized or vulnerable groups – immigrants, asylum seekers, refugees, welfare claimants terror suspects and so on – so the social sorting such systems enable will likely affect them first. Where we do have evidence, historically, of pre-electronic ID systems, the record is uniformly stained with abuses and misuses.

New national ID systems play a crucial, pivotal role in the development of contemporary surveillance societies. Given the spiralling media-amplified public fears, the making of political mileage out of conspicuous and expensive 'anti-fraud' and 'anti-terror' schemes, and the corporate pressure from persuasive high-tech companies, the struggle for human security and against civil liberties-compromising measures such as ID systems is likely to be long and tough. But for the sake of common humanity it is a struggle eminently worth engaging.

References

Abercrombie, N., Hill, S. and Turner, B. (1983) *Sovereign Individuals of Capitalism*. London: Allen & Unwin.

Ball, K. and Webster, F. (eds) (2003) *The Intensification of Surveillance*. London: Pluto Press.

Bigo, D. (2004) 'Globalized in-security: the field of the professionals of unease management and the ban-opticon', *Traces*, 4: 109–57.

Black, E. (2001) *IBM and the Holocaust*. New York, NY: Random House.

Clarke, R. (1988) 'Information technology and dataveillance', *Communications of the ACM*, 31: 498–512.

Clarke, R. (2006a), 'National identity schemes: the elements' (www.anu.edu.au/people/Roger.Clarke/DV/NatIDSchemeElms.html).

Clarke, R. (2006b) 'National identity cards? Bust the myth of "Security über Alles"!' (www.anu.edu.au/people/Roger.Clarke/DV/NatID-BC-0602. html).

Clement, A., Hosein, G., Davies, S. and Boa, K. (2008) 'Towards national ID policies for Canada: federal initiatives and alternative principles', in C. Bennett and D. Lyon (eds) *Playing the Identity Card.* London and New York, NY: Routledge.

Cole, S. (2002) *Suspect Identities.* Cambridge, MA: Harvard University Press.

Galloway, A. (2004). *Protocol: How Control Exists after Decentralization.* Cambridge, MA: MIT Press.

Gandy, O. (1993) *The Panoptic Sort: A Political Economy of Personal Information.* Boulder, CO: Westview Press.

Gandy, O. (2006) 'Quixotics unite! Engaging the pragmatists on rational discrimination', in D. Lyon (ed.) *Theorizing Surveillance: The Panopticon and Beyond.* Cullompton: Willan Publishing.

Giddens, A. (1987) *The Nation-state and Violence.* Cambridge: Polity Press.

Grayling, A.C. (2005) *In Freedom's Name: The Case against Identity Cards.* London: Liberty.

Guardian (2008) 'FBI wants instant access to British identity data', 15 January.

Hacking, I. (1993) *The Taming of Chance.* Cambridge: Cambridge University Press.

Hacking, I. (2002) *Historical Ontology.* Cambridge, MA: Harvard University Press.

Haggerty, K. and Ericson, R. (2000) 'The surveillant assemblage', *British Journal of Sociology*, 51: 605–22.

International Civil Aviation Organization (2008) *Machine-readable Travel Documents* (www.icao.int/icao/en/atb/fal/mrtd/overview.htm).

Kaldor, M. (2005) 'What is human security?', in D. Held *et al.* (eds) *Debating Globalization.* Cambridge: Polity Press.

Lessig, L. (1999) *Code and Other Laws of Cyberspace.* New York, NY: Basic Books.

Lewis, N. (2005) 'Expanding surveillance: connecting biometric information systems to international police cooperation', in E. Zureik and M. Salter (eds) *Global Surveillance and Policing.* Cullompton: Willan Publishing.

Longman, T. (2001) 'Identity cards, ethnic self-perception and genocide in Rwanda', in J. Caplan and J. Torpey (eds) *Documenting Individual Identity.* Princeton, NJ: Princeton University Press.

Lyon, D. (2003) *Surveillance after September 11.* Cambridge: Polity Press.

Lyon, D. (2004) 'ID cards: social sorting by database', *OII Issue Brief* (www. oii.ox.ac.uk/).

Lyon, D. (2007) *Surveillance Studies: An Overview.* Cambridge and Boston, MA: Polity Press.

Marx, G. and Reichman, N. (1984) 'Routinizing the discovery of secrets', *American Behavioral Scientist*, 27: 423–52.

Mattelart, A. (2007) *La Globalisation de la surveillance*. Paris: La Découverte.

New York Times (2006) 'Plot shows need for more passenger data, officials say', (www.nytimes.com/2006/08/15/world/europe/15visa.html?_r=1&oref=slogin).

Pugliese, J. (2005) '*In silico* race and the heteronomy of biometric proxies: biometrics in the context of civilian life, border security and counter-terrorism laws', *Australian Feminist Law Journal*, 23: 1–32.

Rule, J. (1973) *Private Lives, Public Surveillance*. London: Allen Lane.

Salter, M. (2003) *Rites of Passage: The Passport in International Relations*. Boulder, CO: Rienner.

Scott, J. (1998) *Seeing like a State*. New Haven, CT: Yale University Press.

Select Committee on Science and Technology (2006) *Identity Card Technologies: Scientific Advice, Risk and Evidence* (www.parliament.uk/parliamentary_committees/science_and_technology_committee/sag.cfmb).

Stalder, F. and Lyon, D. (2003) 'ID cards and social classification', in D. Lyon (ed.) *Surveillance as Social Sorting: Privacy, Risk, and Digital Discrimination*. London and New York, NY: Routledge.

Staples, W. (2000) *Everyday Surveillance*. Lanham, MD: Rowman & Littlefield.

Torpey, J. (2000) *The Invention of the Passport*. Cambridge: Cambridge University Press.

van der Ploeg, I. (2005) *The Machine-readable Body*. Maastricht: Shaker.

Zureik, E. and Hindle, K. (2004) 'Governance, security and technology: the case of biometrics', *Studies in Political Economy*, 73: 113–37.

Chapter 11

A view of surveillance

Peter K. Manning

Introduction

Strong evidence from ethnology and zoosemiotics suggests that monitoring the behaviour of others in the immediate sensorium of animals is the result of deeply embedded genetic patterns and adaptation to the environment (Sebeok, Lorenz, Tinbergen, Hine). This monitoring behaviour is in part related to the survival needs, food-gathering and group solidarity requirements of all higher mammals. The role of monitoring, watching and surveillance is well documented in these studies and, by extension, we can easily extrapolate that it is probably also part of human equipment. Even plants, however, engage in deception – they use scent, hidden traps and coloration to lure insects to their death.

While such capacities have relevance to zoological and evolutionary studies, a sociological equivalent can exist only when the objects of interest are recognizable and available for repeated orientation. These objects are not self-defined nor given; they are the result of actions directed towards them, which in time become patterned and known for continued use and manipulation. As discussed later in this chapter, confusion in the current wave of essays about surveillance, watching and the like, arises in so far as *capacity* is confused with *competence* in respect to identifying, culling, sorting and using again the recognizable objects of concern. These can be patterns of messages, information, visuals, auditory records or anything that can be traced to human endeavour. While historical analyses of spying, surveillance and mere watching have focused on developing capacity

– training, bureaucratic organization, technological advances, changes in political-economic growth and decline – the phenomenological question is: what is worthy of watching?

The objects of concern must be available to the senses, memorable, repeatedly accessible, defined, known to be known and socially labelled. They are the products of routines that sustain their presence. These objects of concern, in turn, mobilize and become centred as matters for control, topics of conversation, oriented-to-objects for agencies and the targets for accountable activities. In other words, agencies-of-control-as-bureaux must know what they are looking for in the social world: something named, objectified, available and countable such that, in the end, they can produce evidence that they are active. Organizations, as a result of their monitoring, coding and classification systems, produce recognizable objects. Note that the *capacity to know* and the socially warranted *ability to know*, to produce objects in context, are noticeably different. As Mary Douglas (1991), following Durkheim, has so often argued, the contours of the social world must be drawn out and up in order for it to be monitored. While the capacity to monitor can produce the array of possible objects of concern – that is, while technologies can run ahead of practice and simulate practices – technology alone cannot produce objects. The recent literature on security, 'technocrime', surveillance and intelligence has mistaken the subject for the object. The focus of this chapter is surveillance, its social and organized forms, its connection to the national state and its interests and, finally, the actual targets of surveillance – the poor, the disadvantaged, the powerless and those society has otherwise abandoned. The argument developed later in the chapter is that the primary targets and activities of the police remain unchanged. The chapter then finishes with an overview of the characteristics of police surveillance.

Background

There is a historical dimension to the production of objects of concern. Because the focus of socially embedded watching shifts contexts from the local, immediate and what is perceptible in the environment by the senses, to the unknown, the suspicious, the suspected and dangerous – however defined – it is necessary to refine the ways in which shifts in contexts take place. This watching can be captured, transmitted, stored, analysed and reproduced in many ways.[1]

While secrecy, codes and observation were practised at least from the time of the first Roman Caesar (Keegan 1994), let us first consider systematic attempts in the premodern world to gather information in the interest of the nation-state. Spying has a long history, but *systematic spying* became a necessity with the coalescence of the nation-state in England, France and Spain in the sixteenth century (Budiansky 2005). The first spying, as an organized social endeavour, was undertaken in Queen Elizabeth's time and has persisted infamously since. Societies soon employed spies and counter-spies, invigilators and informants, and sought coerced information from captured enemies, turncoats, double agents and civilian non-combatants. The means by which this information was gathered, including sex, money and immunity, sanctuary and torture, has been and remains controversial. The development of mass armies, invasions carried out at a distance with speed and new forms of technology that arrived around the turn of the century and escalated during the First World War precipitated the use of spies and counter-spies as a tactic and counter-tactic. It was now necessary, and possible, to anticipate movements and to foil, deter or destroy planned invasions and to refine battle tactics (Keegan 2003). It was also possible to dissimulate and mislead by emitting false signals. By the First World War, the English, French and German governments, with some reluctance perhaps, ambivalently moved towards more systematic information gathering, recruiting and training spies and counter-spies. All these were governmental or quasi-governmental agents acting on behalf of the citizenry at large to protect citizens' security from (primarily) foreign enemies. In these dynamics of developing information that make a difference in context, individual spies were made semi-tragic heroes, even though their role was and is to confirm information already made available through other means (Hitz 2004: 91).

An important distinction must be drawn between the reactive, *passive gathering* of facts based on information received, observation or informants, and the *active gathering* of intelligence, which is a priori gathering of facts in anticipation of a crime, threat or risk. It can also be construed as facts within a context for which connections have not been drawn. In the intelligence world, this is what is called 'connecting the dots'. Whether the facts are gathered in an ad hoc fashion or systematically, a context must be present: context is that which is brought to the facts or, in a sense, what questions are asked of such facts. Context and querying create information from facts. Given either passive or active gathering of materials, nations can interfere, distort, deceive and provide false information to those attempting to spy. Much of the classic literature (summarized neatly by Hitz 2004) focuses on the interpersonal 'strategic interaction' (Goffman 1969) and the way in which modern post-First World War I bureaucracies create their own self-serving aims, classic moral dilemmas and fabrications tailored to their organizational interests, rather than those of the state, their agents or agent-operatives (Hitz 2004). While the traditional paradigm of spying was spying on behalf of a nation-state and loyalty thereto, post the Second World War this consensus has vanished and betrayal is now patterned more by money, envy and revenge and less by ideology (Hitz 2004: 119, 121). The attributable motive for spying and betrayal has shifted from ideology to personal gain. As Goffman has written extensively under the title of fabrication (1974: ch 6), counter-espionage mirrors espionage and they both have 'game-like' properties that lead to autotelic interests in betrayal, manipulation and 'winning' (Hitz 2004: 143).

In democracies, since the primary focus is on threats from abroad – with periodic inward turns of demonizing immigrants, foreigners and guest-workers – intelligence-gathering has been restricted by law and tradition to external enemies of the state, and policing, other than specialized units, has defined its role as reactive. Even at the federal level, the line between the activities of the Central Intelligence Agency (CIA) and the Federal Bureau of Investigation (FBI) within the USA, although always blurred and negotiated, is based on the location of the threat: domestic or foreign. Thus, the CIA must call the FBI to investigate suspected spies in its midst and, while the FBI operates in some 53 stations abroad, it has limited or at least debatable powers to act internationally. The assumption that espionage and counter-espionage, almost by definition, require law-breaking within and without the nation-state has placed intelligence agencies in the western world in an odd liminal position: they are to be regulated, audited, made to conform to legislative oversight, yet are to operate at the edges of national and international laws (Hitz 2004: 162, 183).

New forms of surveillance that target domestic civilian populations in wartime or in announced non-wars – such as the current 'war on terror' – have been refined to a high degree. Yet the threat of terrorism – distant, invisible, non-national in origin, devious and driven by absolutistic ethics – has blurred the growth of insidious forms of watching and self-monitoring. These forms are an entanglement characterized by four features that have given the sociological problem of surveillance a new face: most are *invisible*: unknown as to time, place and channel; they are *consequential*: the fatefulness of being watched, even if known, is unknowable in advance; they are almost *universal*: cheap, available, growing in capacity and shrinking in size. They engage the *person*, knowingly and unknowingly, in self-monitoring and self-revelation which in turn has commercial and/or criminal aspects (see Chapter 7, this volume). In short, these new modes of surveillance are powerful. Modes of detection and resistance are still emerging and not generally known (see Dupont forthcoming; Marx forthcoming). These modes are both intra-Internet and extra-Internet (Dupont forthcoming).[2]

Presently, while surveillance creates widespread anxiety, its actual, consequential impact is as yet unknown. Most of the commentaries on surveillance are based on assumptions of the power and efficient use of these new forms of surveillance and their reliability, but there are few studies of the actual operation of such modes of watching. There are studies of visual surveillance of public places such as studies of CCTV (see below and Chapter 3, this volume), but there are no systematic studies of the functions, successes or failures of federal or state systems of surveillance. We are left with media reports, the occasional government document and quite a few guesses. Upon reflection, of course, it is likely that watching is focused, targeted in some fashion rather than universal and operates with some design. The Internet in particular is an icon of surveillance: its worldwide status, standardized modes of entry and exit, usually via a Windows platform, simplicity and apparent transparency make it almost universal. Aspects of these changes, particularly as they have become part of the routines of citizens and the operations of the agents of the nation-state, are summarized by many social scientists (Poster 1990; Lyon 1994; Ericson and Haggerty 1997; Staples 1997; Dupont forthcoming). The complicity of us all in the surveillance and watching, a psycho-sexual excitement for many, is equally worrying to observers.

The nature and range of types of watching have changed, but the focus and targets of the controllers may not have. The targets of officialdom are always the other, the stranger, the outsider and the marginalized. While *watching* connotes casual, almost adventitious looking, *surveillance* denotes a specific target, a recognizable, reproducible object and at least an implicit purpose. This change is from a focus on the immediate – the range of the human senses – to the local, and from the local to the national and international; from reliance on the human senses to powerful extensions of the senses; from using a few channels with no memory – mere dumb cameras – to channels with many expansive memories, storage capacities,

213

linked databases and the capacity to reproduce and analyse data; from monitoring known and common threats to monitoring the possible and the unknown. This sequence outlines a wandering and complex pathway.

Unfortunately, these summaries are misleading. The language and theatrical-theoretical paradigm of Foucault have shaped the language of much contemporary social theory. The anecdotal evidence is everywhere, seized on easily, that surveillance has become universal and by implication a threat to civility, if not to civil liberties. Yet if one examines the work of the most present and visible agents of democratic states, the police, close analysis of the surveillance they carry on suggests a different focus and concern. Police surveillance is not a universal matter with equivalent risks for all but a tool for monitoring selected others: the poor, the powerless and those who lack resources to dissemble, to avoid surveillance and to reduce the risks to their wellbeing. To what extent is the new interest in 'surveillance' a product of the fears of the rising middle classes rather than the documentation of surveillance? Who is being watched these days?

Surveillance as an evolving social function: constraints

Surveillance operations can be characterized by a number of constraints that arose from the cultural context shared by western industrial democracies. The first constraint was moral and cultural in nature. This cultural context was that spies and counter-spies were in effect quasi-governmental agents, lacking the protection of the Geneva Convention and thus were vulnerable to immediate execution. By and large the tradition that continued until later in the twentieth century was to recruit these agents from the well educated upper classes, and specific universities such as Yale and Princeton in the USA and Oxford and Cambridge in England (Winks 1996). The social control of their behaviour in this sense was more a function of elite values than of skill, training or even penchant (see Philby 1968). The cult of amateurism in spying was a function of social embeddedness – the social class of the gentry was a surrogate index of loyalty (the shock of finding Cambridge graduates, MacLean, Philby and Burgess, were spies, as well as the Queen's Keeper of Pictures, Anthony Blount, was based on the betrayal of class as much as the nation). The idea of spying on citizens internally was not considered before the First World War, except when based on stereotypic group/categorical characterizations. This included imprisoning first-generation Japanese in the USA, for example, and suspicion of German-origin people in England in the First World War. Post the Second World War, the perceived risk of betrayal was a mixture of jingoism, anti-Semitism and anti-communism. Proving the guilt of those who betrayed American secrets was a result not of assiduous work of FBI agents but of information given by fellow travellers who had once been members of the Communist Party or by informers who were coerced to betray others to reduce their sentences.

Tacit notions about those who were active in warfare constrained the range and kinds of surveillance of citizens. Close and organized surveillance of civilian populations was not considered a part of the war effort in democracies although, with the rise of the totalitarian police state in Germany after 1933, the Nazis quickly developed an infrastructure based on the efforts of the Gestapo, the SS and citizen co-operation (Evans 2005 shows this was a failure). The exception to this was the police use of informants, double agents, undercover or plain-clothes police officers and surveillance carried out by the naked eye, camera or hidden microphones. Wire taps and hidden microphones were in wide use by counter-espionage agents in the UK (Wright 1988).

In the USA, in cases of suspected espionage, warrants were technically required for the surveillance of a citizen (until the passage of the Patriot Acts I and II and their extension later in 2007). Note that 'espionage' in French means spying, and the purpose of previous laws was to prevent *spying*, which connotes information-gathering for a foreign nation or for the overthrow of the legitimate government. In contrast, the Patriot Acts cover all forms of actions that might damage the USA, and are not restricted to purposive spying with a ideology, aim and national location and origin. In this guise, buzzwords such as terrorism justify indiscriminate fact-gathering. The extent to which a paradigm shift has radically changed actual practice is unknown yet, the new powers being still under debate in the USA and being reviewed by the federal courts. The concern, in wartime and in the cold war, was biased towards sensitivity to the civil liberties of US citizens because the space, distance and cultural barriers that separated the USA from foreign enemies provided the concrete protection of time and space. Only in the case of the Mexican border was a threat seen nearby. The long and dubious history of the Texas Rangers shows how those fears lead to violent vigilance at national borders (Webb 1935).

There were technological as well as legal and cultural limitations on postwar surveillance. These inhered in the expense of such equipment as listening devices; the size and cumbersome nature of microphones, cameras and other equipment; the low power, sensitivity and capacity of recorders radically limiting their range; and legal and semi-legal limitations on wire taps and on the tracing of phone calls that required a warrant, considerable time on the line to trace the call and the co-operation of the phone company (primarily Bell Canada and AT&T) to make the trace. Cameras, with a few expensive exceptions, were large, and noisy and thus not easily concealed, and states varied in the legality of one-party consent recordings of conversations. Federal law required strict supervision and reporting to a judge even when a warrant had been granted. These restricted surveillance to eye-ball following with automobiles or on foot, well established legally anchored operations or private corporations' security operatives.

The growth of massive intelligence-gathering organizations, especially in the USA – the Office of Strategic Services (OSS) which became the CIA (Thomas 1995; Weiner 2007), the Special Operations organization in the British government that was later transformed into an aspects MI6 (Foot and Daniell 1984), the National Security Agency (NSA) and now the Directorate of Intelligence and Homeland Security Agency – is now big business, especially when contracts for the interrogation and redirection of suspects for torture and for the protection of diplomats and infrastructure are out-sourced to ever-growing corporations (e.g. Blackwater).

This growth was stimulated in large part by the 'cold war'. The period prior to the Vietnam war was a time in which the nation poured money into military versions of surveillance technology. Both the Second World War and the Vietnam conflict stimulated the creation of a variety of high-tech weapons systems (as they began to be called) associated with aircraft firepower and bombing and, to a lesser extent, with firepower for the foot soldiers fighting what was a guerrilla war. As Kraska and Kappeler (1998) and Haggerty and Ericson (2001) have very persuasively argued, there is both a 'trickle down' (the diffusion of tools developed for the military adapted to civilian products and sold) and a direct effect (tools created as a result of contracts that are planned to produce tools with a dual civilian and military purpose) of military technology on policing and security work generally. These weapons systems reflect a general trend in technology, particularly information-surveillance technology: a movement to cheaper, lighter, more efficient tools clustering around various kinds of computers. Their argument is that the diffusion into the corporate world of a technological capacity developed in military procurement enlarges the capacity of the public police to track, gather information on and monitor movements. Implicit here is that such data would then be stored, analysed, refined, applied in future operations and, in turn, further refined or abandoned as a failed extension of the senses. The efforts of the Defense Department (through the creation of ARPA or the defence net, which was later privatized after being shifted to the National Science Foundation) drove further the technologically based Internet. Conversely, the lurch towards systemic management, management by objectives and strategic management was brought to the Pentagon via Harvard and the Ford Motor Company by Robert McNamara.

The new wave of electronic computer-centred surveillance

The technology-driven wave of new forms of surveillance arrived in the 1980s as computers, at first mainframes, desktops and servers, and then 'personal computers', made possible the new passive forms of data gathering, analysis and storage now used universally in business, management, public services and universities. While the interest in national control systems and rational planning had been stimulated by the technological needs of the beginning of 'high-tech war', there was no social science theory easily adapted to the question of the new changes reshaping industrial societies. As Bogard (1996) observes acutely, the tradition of social science, manifested in the work of Weber and later Giddens (1984), was to see surveillance in an organizational context as a pale reflection of the controlling interests of the nation-state – monitoring and partially disclosing information, tracking and making 'visible' places and people.

The breakthrough for many observers was the translation and distribution of the works of Foucault, more than 10 years after they had appeared in France. The most important of these, in connection with surveillance as an emergent buzzword, was *Discipline and Punish* (1977), a metaphoric history transposed from the early nineteenth century in France to the twentieth century in western democracies. Foucault's question was how do diverse, conflicted, ever-fragmenting nation-states produce constraint and order without physical, visible, dramatized public forms of degradation and punishment. Foucault's model was the development, in France, of the prison system, which created routines, hierarchies, observation, examination and recording. Through the social practices of ordering via indirect means, socialization took purchase. The result was an orchestration of bodies in space and time and, in time, too, mutual socialization and control. These manoeuvres, socialization and mutual monitoring, were attributed to the order and ordering taking place in the context of the prison, which produced an emerging mode of societal control. As Bogard (1996: 18) writes: 'Beyond incarceration and the prison, one and the same method now will come to serve a variety of institutional functions at the opening of the modern age – from instruction and training, testing and preparing, credentialing and selection, to care, rehabilitation, security and deterrence, production and consumption.' As Bogard correctly argues at the end of his summary of Foucault's *Discipline and Punish*, Foucault generalizes by metaphor and analogy, not historical fact,[3] positing the future as a reproduction of the prison in unknown, subtle, almost sinister modes unrecognized by those wrapped in the web of docile self-control. The pervasiveness of surveillance is attributed by Foucault to the willingness of all to survey, watch and report all. This metaphor became a new factual condition of postmodernity, and the task remaining for many social scientists, to be considered below, was to specify the conditions of such a spread rather than to probe its generality or existence. The Foucault solution was, in lagged version, a response to the era of 'postmodernity' stimulated and amplified by the writings of Baudrillard and Lyotard, ten years earlier in France. The metaphor, of course, is misleading with respect to the capacity of the Internet and related electronic modes of surveillance. Mark Poster's work (1984) is perhaps the most scholarly interrogation of the extent to which this new networking and electronic surveillance is consistent with the claims made by the primary authors (Baudrillard, Foucault, Lyotard). While it is a deep and trenchant analysis of the limits of their arguments, Poster's position is philosophically, not empirically, based. The details of these postmodernist arguments, as they trickled into criminology and criminal justice, are less important than their massive acceptance, especially among the theorizing trades, history, English, literary criticism and philosophy, areas of study in which the 'known' and the written about trumps the empirical.[4]

Changing social relationships

The nature of social relationships in postmodernity has changed the social web: it is looser, more porous and, while 'thinner', it is quite widespread and more easily accessed. Our theories are mostly derived from late nineteenth-century works – those of Weber, Marx, Durkheim and Freud – while we live somewhere in the midst of the twenty-first century. A broad sketch (see also Manning 1989: 18-19) of social relationships found in high modernity or 'postmodernity' would include features such as the following:

- A heightened reliance on trust in interactions, a wait-and-see posture in social interactions, especially among strangers.

- A snapshot view of individual performances – heavily burdened with concern for managing the here and now in interactions.

- The predominance of the visual in everyday life – screens on which one is observed, observes others and observes others observing self and others and so on now suffuse daily experience.

- An absence of biography, history and kinship as factors in establishing social fit between each other when interactants ('actors') encounter each other.

- An acceptance of the 'to get along, go along', style in interpersonal matters, and the assumption of a working consensus view of interaction rather than a consensus-based or normative gyroscope guiding choice.

- A wide variety of well-known symbols and images that refer to other symbols and images rather than to material matters.

- Non-referential, sensate and surreal-virtual experiences – compete with concrete everyday personal experience for salience.

- Media and games confound the symbolic and the real and create real events from the imaged and imagined events from the real.

- A powerful media and information-based network within and across societies. The media effect and shape interactions and imageries of interaction and these in turn become a possible basis for judging the veracity of images and stories.

- New forms of crime and deviance that surround electronic communications – phishing, hacking, stalking, luring, spamming or otherwise importuning others (males and females, children, the naïve and lonely); identity theft and cybercrimes of all sorts; and life online as an alternative to other realities (see Chapter 6, this volume).

- The rapid movement of peoples in brief time periods and population movements between poorer and wealthier nations that fragment the 'cake of custom'.

These ideas percolated slowly through the social sciences and drifted into criminology. The notion driving new observations about control and surveillance was that the technological capacity now available was a confirmation of the Foucauldian analogical premise. It took this as a given – that is, that mutual co-ordinated socialization, driven by the gaze, the routines, examinations, records, self-surveillance and the visible docility of the other, produced a vast reservoir of self-governance in the interest of authority and power. While Foucault did not identify this entirely with the nation-state and in fact made efforts to temper his ideas, it became a mantra and a gloss for the instances of surveillance then revealed of identified regardless of their actual social consequences.

The ideas that emerged from an exposure to Foucault's ideas in the non-Francophone world, even after his death, were complex and were often overstated as literalisms. I state these as propositions in the following form:

- A network of monitoring and watching systems existed within and across nations, and these were periodically linked and co-ordinated but, for the most part, were competitive and partial (Ericson and Haggerty 1997).

- This multi-headed network altered and shaped lives and turned reflexivity into a system-based matter (monitoring the other in the interest of the self, mediated by large organizations, the state and the Internet).

- By examination, by aural, visual and sensate tracking (smells, emissions, bodily fluids, body parts and samples of hair), organizations altered the life chances of citizens across the class spectrum (Staples 2000).

- Governance was possible now through raising fears and encouraging a mutual surveillance that would substitute for direct violence and sanctioning, and this in turn obscured the degree and kind of actual intrusion of governments into private relations.

- Policing is in some sense less dependent on violence and the threat of violence. This is a result of increased citizen complicity in self-regulation and self-regulating practices, community policing and perhaps the staggering number of people in prisons and jails.

- That everyday foul-ups, incompetence, wilful laziness, ignorance and error, as well as technological limitations, malfunctions, breakdowns, disconnects, inoperability of systems and database incompatibility, are absent or irrelevant.[5]

The implicit theme in this misapplied metaphor was a modern paranoia cast in the language of the social sciences. That is, fear of the unknown, the unseen, the invisible that penetrates the body, alters the self and resounds in unknown ways beyond the control of the individual. This self-centric idea is consistent also with the focus in American mass books: 'take control of your [fill in the blank]: appetite, weight, time, health, family, spouse, lover, bills, credit, etc.' The implication of this is that, without external intrusions, one could control life, others and the deeper meanings of life. Of course you cannot take control of something you cannot see. The imputation of flawless performance and the conceit of technological omnipotence are very persuasive ideas, especially in North America.

Visualization and surveillance

The late twentieth century brought a new awareness of the capacity of the state and the corporate world to watch others. The argument was posed by observers of the 'visualization of social control', whose concern for visual surveillance as a means of social control included all forms of watching, tracking and monitoring that are unknown to the viewer – and perhaps cannot be known (Bogard, Staples, Gary Marx, Baudrillard, Kellner among others). Writers in this tradition all reproduced a modified Foucauldian argument. They believe that visualization of control is built into the temporal and spatial aspects of modern life, almost assumed as a thereness that is always there. They also present technologies as forces driving change, and as fundamentally dangerous.[6] Gary Marx has been systematically alerting us of the dangers of such surveillance, and complementing it with a myriad of rich examples of foul-ups, banalities, ignorance and error, and modes of resistance he refers to as the 'tack in the shoe'. This concern reflected changes in the material world of communication electronics, the preoccupation of the media with the visual and the new, and the absence of a theory of control based on absent others. We have no careful ethnographic studies of these agencies and their operations (I include here the FBI, the CIA, the NSA, agencies now included in the Department of Homeland Security (DHS), the former MI5 and MI6, the Department of Defense and intelligence-gathering units within the several armed forces).

The interaction between the explosion in cheap electronic equipment, the Internet, inexpensive travel over long distances and the displacement of huge numbers of people from developing to developed nations caused by economic opportunity, war and genocides (Bosnia, Kosovo, Darfur, Rwanda) produced new kinds of *others*, or non-specific groups that represent threat. These were dramatized by the horrific terrorist attacks of 11 September 2001. These same disruptions were accompanied by the efflorescence of all forms of the visual. The interaction between the theorizing of Foucault and others and the instances of visualization that could be seen and described, certainly presented widely by the media – themselves reflexivity oriented more than anything to themselves – produced the idea of a new society preoccupied with watching itself, and watching itself watch itself.

Most of the taxonomies of types of surveillance that have developed are unsystematic and seem to have just grown by example. Top-down, descriptive taxonomies adopt a cyclical representation of surveillance: 1) a recipient instrument, or tool for gathering data, which is an extension of the human senses (hearing, seeing, smelling, touching), comes online. 2) A processor, which may be human, electronic or mechanical, monitors the gathered data. This may involve the conversion of the raw data to a code or not. 3) The data are subject to some form of analysis. 4) A conversion process produces *output*. 5) Various means are used to pass on this output, for immediate use or potentially for other means, such as 6) evaluation, implementation, refinement and consideration for 7) an alteration of the recipient instrument (feedback). This is a misleading characterization because it represents a closed, linear and cybernetic system – which the Internet is not. As will be discussed further below, this sequence assumes that the watched group or the potential target has no capacity to resist, to alter the sequence, to mislead and undermine the apparatus, to corrupt the machinery of the people in charge or to use the system to destroy itself. It is also a naïve version of the functioning of the Internet which, as everyone well knows, is flawed and often notoriously frustrating.

Monitoring, watching and surveillance can look into people, places or things, can look out at things in a field of vision or can exist in an interactive or dynamic relationship. *Looking out* (either scanning or focused on activities, sounds, movements, places or groups) can be contrasted with *looking into* something (animal or human bodies). Looking into the body can be done simultaneously, online or after an operation by viewing and re-viewing the recordings of the operation later. The domain primarily of medical operations using cameras and other technologies that can visualize interventions and permit cutting and suturing at a distance, or simply monitoring internal states or functions, looking into the body, is not, presently, seen as a threat to individual liberties. This is in part a result of the presence of 'informed consent' procedures. Vast networks of police-controlled television cameras in London and Istanbul do permit looking into windows, cars and open doors. Satellites and helicopters allow looking on roofs. Selected areas in Boston (Chinatown, Roxbury and Dorchester) are watched by concealed cameras, as are parts of Boston harbour, the financial district and municipal buildings (*Boston Globe*, 2007). These cameras permit both looking in and looking out. In Istanbul, headquarters can zoom in or out, pan and tilt in response to a joy stick controlled by a headquarters officer. Robotics permit sending in robots to explore dangerous sites, to survey for bombs, to observe and to record. These 'looking into' approaches are launched to watch an area or place, not to target specific groups or activities. Private cameras, in some unknown numbers, monitor everything within homes and buildings, from bathrooms to outside buildings.

Looking out can be active, passive or interactive. Active looking, or tracking, applies to signals such as those from a beeper, an electronic tether or a mobile phone connected to a transmitting tower. Such devices can produce texts, sounds, and images or still images, sounds and full motion video, either recorded or in the form of continuous streams of data (such as produced by webcams). The recording device can be personal (mobile phone/Blackberry) or corporate (media, business). It can be carried out by satellites, people, robots, dogs or horses or other moving, tracking devices. Interactive looking out is perhaps epitomized by the police use of video cameras with sound and image, in cars that monitor traffic and for other stops.

Once recorded, these packages or streams can be processed locally or networked through the Internet, satellite systems or servers that relay data to storage points. The channels by which the information is processed vary from phones, computers, faxes, copying machines and scanners to various hand-held personal devices. All these processing/ channelling devices are in turn possessed of memories, and can be linked to larger, denser and semi-accessible networks and databases (which themselves can be copied, sold and resold). Once stored, of course, such data can be analysed, reanalysed, coded and recoded, packaged and repackaged, sold and resold. Amazon.com's reflexive profiling sustains a constant information exchange in the interest of consuming (see Chapter 7, this volume). Yet another example here is buying and selling lists of people to whom loans are sold, lists of credit card holders or phone lists used to solicit. The iterations of this are untold, and the consequences of theft or loss of those lists, such as the TJMAX credit lists lost in the spring of 2007, are still unknown and worrying. With this comes the spectre of 'identity theft', a media-created misnomer which increases the fear that losing one's credit cards or having its numbers lifted is the equivalent to losing ones anchorage as an embodied person in the social world.

Passive looking out consists of watching places more than people, but with an identified target or objective; it is thus more focused than 'looking in'. In this case, the place is identified and labelled as a 'hotspot', or specifically dangerous area. Finally, interactive watching out is the monitoring of one citizen by another, and is done by various means, such as webcams that are either periodically used or running constantly in homes and businesses. In this case, talk and images can be exchanged, edited and altered when sent back and forth. Mutual, and what Dupont (forthcoming) calls 'democratic' surveillance arises: the distinction between the watchers and the watched becomes moot. The simple version of this is interaction websites that features hyperlinks to other people's websites, etc. There are extensions of this technology, as pointed out by Dupont: information can be plugged into the electronic network from extensions of the network. Here he includes YouTube (www.youtube.com), Google Earth and Virtual Earth, which enable observations channelled into the Internet for mass distribution, thus escalating the capacity to observe. These new extensions of media greatly expand the watchers' 'virtual protection', since those observed cannot detect they are being watched. The combination of functions and files, as happens in mobile phones, calculators, date books, Global Positioning System (GPS) locators and other devices (especially those with mapping functions), also permits combining these data into new forms and files and redistributing them.

To a large extent, the thrust of the 'visual surveillance' critique comes from the fears of the imagining classes. The middle classes and above now have computers, interactive televisions and wireless connections everywhere, Bluetooth in their car and a Blackberry earpiece in their ear. As property shifts from the material to the symbolic, modes of communication, money, intellectual property and entitlements lodged in stock, bonds and investments, risk becomes indirect and mediated. The actual monitoring capacity of corporations and governments has radically increased with respect to the workplace and the virtual workplace. The fear that aspects of behaviour, feelings, movements, sounds and pictures can be captured and reconfigured in new and unknown ways is a product of this new era. Rapid mobility or movement between homes is as high as 25 per cent a year in the USA: most people now live in suburbs, not large cities, and their social life is more privatized (Putnam 2000). The notion of 'community' is certainly under debate, as it has been for more than 50 years in the USA. Stranger–stranger interaction is the norm.

The new surveillance systems appear to target the electronic impedimenta of the middle classes, but the operations of particular systems, in particular places with particular consequences in human lives, are left unexamined. The few studies that have been done on the impact of CCTV are inconclusive (Ditton and Farrall 2000; Newburn and Hayman 2001). On balance, it does not reduce crime significantly, has mixed impacts on individuals' sense of security and is plagued with malfunctions, misunderstandings and unintended consequences (Norris and Armstrong 1999; Ditton and Farrall 2000; Newburn and Hayman 2001).

The sort of surveillance that does 'work,' is not mentioned in the passionate overviews of surveillance reviewed above (Lyons, Staples, Bogard, Ericson and Haggerty), and yet is the oldest and most common: the pattern of policing, from the beginning, in Anglo-American societies. This is policing focused on the disadvantaged, in disadvantaged areas of large cities, and rarely on the middle class (Friedman and Percival 1981).

Studies of control via new modes of surveillance

The most prominent advocate of the new surveillance position in social control is Richard Ericson (with associates Kevin Haggerty, Aaron Doyle and Dean Berry). His argument, made famous by his book in which he calls the police 'knowledge workers' (Ericson and Haggerty 1997), shifts attention from 'crime control' on the streets to the ways in which the police liaise with other institutions, such as schools, banks, insurance companies and other government agencies. Ericson and colleagues see these transactions within a metaphor of risk communication. That is, policing as an institution is interdigitated with other institutions to communicate about and manage risk (unwanted external dangers) and, in so doing, produces governance. Security they call 'guarantees against loss'. Risk is communicated about and managed through rules, technologies and formats (1997: 3). They focus on risk communication systems 'that institutions develop to identify and manage risks and how the police become involved in these systems'. Through participation in these communication systems the police are embedded in a larger world of logics and processes that '*direct* how the police are organized and assessed' (p. 4, emphasis in original). The police are knowledge workers in the sense that they respond to demands from other institutions and are thus 'shaped by external institutions' (p. 4). Most of their information is not about crime; it is not entirely territorial, but is in part extraterritorial (abstract knowledge about economic and exchange relationships, careers of persons and their identities). The police role in the mapping and distribution of risk is through 'risk communication systems designed or territorial surveillance and security' (p. 7). They advise on risk and co-operate to produce a kind of subtle coercion (p. 7). They subject themselves to surveillance and scrutiny through rules, formats and technology directed to police work itself. They reject the conventional stereotype of the police as law enforcement officers fighting crime within a paramilitary organization (p. 13).

Unfortunately, the book does not provide evidence by which one could judge its claims about the reorganization of policing. While the authors reaffirm the view that the resources, time and energy devoted to 'crime' are not substantial – and they do not claim it is more or less than it was 30 years ago – the metaphoric shift is drastic: in the book, the police are no longer characterized by their use of force, their legitimate mandate to control crime via various tools or their longstanding claims to be 'crime-fighters' but, rather, by their information-processing centrality, which has become definitive. Either this new position has not been understood by the public and by scholars or this information-processing-services approach has gained new status as a grounding for the mandate of police organizations. Let us look further at the evidence presented. The data, passed off in a few sentences (p. 128), consist of 155 interviews with police officers across Canada and fieldwork in a number of departments (unnamed). The rank, duties, place of employment, years of service and any special qualifications are not stated, either in aggregate in a table or at the time the officers were quoted. The social characteristics of the officers are not noted. The organizations from which data are gathered are not named nor are any of their characteristics (size, location, civilian employees, technological capacities, age). These omissions mean that the context of the reported anecdotes, quotations, programmes, operations, claims, narratives and complaints cannot be located in social space. They cannot, therefore, be refuted, replicated or disproved. This is a fascinating essay in organizational analysis, yet heavy on metaphors, light on evidence and laden with claims. Further, the methods in which the gathered information is organized within and between police forces are never described. Yet a number of very systematic studies (Abt Associates 2000; Dunworth 2000; Manning 2003, summarized in Manning 2008) show that integrated information processing cannot exist at present in police departments, given the state of the databases; the level of co-operation; the varied software and workstations that exist; the various unintegrated national and international databases; the lack of analytic skills; the multiple and not integrated channels for communication to and from the public (311, 911, crime stoppers and other ad hoc 800 numbers, 10-digit numbers and numbers of specialized investigative units); and disinterest in non-crime information in general.

Police technologies are clustered and dramatized by the extent to which they connect to the patrol officers' notions about crime and detectives' interests in the same. The filming of interrogations is unevenly practised across the USA, and often resisted (such as is the case of the Chicago PD, for example), though it is common practice in western European nations. The information gathered is screened, coded and decoded in terms of police categories and classification systems that crudely reflect legal categories of offences or disorders. Such classification systems are relatively impervious to changes in law, social conventions or local knowledge. In spite of the growth in surveillance technologies such as CCTV, mobile phones/cameras, fixed cameras to record car number plates on turnpikes and toll roadways, facial image databases and satellite systems that can be used with GPS to locate calls and callers' movements, Anglo-American policing remains reactive and crime focused. Local police departments are little capable of focusing on surveillance and preventive actions (e.g. anti-terrorism and homeland security) because they have no training or experience in such policing. With the growth in reflexive communication and the surveillance of the police by citizens (the use of mobile phones/cameras to record police violence, crimes in progress or suspicious activities, or lightweight cameras used by various media organizations, connected worldwide via satellite feeds), police activities are more transparent than ever. As a result of the use of computers and other devices linked to the Internet that, in turn, leave traces and data-trails that can be tracked, policing will soon be forced to reckon with the sources and kinds of data it should gather, within its historical, common law, responsive mandate. At present, the police are overwhelmed with facts, images and other forms of data, without the capacity to convert these facts into information –

227

that which makes a difference in future resource allocation decisions. In addition, it is fair to say that, at present, no police department has yet devised a systematically integrated collection of technologies that can facilitate problem-solving, crime prevention, policy analysis or community interfaces.

The police have focused publicly, in their rhetoric, on their crime-fighting capacities, their network of online databases and immediate, short term applications, rather than developing their capacities. Studies of 'Compstat' schemes, for instance, have failed to examine the infrastructure (the work, if any, of crime analysts, the linked databases, the feedback or the evaluation of results) that is claimed to make this change in police practices possible (Manning 2008). This infrastructure is limited in regard to 1) analysis – the ability to integrate, reflect upon, change and refine databases; 2) interoperability – the ability to talk to, merge and integrate analytically databases and software; 3) 'house-keeping' – the ability to clean and eliminate faulty or misleading data rather than simply gathering more; 4) data sharing – with other agencies, integrating and distributing it, and mutually defining data uses, protection, security and other constraints on use; and 5) developing records management systems – the ability to integrate past and present records. For instance, the evidence in larger databases, such as those kept by the Federal Emergency Management Agency (FEMA), the Occupational Safety and Health Administration (OSHA), the FBI or the CIA (those that are quasi-public or could be shared), shows an unfortunate list of flaws, including a failure to clean the data from past entries or to determine the current validity of the data entries (FBI); a failure to integrate data systems within the organization (FBI); databases that are incompatible because they use separate and distinct operating systems (Linux, Unix, Windows); and an overwhelming data influx without a reliable, shared coding system and schema that could permit computer systems to communicate and transfer data (NSA).

Formalizing, in any form, reduces complexity to banality. What is lost in this growing web of intermeshing data sets is the sense of chaos and on-ground loose coupling between the events, the organizational encoding of information and the decisions to act. My observations, based on fieldwork in several American cities, suggest that the complexity of information technology has not been met by an increased capacity of the police to use such devices to their own benefit (Dunworth 2000). The potential for the weaving together of a 'surveillant assemblage' does exist. But it is not in place. The web of control is technically flawed on the ground because the databases are not wedded or linked; the software is incompatible; the management information system is a hodge-podge of ad hoc arrangements assembled over the last 30 years; and the introduction of new technologies, geo-coded data, enhanced 911 and 311 non-emergency call systems has created new complexity and incomplete linkages. The several 'silos' containing unique data that exist in all organizations are not linked within, or across, organizations. This incompatibility of the electronic infrastructure is compounded by the inadequacy of the support, maintenance and upgrading and updating of systems themselves. The investment in the present expensive mélange of systems makes full-scale revamping too expensive. The transformation of organizational systems into compatible and operationally integrated units in general cannot be undertaken because of costs. In any given area of the USA the 911 systems, fire alarms and/or police or private emergency systems are multiple and overlapping and, as a result, officers cannot talk directly to each other. Communication requires phone calls, by landline or mobile phones, between agencies. When interagency co-ordination is required in a major case, such as a hostage situation or an unfolding crisis, the phone systems themselves are not able to bridge the 154 megahertz (local radio systems) and 800 megahertz (now carried by federal agencies and in some large cities) radio channels. Very often, change is confounded by the power bases of those who collect the data, those who mind the data and those who wish to use them. Furthermore, ethnographic work (Sanders 2007) suggests that several systems of response (EMS, fire and police) are not directly co-ordinated but are patched together on an ad hoc basis; that priorities and working assumptions about service are not shared (the police are concerned about risk and crime, EMS and fire about service and prevention); that the claims of efficiency from the suppliers (Bell Canada) are rhetorical; that much duplication of records exists; and that interoperability, even within cities, is not functional. As a result, the services are parallel rather than complementary functions. The fact that some services are privately owned, and some are public agencies, of course, does not help.

The sustaining ideology and practices

The assumption of the Foucaldian argument, as transformed by Ericson and Haggerty, is that the new work of policing is risk management, based on a tacit notion of what is 'bad', or a risk, and what is not. What is good is not surmised. The police targeting of activities and people is not inflexible but endlessly elastic, and can include the control of the rising classes and their challenges to the status quo, as well as marginalized or falling classes and status groups. The absence of compliance with any rule provides yet another tool for sanctioning and constraining, regardless of the viability or logic of the rule itself. The constant, redundant sanctioning envelops groups. Activities in places are merely representations in various shifting and changing forms of acceptable behaviour. They are a distorted mirror of the dominant activities in a society. This means that a focus on 'law breaking' and 'crime' as an indication of behaviour is only a partial truth.

The police are, of course, captured by their own beliefs about the location, meaning, social placement and consequences of crime. In every way a dependent force that, on the one hand, is required to enforce the status quo – whatever that may be, and as politically defined – and, on the other, is dependent on public compliance for success and indeed for the sustained mandate to police at all, may rarely see its own, rather ambiguous role, in order and ordering.

The police, in the modern urban environment, have developed what might be called a *métier*. In one sense, they reflect the assumptions of modern policing: that effective policing is patterned by 1) the random patrol of units differentially allocated to areas of the city based on 911 calls, or district or police-defined areas (not natural areas, neighbourhoods or socially constituted places – though they are often shaped by natural areas or transportation lines: rivers, parks, lakes, interstate highways and freeways or railroad tracks); 2) by some investigation of crime; and 3) by a rhetoric of service and crime control. These standing patterns of behaviour are complemented by three other activities: 1) wide-ranging services to disadvantaged sections of the city (emergency medical help, mediating conflicts); 2) periodic drug investigations and arrests; and 3) specially mounted periodic 'operations': crackdowns, saturation patrols, the targeting of special squads focused on disadvantaged areas. These are uniformly and unequivocally considered necessary, a result of present crime, justified by events, and always directed at the same places, people and lifestyles. This persistent *métier* survives in spite of abundant evidence that short-term crackdowns are only marginally and briefly effective; that they are never evaluated (unless they are planned and directed by social researchers); and that negative consequences are never discussed, measured or publicized or are part of the public–police dialogue.

This cluster of practices leads to the formation of boundaries in the types of activities sought by the officer, which are relative to the area in which he or she is assigned (this may be the result of a requested transfer); a division of labour among officers, based on their skills and preferences (which vary from driving skills to traffic ticket skills to handling domestic violence); a differential focus on crime and arrests, based on proactive policing (most common in highly disadvantaged areas); and an 'ideology of areas' that represents these areas as dangerous, crime ridden and full of criminals (usually elaborated with ideas about drugs, gangs, gun shots and other commonsense indices of violence potential). This everyday working conception of the police is complemented by the ideology of the top command, which can be summarized in general as a belief in the need to show the flag, to keep homicides down, to punctuate everyday patrolling with crackdowns, warnings, threats and shows of force, to pacify the troops and to negotiate all changes as concessions in the contract terms (wages, overtime, conditions of work). The core of the public rhetoric is crime control balanced with an emphasis on community policing.

There is a deep set of assumptions, accounts and rationales that sustain this *métier*, and these unexamined matters are driving forces behind present police practices. First, the police assume they know local areas and their dynamics. These dynamics, cross-neighbourhood processes, are shaped by and shape policing. This is implicit in the data shown on crime rates, trust in policing and collective efficacy, which tap people's sense of security and empowerment in their neighbourhoods (Sampson and Raudenbush 1999; Weitzer 2000; Weitzer and Tuch 2006). Secondly, while the police eschew any attempt in practice to alter the deeper and more profound structural features and dynamics of these areas (Kefalas 2003; Carr 2005; Manning 2008), they feel supported by the false notion that disorder can be altered superficially by local and personalized 'treatments' and pragmatic, order-based policing (Wilson and Kelling 1982). Thirdly, the police assume that social, structural features produce the morality or lifestyles that are criminogenic in the extreme (Klinger 1997; Herbert 2000). Thus, commonsense morality and sociology provide the public rationales for sweeps, crackdowns, the saturation of areas with plain-clothes and uniformed patrols and intense patrolling of areas seen as 'high crime'. This label, in turn, of course, refers only to the crimes of the poor and the marginalized, not to the crimes of the middle classes and the elites, the 'white-collar crimes' that are violations of trust. Fourthly, policing in local areas or neighbourhoods is differential, based on ethnicity, class, time of day and the political context (Klinger 1997; Anderson 1998, 2000; Weitzer 2000). Fifthly, the police, as an organization, produce differential impacts in neighbourhoods since they provide different services to victims, to citizens at large, to those who violate the law and to other audiences.

These studies show convincingly that the police are not 'knowledge workers' to any measurable degree, whether on the basis of ideology, practices, record-keeping or justifications offered the media, city councils, mayors or managers. The actual surveillance and risks that are managed are 1) visible, 2) concrete in the here and now, and 3) largely in marginal areas of cities in which immigrants, African-Americans, the poor and homeless live. Detectives deal with much the same population and are largely reactive in their work rather than 'investigative'. These disadvantaged areas are the primary focus of 'risks', and that is where attention is directed.

Police practices

The standard police strategies – random patrol, answering 911 calls and investigating crime – have not been modified by 30 years of research pointing out their inefficacy, or by reading Foucault. Policing is episodic as a result of a long history of reactive policing, of refining of the means and of the displacement of effort into them (e.g. by keeping elaborate records of officially recognized crime, focusing on response time or responding to media displays of crimes, especially sequences of visible crimes). This rhetorical position is reified daily by the slavish echoing of the police version of events, their unquestioned position as 'experts' on crime, their control of the relevant information concerning crime and their management of information in their own interest. Given the present position of professional policing – that is, scientifically based, responsive, available, crime focused and visible, and their commitment to traditional strategies (unaltered since the late nineteenth century) – it is not surprising that their surveillance is concentrated, as it has always been, on anomalous matters in well-known areas of extreme disadvantage. These are the others, at the edges of society. It is this surveillance and its consequences that are the most fundamental and that have the greater effect on the life chances of individuals and on current inequalities. I draw on several recent public descriptions of police surveillance and raids (Rose and Clear 1998; Silverman 1999 on the New York PD crackdown; and Kane 2003, 2005). In outline, the police *métier*, in regard to surveillance, takes the following form:

- Disadvantaged areas, known as being high-crime areas as a result of past patrol, field stops, arrests, raids and the work of special squads, such as the gang squad, the tact squad and the SWAT teams (or 'dynamic entry teams' as they are euphemistically called in Boston), are targeted for continued scrutiny (Kane's qualification).

- Additional information is added by the oral culture of patrol concerning 'bad areas', where the dope dealers hang out, where gun shots are heard and, in particular, where recent homicides are concentrated. These are amplification effects on the deployment patterns and the focus of these special squads.

- Interactions between uniformed officers and the special squads, visible arrests, warrants served and drug raids reaffirm the presence of inordinate criminal activity in these areas.

- In large departments that host crime analysis meetings, maps are produced showing the location of these crimes and raids, pictures of those arrested are shown, gun shots and homicides are mapped and gangs' turfs discussed.

- The concern are known, classical nineteenth-century street crimes – visible, violent, carried out by uneducated young men on each other, as well as drug crimes of various sorts. While homicide in general is not a crime committed in public, when it is carried out in these areas it is well publicized, especially if strings of more than three occur over several days. Other crimes of major concern do not result in targeting areas to respond to them (e.g. the homicide of a child, an older person or a white high-status person).

- Other matters seen as bad behaviour – gangs, drinking, using drugs in public – are targeted periodically when the police publicly attribute crime and violence to them.

- Raids, operations and sweeps are designed like terrorist attacks (unannounced, affecting the innocent and guilty alike), are public, well publicized after the fact and are named dramatically in militaristic terms: 'Operation 13'.

- The sole announced aim of these interventions is to arrest the bad guys. They are the result of recent spikes in crime or reports of such in the media. Further spikes in crime in the coming year, correlated with 'crackdowns', sweeps and intense surveillance in an area, as indicated by drug arrests figures, are of little interest because such results are not tracked or evaluated (Kane 2003, 2005).

- The focus is arrests. They are seen as deterrents, and other, perhaps more long-term or subtle matters, unintended or intended consequences, are ignored (e.g. divorce, family break-ups, children sent into foster care, the changed employment status of men, false arrests, fear of the police by other community members, a long-term unwillingness to testify or to inform the police of criminal activities, distrust of the police and distrust of more benign efforts at partnerships, community policing and problem-solving, etc.).

- Interventions are brief, short term and a few hours or days, typically involving a concentrated effort of uniformed officers saturating an area, serving warrants and making arrests. Later results of the raids in general – such as the release of innocents, the failure to charge by the district attorneys and the impact on gang behaviour, homicides or the matter of interest – are either never reported in the media or are reported in reference to the police assessment of the results.

- When the raids are co-ordinated at a given time by federal, local and state agencies, they are managed because of personal contacts and relationships that vanish when the officers in the organizations involved are promoted, transferred, retire or change agencies. Task forces focused on drugs or gangs funded by the federal or state government only exist as long as they are funded.

- The periodicity of the raids is based on the assumption that crime always rises, the bad guys are always out there, the police can only do so much and it is necessary therefore from time to time to crack down again. The existence of the crackdown and the arrests validates the concern that led to the raids and is seen as evidence of the need to continue these tactics: these areas must be patrolled and watched for the inevitable new spike in violence.

These syllogisms have tenacity and fit the police ideology as well as the assumptions of the middle classes about danger and crime. They reflect what might be called the *accountable objects of policing*. The areas are known areas, the tactics are known tactics, the practices surrounding the tactics (generalizations about tactics) are accepted as legitimate and the outcomes predictable. Thus, the surveillance mounted by the police is not news, not new nor innovative except that new *channels* (visual and aural-extensions of the senses) for gathering materials have been added to their repertoire. Though the technology advances, the *ex post facto* tactics remain.

In 2006, the Boston Police adopted crime mapping as an anti-gang tool. Over the period 2005–6, the *Globe* had run a series of stories with maps pointing out the concentration of homicides in specific areas of the city – now called 'hotspots'. These stories and maps reinforced the conventional wisdom about where violence takes place, who does it and why. This is normally accompanied by media quotations from family and neighbours explaining how the victim is a 'good boy' and innocent (*Boston Globe* 2007a). Police crime mapping also allowed the department to locate the addresses of crimes with a particular interest for gun shots, gun crimes and arrests with guns involved, the addresses of members of gangs (information supplied by the gang squad, based on their observations and interviews) and the names of the gangs of which they were members. These names, addresses, crime locations and arrests involving guns were printed out on a series of maps, some 'zooming' in on small, known areas (a few contiguous blocks) and some covering areas more than a square mile. These were done for a number of 'high crime' areas of the city (see above for how these labels were arrived at). The plan devised by the then Deputy Superintendent was to identify and target 'key players', to watch their movements by visual surveillance and to intervene from time to time to prevent conflicts between members of opposing gangs. Even though the plan was never actually put in practice (the superintendent was demoted and the plan scrapped), the idea was to monitor gang members to incapacitate them (sometimes by pretext arrests or stops), to make them aware of police attention and to use the maps as a kind of programme, much like the sporting-event programmes sold at Fenway Park or the Boston Garden. While the capacity to locate violent crime and to watch and monitor the named 'key players' was new, this information did not alter the tactics that had been developed during 'Operation Cease Fire' in 1990–1, already in place for more than ten years.

Following 9/11, and as a result of the Democratic Convention held in Boston 2004, the city, in co-operation with the DHS and corporations in the financial district (which abuts the harbour, the mouth of the Charles River and the federal courthouse), installed a record number of surveillance cameras. The Boston PD can also access cameras installed by the DHS to monitor evacuation routes, the harbour and parks. These remain in operation for 'special events' and, for instance, monitored the Caribbean Carnival (in Roxbury) and the celebration after the Red Sox won the World Series in 2004. The Boston PD itself owns 25 cameras, each costing about US$ 20,000, that can pan, tilt and zoom and can be quickly attached to a wall or roof (Ballou 2007). They are installed in two areas of the city. The first is Chinatown, which abuts the financial district and was formerly called the 'combat zone' because it was a place for strolling male and female prostitutes, bars with 'working women', drug dealing, porno theatres and various entertainment possibilities. The second area in which they are deployed is a series of 'hotspots' (see above) in Roxbury (Ballou 2007). As other research has reported, the Boston PD only use the recordings – when they use them at all – after a crime has been committed, in hope of identifying the perpetrator (Ballou 2007). Their deterrent-preventive value has not been determined.

In the late spring of 2007, Mayor Menino of Boston proposed that the city buy and install a sound-sensitive, 1,5 million dollar surveillance system, manufactured by ShotSpotter, that would identify and locate gun shots in high-crime areas (primarily in Dorchester and Roxbury). By October 2007, some 91 sensors had been installed. The claim was that this would improve the police response to shots fired, be a deterrent to shootings and be the first step in the creation of a sophisticated monitoring system in the most violent areas of the city (according to homicides and shots fired; *Boston Globe* 2007b). The City Council supported buying and installing the complete system, but at the time of writing it had not yet been installed (October 2007). In early October, Boston police fired blanks in a '6.2 mile area of Boston that has been blanketed with gunshot sensors, designed to alert police dispatchers in 10 seconds to the location of the gunfire within 30 feet of its origin' (Drake 2007). A member of the top command, Superintendent Daniel Linsky, then said that 'We're hoping to stop gunfights and people using guns in the city of Boston ... We're hoping to do that by showing up on crime scenes in a timely fashion'.

Like the CCTV studies in England, the results of previous 'experiments' with these systems in Dallas, Texas and Redwood City, California, were not promising. The ShotSpotter website reports anecdotal and thin evidence that the system works to reduce crime, with no analysis of how that takes place or why. These studies, funded by the National Institute of Justice (NIJ), were supposed to detect the location from which a gun shot occurred. One study made in Redwood City produced somewhat problematic results. Since the level of detection can be set within a range, the lower the threshold, the greater the number of false positives (jack hammers, car backfires, fire crackers) detected. Higher thresholds produce fewer detected explosions. Findings from another study conducted in a small area of Dallas – a low-income Hispanic neighbourhood with relatively high numbers of discharges (in the absolute they were very small, representing less than one per cent of calls for service) – revealed that response time was unaltered, but that officers sped up their investigations, and had more calls to answer. It increased the total number of detected shots fired by five times that of the previous two months (before the experiment), while citizens' calls concerning shots fired remain stable. It was found that shots were under-reported 23 per cent by citizens (when compared with the monitors). The net consequence was increased workload, with no other obvious benefits. The Boston system has been rationalized as a preventive-deterrent device, but it is used, as is CCTV (4 million of which are now perched around metropolitan London), to gather evidence *after* a gun shot has been fired (the same is true for the video devices noted above). It is likely that the consequence of the new system will be to increase the detection of 'shots fired' incidents (recall this differs from the number of citizen calls), to increase responses to such incidents, to increase workload and to have a negligible impact on crime, reported crime, actual gun shots fired or gun-related crime. Other than increasing workload in already busy periods – nights and Friday night to early Sunday mornings – the other consequence of such a system is to increase the surveillance and police presence in these areas. The symbolic presence trumps any discernible instrumental effects, and it is unclear whether the audience of the new technological conceit is the middle classes and others who live *outside* high-crime areas or those living in the disadvantaged areas being watched (see Chapter 3, this volume).

One final example is the 'consent search' initiative. In the late autumn of 2007, the Boston Police advanced the idea of a consent search programme (it is still pending before the City Council, as of 21 December 2007). The theory is that this operation would permit the parents of children to ask the police to search their homes for guns (any gun found would not be the basis for prosecution, unless it had been used in a crime; if that was the case, and could be proven, no immunity was to be offered). The operation was again targeted to a small area of Dorchester and Roxbury, in practice restricted to lower-class and disadvantaged areas of the city, and was a means to gather information on crimes and offenders more than to seize guns. The previous use of this pretext, in St Louis (Decker 2004), found that the results (defined in terms of the number of guns seized) declined rapidly as information on the searches spread.

In each of these examples, the technology follows prior oral knowledge embedded in the police patrol culture about where danger lies, who is dangerous, what should be done and how it is known. The technology is a tertiary adjunct, laid on to extend the current practices but not used to prevent or alter the probability that crime will be committed. Watching may increase the chances of arrest or charge after the fact.

Conclusion

Watching may be a pan-species trait, but surveillance, watching with a purpose, is a feature of organized communal life. When the agents of nation-states shift from observing external enemies to monitoring their citizens, the nature and implications of their surveillance shift. It becomes unknown, secretive and unaccountable, and the modes of being watched have an unknown, and perhaps unknowable, purpose. The top-down view of surveillance assumes that capacity and practice are equivalent, and that generalized surveillance has an aggregative and analysable effect. This is perhaps mistaking the ongoing monitoring with purpose, analysis and reproducible results. The growing capacity of monitoring systems to link databases so that an address can be associated with previous calls for service, the results of prior stops, residents' characteristics, sex offender information, gun possession, flammable materials and, in the private sector, pizza preferences, is incontestable. Whether it can be applied and the extent to which such data can be applied is unknown. Turning to what is known about surveillance in the modern city, surveillance remains *targeted* on specific people ('players' is a singularly inappropriate label for people who are seen as violent and dangerous) and places – disadvantaged areas. It is multiple, including eye-ball observation from bicycles, cars (both marked and unmarked) and on foot, cameras, sound sensors, other citizens, and it reproduces the already intense patrol and observation of the people in these areas.

Notes

1 Each of these functions has a history: observation, transmission, encoding and decoding, espionage and counter-espionage, and the forms of deception associated with each facet. The 'surveillant assemblage', so

named by Haggerty and Ericson (2000), is based on their inference that such activities now form a network of linked functions with a potential for virtually universal surveillance.

2 Ironically, while people may be aware of the threats of 'identity theft' and being watched by others indirectly via traces of computer activity, for example, subtracting themselves for surveillance requires technical knowledge they may not have. When modes of watching are not known they cannot be deflected.

3 See Scull's (2007) scatching remarks on Foucault's factual errors with regards to mental asylums in France and England, as cited in the new full English edition of *Madness and Civilization* published in 2007 by Routledge.

4 There is a theoretical solution, a mode of understanding these matters, best exemplified by the work of Garfinkel and Rawls (Garfinkel 1967; Rawls 2002, forthcoming). In summary, the argument is that, in the modern world, beliefs, values and shared 'deep understandings' are fading as sources of integration, as a result of the globalization of economies, rapid transportation and immediately available cheap communication, and experiences that are broadened if not altered in depth. Such conditions suggest a move to understanding practices and displays that enable concerted action. It requires an examination of how symbols (both material and non-material) are selectively presented in order to impress or maintain the trust of an audience. This implies a temporal dimension and requires an analysis of the relationships between audience and groups of loosely co-operative teams of performers. Such an idea, by emphasizing the role of symbols in the representation and management of appearances, links social structure and associated symbols with interactional and collective dynamics (Goffman 1983; Wagner-Pacifici and Schwartz 1991). This is a perspective on how performances are given credibility and legitimacy, and how trust manifests itself in everyday life.

5 The constant refrain in the elite mass media has been the failure, on the one hand, of large governmental databases to 'shake hands' – to connect and exchange information – while at the same time engendering fears of the total surveillance of every form of communication, especially via phones and the Internet.

6 These top-down theorists echo a kind of technological lag theory that has been the commonsense explanation for the anomalies of social change since Ogburn's work was published 80 years ago. It assumes the power of technology and gives it putative efficiency and the ability to convert energy into action and outcomes; it assumes the resistance of folkways and the mores to change; it assumes the investment of societies in stability in social relations; and it assumes that the leading source of innovation is technology. Posed in this way, the critic has to provide evidence to the contrary.

References

Abt Associates (2000) *Police Department Information Systems Technology Enhancement Project (ISTEP)*. Washington, DC: Department of Justice, COPS Agency.

Anderson, E. (1998) 'The social ecology of youth violence,' *Crime and Justice*, 24: 65–104.

Anderson, E. (2000) *Code of the Street*. New York, NY: W.W. Norton.

Ballou, B.R. (2007) 'Police to widen use of cameras,' *Boston Globe*, 23 September.

Bogard, W. (1996) *The Simulation of Surveillance: Hypercontrol in Telematic Societies*. Cambridge: Cambridge University Press.

Boston Globe (2007a) 'Sweeps strike at criminals', 24 September.

Boston Globe (2007b) 'Cameras to watch city', 27 September.

Budiansky, S. (2005), *Her Majesty's Spymaster*, New York: Plume.

Carr, P. (2005) *Clean Streets*. New York, NY: NYU Press.

Decker, S. (2004) *Reducing Gun Violence: The St Louis Consent to Search Program. National Institute of Justice Final Report*, Washington, DC: Office of Justice Programs, National Institute of Justice.

Ditton, J. and Farrall, S. (2000) *The Fear of Crime*. Aldershot: Ashgate.

Douglas, M. (1991) 'Witchcraft and leprosy: two strategies of exclusion', *Man* NS, 26: 723–36.

Drake, J.C. (2007) 'Police fire blanks in park as part of a test', *Boston Globe*, 4 October.

Dunworth, T. (2000) 'Criminal justice and the information technology revolution', in J. Horney (ed.) *Criminal Justice*. Washington, DC: NIJ/Office of Justice Programs.

Dupont, B. (forthcoming) 'Hacking the panopticon: distributed online surveillance and resistance', in M. Deflem (ed.) *Sociology of Crime Law and Deviance*. Bingley: Emerald.

Ericson, R.V. and Haggerty, K.D. (1997) *Policing the Risk Society*. Toronto: University of Toronto Press.

Evans, R.J. (2005) *The Third Reich in Power*. New York, NY: Penguin Books.

Foot, M. and Daniell, R. (1984) *SOE: The Special Operations Executive, 1940–1946*. London: BBC.

Foucault, M. (1977) *Discipline and Punish*. New York, NY: Random House.

Friedman, L.M. and Percival, R.V. (1981) *The Roots of Justice: Crime and Punishment in Alameda County, CA, 1870–1910*. Chapel Hill, NC: UNC Press.

Garfinkel, H. (1967) *Studies in Ethnomethodology*. Englewood Cliffs, NJ: Prentice Hall.

Giddens, A. (1984) *The Constitution of Society: Introduction of the Theory of Structuration*. Berkeley, CA: University of California Press.

Goffman, E. (1969) *The Presentation of Self in Everyday Life*. London: Allen Lane, The Penguin Press.

Goffman, E. (1974) *Frame Analysis: An Essay on the Organization of Experience*. Cambridge, MA: Harvard University Press.

Goffman, E. (1983) 'The interaction order', *ASR*, 48: 1–17.

Haggerty, K.D. and Ericson, R.V. (2000) 'The surveillant assemblage', *British Journal of Sociology*, 51: 605–22.

Haggerty, K.D. and Ericson, R.V. (2001) 'The military technostructures of policing', in P. Kraska (ed.) *Militarizing the American Criminal Justice System: The Changing Roles of the Armed Forces and the Police*. Boston, MA: Northeastern University Press.

Herbert, S. (2000) *Citizens, Cops and Power*. Chicago, IL: University of Chicago Press.

Hitz, F. (2004) *The Great Game*. New York, NY: Knopf.

Kane, R. (2003) 'Social control in the metropolis: a community-level examination of the minority group-threat hypothesis', *Justice Quarterly*, 20: 265–95.

Kane, R. (2005) 'Compromised police legitimacy as a predictor of violent crime in structurally disadvantaged communities', *Criminology*, 43: 469–98.

Keegan, J. (1994) *A History of Warfare*. New York, NY: Random House.

Keegan, J. (2003) *Intelligence in War: Knowledge of the Enemy from Napoleon to Al-Qaeda*. Toronto: Key Porter.

Kefalas, M. (2003) *Working-class Heroes: Protecting Home, Community, and Nation in a Chicago Neighborhood*. Berkeley, CA: University of California Press.

Klinger, D. (1997) 'Negotiating order in patrol work: an ecological theory of police response to deviance', *Criminology*, 35: 277–306.

Kraska, P.B. and Kappeler, V. (1998) 'Militarizing American police: the rise and normalization of paramilitary units', *Social Problems*, 44: 1–18.

Lyon, D. (1994) *The Electronic Eye: The Rise of Surveillance Society*. Minneapolis, MN: University of Minnesota Press.

Manning, P.K. (1989) *Symbolic Communication*. Cambridge, MA: MIT Press.

Manning, P.K. (2003) *Policing Contingencies*. Chicago, IL: University of Chicago Press.

Manning, P.K. (2008a) *Police Technologies*. New York, NY: NYU Press.

Manning, P.K. (2008b) *The Technology of Policing*. New York, NY: NYU Press.

Marx, G. (forthcoming) *Surveillance*. Chicago, IL: University of Chicago Press.

Newburn, T. and Hayman, S. (2001) *Policing, Surveillance and Social Control: CCTV and Police Monitoring of Suspects*. Cullompton: Willan Publishing.

Norris, C. and Armstrong, G. (1999) *The Maximum Surveillance Society*. Oxford: Berg.

Philby, K. (1968) *My Silent War*. New York, NY: Grove.

Poster, M. (1984) *Foucault, Marxism and History: Mode of Production versus Mode of Information*. Cambridge: Polity Press.

Poster, M. (1990) *The Mode of Information*. Chicago, IL: University of Chicago Press.

Putnam, R. (2000) *Bowling Alone.* New York, NY: Simon & Schuster.

Rawls, A. (2002) 'Introduction', in H. Garfinkel (ed.) *Ethnomethodology's Program: Working out Durkheim's Aphorism.* Boulder, CO: Rowman & Littlefield.

Rawls, A. (forthcoming) *Toward a Sociological Theory of Information.* Boulder, CO: Paradigm Publishers.

Rose, D.R. and Clear, T.R. (1998) 'Incarceration, social capital and crime: implications for social disorganization theory', *Criminology*, 36: 441–80.

Sampson, R. and Raudenbush, S. (1999) 'Systematic social observation of public spaces', *American Journal of Sociology*, 105: 603–51.

Sanders, C. (2007) 'Is anyone there? The collapse of information and communication in technologies in the social worlds and arenas of police, fire and emergency medical services.' Unpublished PhD dissertation, McMaster University, Hamilton, Ontario.

Scull, A. (2007) 'The fictions of Foucault's scholarship', *Times Literary Supplement*, 21 March.

Silverman, E. (1999) *The NYPD Battles Crime.* Boston, MA: Northeastern University Press.

Staples, W. (1997) *The Culture of Surveillance: Discipline and Social Control in the United States.* New York, NY: St Martin's Press.

Staples, W. (2000) *Everyday Surveillance.* New York, NY: Rowman & Littlefield.

Thomas, E. (1995) *The Very Best Men.* New York, NY: Simon & Schuster.

Wagner-Pacifici, R. and Schwartz, B. (1991) 'The Vietnam veterans memorial: commemorating a difficult past', *American Journal of Sociology*, 97: 376–420.

Webb, W.P. (1935) *The Texas Rangers.* Austin, TX: University of Texas Press.

Weiner, T. (2007) *Legacy of Ashes: The History of the CIA.* New York, NY: Doubleday.

Weitzer, R. (2000), 'Racialized policing: residents' perceptions in three neighborhoods', *Law and Society Review*, 34: 129–55.

Weitzer, R. and Tuch, S.A. (2006) *Race and Policing in America.* Cambridge: Cambridge University Press.

Wilson, J.Q. and Kelling, G. (1982) 'Broken windows: police and neighbourhood safety', *Atlantic Magazine*, 249: 29–38.

Winks, R. (1996) *Cloak and Gown.* New Haven, CT: Yale University Press.

Wright, P. (1988) *Spy Catcher.* New York, NY: Dell.

Chapter 12

Afterword: technopolice

Stéphane Leman-Langlois

Technology has always been a central element in warfare. The army with the best equipped soldiers, all other things being equal, had an edge over enemies less technologically advanced. This applies to weapon and defence systems, of course, but also to support equipment, to information systems and to the logistics line needed to move, distribute and maintain the battle technologies.

The war on crime, no longer a metaphor – like the war on poverty or the war on cancer – also shares this preoccupation with the enemy's capabilities and with the question of whether 'ours' will provide the clear, lasting superiority we seek. Sometimes this preoccupation comes from a rather straightforward contrast between the technologies used by criminals and the technologies available to police. For instance, it is easy to compare the firepower of criminal gangs with that of police, or the abilities of Internet paedophiles with those of the cybercops who chase them. However, one must bear in mind that, while the police adoption of technology is quite a deliberate, organized, often debated, delayed, mediatized, etc., process, those who engage in criminal, forbidden or otherwise irritating behaviour with the help of technology are in a much more spontaneous, opportunistic and 'natural' dynamic. Today's credit card skimmer is not yesterday's mugger. Criminals do not adopt new technologies; they do not modify their trade. New criminals are seduced by the opportunities offered by the new technologies that suffuse their world – just like technopolice advocates and practitioners.

At other times the contrast in technology mobilization is more indirect: in a recent Royal Canadian Mounted Police (RCMP) experiment to use the spectrographic analysis of satellite images to detect marijuana plants, one technology (the peppering of small clutches of marijuana plants in the middle of large cornfields) won over the other (the insufficient 4 m resolution of the imaging satellite available to police) (CCRP 2002).

Finally, in many instances police technology is contrasted not to the technologies or tactics employed by criminals but to a type of crime, or sometimes to 'crime' in general. The involved technologies are guaranteed to impact significant aspects of criminality and to improve the general security of citizens. Video cameras are among such technologies. Their connection with their objective is a pure abstraction, based on symbols (that which is hidden must be revealed), theories (surveillance deters) or faith (technology *works*; it will work here as well).

For all these reasons, we can conclude that technocrime and technopolicing are not geometric opposites, mirror images; in fact, the two sets of representations merely overlap in some technologically minor, yet sociologically highly significant aspects. Technopolicing is not simply an answer to a growing or increasingly dangerous body of technocrimes. Technocrime is not the only response crooks can make to the better policing of their previous, low-tech activities. Technocrime is, of course, a spectre raised by politicians, civil servants or industrial entities to justify more technopolice, but it is not limited to that.

What we can say about the relationship of technocrime to private, public and hybrid forms of technopolicing is as follows:

1. They both have objective and constructed aspects. As is the case with conventional forms of crime, crooks, swindlers and abusers online and off are absolutely convinced that their actions do not create 'true' victims, especially when insurance, credit-card policy or bank practices end up mitigating the negative effects of their exploits on their victims. From the policing point of view, some technologies benefit from what might be described as axiomatic effectiveness. Their ability to fulfil their objectives is, in a way, built into their very definition. Such is the case of surveillance cameras. Like homeopathy and acupuncture, these technologies are evaluation-proof: no amount of negative findings will affect their image, and placebo-level positive findings will always be available.

2. The constructed aspects always trump the objective. Police administrators and politicians are more likely to use the technology discourse in what Edelman would call a hortatory effort to reassure

and to appear in control, and police officers on the ground are more likely to feel sceptical about high-tech approaches to crime-solving. As Manning shows in Chapter 11, street-level police intervention remains decidedly low tech. Brodeur (Chapter 9) demonstrates that the equivalent phenomenon dominates in police investigations, and Lemieux (Chapter 8) in the realm of criminal intelligence outfits. Yet police objectives, budgets, organizational structure, tactics and strategies are decided elsewhere.

3. At the same time, Lyon (Chapter 10) shows how the 'freeloader' government discourse pushes the policing of social entitlements into increasingly intense generalized surveillance. Whether or not first-line government agents (as well as private enterprises) actually apply the new surveillance technologies the politicians bought in precisely the intended way, they *will* use them. Regardless of the adaptations, incompetence, system failures and other shortcomings pointed out by Manning, the new tools will find new users.

4. They are constructed both by individuals and groups who are engaged in either form of activity, as well as by individuals who are not. Our perceptions of various technocrimes are the result of massive quantities of discourse coming from all directions; cybercrime is an especially good illustration of this phenomenon. Between commercial, government, institutional, police, military, media and expert constant *talk* about cybercrime, we are bombarded with various versions of exotic threats to our jobs, families, savings, water supply, etc. (The most exotic is that of Second Life miscreants who prey on other virtual visitors, as described in Chapter 6 by Whitson and Doyle.) These claims are often contradictory, as is apparent in the chapters by Nhan and Huey (Chapter 5) and Gagnon (Chapter 4), as they are contingent on particular social and economic factors unique to each claim-maker.

5. Private industry remains ahead of the public police. In a way, that developmental differential is easy to explain, since most technologies (civilian and military) are developed by the private sector. While low-tech, traditional forms of policing were closely enmeshed with legal and political demands, expedients and operational frameworks, technopolicing hinges on the decisions, discoveries and market strategies of private enterprise. Today this is most apparent in the aggressive marketing/lobbying of Taser International for the acceptance of its products, for instance.

6. As Brin (Chapter 2) describes our transparent future, many will find little comfort in the idea that individual spying cancels out, or makes up for, personal info- or techno-nakedness. Either way, the

tide is indeed in and on the way up, and no amount of legislation, contestation or retreat is likely to stem it or even slow it down. One may not like Brin's version of bending in the wind, but flexibility is going to be the answer. Already, such flexibility can be seen in the rapid redefinition of 'privacy' that is taking place, as described in my Chapter 7. We may not *like* the new privacy, but it is there and offers a number of possible keys to our feeling safe in the next society.

In the 'information society,' technology occupies a central position. Not only is it concretely at the centre of many of our activities, but it also symbolizes the essence of what is still 'modern' in our late-modern culture: the belief that we can voluntarily ameliorate our human condition. Though it also stands for what is wrong with us – pollution, unsafe foods, Beck's nuclear risks – for most of us, technology, whether medical, information, entertainment, transportation or other, embodies the better future. Technocrime, as a perversion of this promise or at least an irritant side-effect comparable with pollution, must always be accompanied by technopolicing and its objective, technosecurity.

Reference

Canadian Police Research Centre (CCRP) (2002) *Operation SABOT and Illicit Crop Information Management Using Satellite Imagery*. Richmond, BC: RADARSAT International.

Index

Added to a page number 't' denotes a table.

Abuse Reporter function (Second Life) 98
Access Card, objections to, Australia 204
active looking out 223
Acxiom Corporation 20
Air Miles 122
amateurism, in spying 214
Amazon 122, 123, 223
American Civil Liberties Union (ACLU) 20, 25
analytical technologies 157–62
anonymity 98–9, 100, 114, 125
anonymous statistics, music management packages 124
applications *see* software applications
Ashcroft, John 25
augmented reality 21, 127
Australia
    criminal intelligence service 147–8
    objections to Access Card 204
Australian Crime Commission (ACC) 147–8
Australian Criminal Intelligence Database (ACID) 147, 148
Australian Identity Protection Register (AIPR) 148
Australian Law Enforcement Intelligence NET (ALEIN) 147, 148
Australian Law Enforcement Reference and Targeting (ALERT) 148
Automated Criminal Intelligence Information System (ACIIS) 150, 163

banking institutions, concern over security of online forms 146
behaviour modification 129, 134
behaviour monitoring 209
Belgium, criminal intelligence service 148–9
betrayal 212
Big Brother 14, 15, 18, 40, 113
biometric identification 18–19, 195, 200
biometric passports 199–200, 201
biometric tests, reliability of 203
Bittner, Egon 188

Blair, Tony 205
BNG *see* national general databank
Boston police 235–7
botnets 79
browsers 125
Bunker, Robert J. 50
Bush, George W. 191

C-CRIS (Computerized Criminal
    Intelligence System) 151–2
California, inter-jurisdictional
    cybersecurity study 66–85
cameras 28
    disguised as jewelry 22
    dispersed ownership 17, 18
    see also police cameras
Canada
    criminal intelligence service
        149–50
    criminal investigation costs 184–5
    cyberspace protection 130
    police videosurveillance study
        29–44
    wrongful convictions 189
Canada Border Services Agency 149
Canada Public Safety Information
    Network (CPSIN) 116, 150
Canadian Police Information Centre
    (CPIC) 149
Canadian Recording Industry
    Association (CRIA) 131
capital, security and mobilization
    of 70
Central Intelligence Agency (CIA)
    212, 216, 221, 228
charged-couple device (CCD)
    cameras 17
children, cyberthreats against 132
China, cybersecurity 59–62
ChoicePoint 20
citizen ownership, security monitors
    17
citizenship
    eligibility and legibility 195–6
    exclusion 200

civil liberties
    objections to ID cards 205
    and technology
        as a new way to encroach on
            3, 18
        as a new way to protect 3
civilian populations, surveillance of
    196, 212, 215
class *see* social class
classification, interrogation
    information 227
clearance time, criminal
    investigations 173–6
closed circuit television (CCTV) *see*
    police videosurveillance
CodeRed worm 79
Cold War
    growth of intelligence gathering
        216
    model, cybersecurity 51
collective responsibility, cyberspace
    protection 130
collectivizing security 104
commercial cyberspace 126
Communications Security
    Establishment 130
community building, Second Life
    102–5
community-oriented policing (COP)
    142
Compstat 6, 228
computer forensics 75–6
Computer Information Network and
    Internet Security Protection and
    Management Regulation 60–2
computer network analogy,
    cybersecurity study 69–70, 71
computer-centred surveillance
    217–18
'connecting the dots' 211
consent search programme 237
consequential feature, of
    surveillance 212–13
consumer need 116
consumers

disposable privacy 112
loyalty programmes 113, 122
personal information
    as currency 115–16
    exchange 223–4
    see also cyberconsumers
control theory 91–2
cookies 123–4
copyright violation 131
corporate world, diffusion of
    military technology 216–17
costs
    investigative 184
    wrongful conviction inquiries 189
counter-spies 211, 214
counter-surveillance 134–5
counter-terrorism 52–3
courtroom evidence 183–4
credit cards 115, 116, 121
crime
    fiction, criminal investigation 170
    impact of police cameras on 38–9
    policing, Montreal 32–5
    in risk society 117
    technological language 4
    trends in literature 2–3
    see also cybercrime; technocrime
Crime Identification Technology Act
    (US, 1998) 140
crime mapping 6–7, 140, 235
Crime Scene Investigation (CSI) 170
criminal convictions, wrongful 189
Criminal Intelligence Service
    Canada (CISC) 150
criminal intelligence services
    and IT
        analytical 157–62
        factors favouring adoption of
            163
        international 152–7
        national 144–52
        obstacles to adopting 163–5
        organizational statuses 156
criminal investigation 169–91
    costs 184

crime fiction 170
dearth of research 169
empirical research
    aims 171
    findings 173–81
    focus 172–3
    method 171–2
    outcomes 185–6
    publications, investigative tools
        170
    scientific policing 170, 178–81
    semantics 182
    technology 184
    theories
        epistemic approach 182–5,
            189–90
        pragmatic approach 185–9
Criminal Investigations Management
    System (CRIMES) 151
criminal prosecutions 131
criminalization 5, 90, 132
cultural capital 70, 78, 80, 81
cumulative disadvantage, social
    sorting systems 201
customization
    cyberspace 128–9
    Internet portals 123
cyber 3–4
cyber attacks 46–7, 53
cyber-witnessing 22
cyberconsumers
    docile 134
    personal profiles 122
cybercrime
    general public
        as an instrument of 79
        as a target of 78
    justification for monitoring 5
    perceptions of 245
    research 90
    risks 131–2
    US fight against 52–3
        key actors 54–7t
        legitimizing as warfare 53
        militarization 63

cybercriminals 131
cyberpolicing, private 118–19
cybersecurity
    China 59–62
    industry 130–1
    United States 48–52
        key actors involved in 54–7t
    see also inter-jurisdictional
        cybersecurity study
cybersoldiers 58
cyberspace
    China, state control 60–2
    economy 127
    emergence of 49–50
    information see information
    monitoring 5–6
    protection behaviours 129–30
    (re-)militarization 63
    risks 133
    as a space of consumption 126
    as a strategic space 50–1
    United States, national strategy
        to secure 51–2
    user-friendly 122–5
cyberterrorists 2
cyberthreats, against children 132
cyberwarfare programmes, United
    States 53
cyberwarfare units, China 59
cyberweapons 53, 58–9
Cyberwise 132
cyberworld see cyberspace

3D applications 128
data
    technology 15–18
    see also information
data aggregators 20
data collection 122, 124–5, 129, 149
    see also information gathering
data entry, limitations to use of IT
    164
data matching 198
data mining
    by police 146

detection of terrorism 141, 162
    pre-crime analysis 161–2
    privacy 120, 144
data protection 199
data retention 133
data security 113, 114
databases
    private individual data 19–20
    searchable 194, 198–9
dataveillance 197–8, 202
dating services, online 20
Defense Advanced Research Projects
    Agency (DARPA) 49, 141
defensible space(s) 36, 80, 85
'delimiting cyberspace' 52
democratic surveillance 224
denial-of-service attack, Estonia 46–7
Department of Defense (US) 52, 55t,
    58, 140, 217
Department of Homeland Security
    (US) 54–5t, 221
Department of Justice (US) 54t
'designing out' behaviours 96–7
detective work 186, 190
detectives 182–3, 187–8
deterrence 29
deviant behaviours
    unauthorized use of personal
        information 132–3
    virtual worlds 90–1
        governing, case study 92–105,
            106
Diamond database 145
digital defensible spaces 80
Discipline and Punish 217–18
disclosure reports (NCIS) 146
disorder 35–7
displacement 38
disposable privacy 112
DNA tests 189
docile cyberconsumers 134
dossier society 198
drug dealing, effect of police
    cameras on 37–8
drug seizures, Diamond database 145

education campaigns, music piracy
131
electrical pulse weapons 7
Electronic Privacy Information
Center 20
electronic surveillance 217–18
Elementary Information System 145
eligibility, ID systems and 195–6,
203
ELMER system 146
encryption 2, 82, 149, 152, 155
end-user licence agreements
(EULAs) 95, 113
epistemic approach, criminal
investigation 182–5, 189–90
Ericson, Richard 225
Estate Level Governance, Second
Life 104
Estonia, denial-of-service attack 46–7
ethnicity 37
Europol 152–3, 155
Europol Computer System (TECS)
153
Europol Convention 152–3
evidence
in criminal investigation 182
see also courtroom evidence; false
evidence
evidentiary technology 187

'failure to enroll' 203
false evidence 188
'false non-match' 203
Falun Gong 62
fear of crime 29
Federal Bureau of Investigation
(FBI) 83, 201, 212, 221, 228
Federal Emergency Management
Agency (FEMA) 228
Federal Trade Commission (FTC)
56t
film sector
law enforcement agencies 81
private security 76–8
software piracy 79

financial institutions
concern over security of online
forms 146
hyper-vigilance syndrome 146
mistakes in recognition of
suspicious activities 146
flagging systems, criminal
intelligence services 146, 148
flexible space, information exchange
126–32
forensics 75–6, 170, 187
'framing the guilty' 188
freedom, trade-off between safety
and 25
'freeloader' government discourse,
technopolicing 245
functional magnetic resonance
imaging (fMRI) 22

game spaces
criminological inquiry 88–92
governing (case study) 92–105,
106
gangs, protection of social peace 35
gated communities, Second Life
103–4
general public
insecurity due to indifference of
37
US cybersecurity 78–80
Global Information Grid (GIG) 58
Global Network Operations (GNO)
58–9
globalized surveillance 119, 200–1
globally interoperable (identification)
systems 201
Google Earth 30, 224
governance
ID cards and social control 199
real/virtual world comparison
(case study) 92–105, 106
see also nodal governance
government
'freeloader' discourse and
technopolicing 245

harmonization of identification
systems 201
ID Cards, significance for 202–3
through technocrime 5–8
US cybersecurity 71–3
websites, cookies 124
Gulf war (1991) 53

hacking 46–7, 53
harms, online 91
Howard, John 204
human security 205–6
hyper-vigilance syndrome 146

I-24/7 system 155
ID cards/systems 194–206
biometric technology 200
challenges to regulators 204–6
citizenship, eligibility and
legibility 195–6
data protection 199
harmonization of procedures 201
multi-purpose 202, 204
national registries 197
non-obligatory nature 205
objections to 204
population classification 203
potential social control 199
reliability of 203
significance for government
activity 202–3
subject to globalizing forces 201
and surveillance 194, 195, 199,
206
unique personal identifiers 199
identifiability, Second Life 100–1
identification
biometric 18–19, 195, 200
criminal investigations 176, 177t
see also ID cards/systems; priority
identification processes; real-
time identification
identity theft 121, 130, 148, 224
ignorance, about privacy-reducing
technologies 120

implanted devices 16
indifference
insecurity due to 37
to risk of victimization 80
individualization see customization
individualizing security 104
inductive approach, to investigation
187
industrial information exchange
119–26
information
control over 113
in criminal investigation 182
encryption 2, 82, 149, 152, 155
secrecy of 113–14
violence as legitimate means of
extracting 191
see also data; knowledge; personal
information
information exchange
consumer data 223–4
Europol 153
flexible space 126–32
industrial 119–26
Interpol 155
MATRIX system 141
real-time identification (RTI) 150
system incompatibility 152, 163–4
information gathering
distinction between passive and
active 211
in policing 227
see also data collection
information revolution 197
information society 117–18
information technology 139–65
anti-crime impact 141
criminal intelligence services
analytical 157–62
factors favouring adoption of
163
international 152–7
national 144–52
obstacles to adopting 163–5
development of pattern-

recognition systems 140-1
law enforcement 139–40, 142–4
national identification systems
194
private security 76–8, 81–2
risks 117
insecurity 34, 37, 41
institutional mistrust, cybersecurity
81–2
Integrated Justice Information (IJI)
initiative 150
intellectual property 77, 95, 118
intelligence, in investigation 182
intelligence gathering 211, 212
intelligence gathering organizations
216
intelligence services *see* criminal
intelligence services
intelligence-led policing 141–2,
142–3
intelligent pattern-recognition
systems 140–1
inter-jurisdictional cybersecurity
study 66–85
method of inquiry 67–9
nodal governance 69–71
nodal clusters 70–1
government 71–3
law enforcement 73–6, 81–2, 83
private industry 76–8, 83
general public 78–80
internodal connections 81–4
conclusions 84–5
interaction websites 224
interactive looking out 223, 224
International Civil Aviation
Organization 201
International Criminal Police
Organization *see* Interpol
Internet
as an icon of surveillance 213
automated loyalty programmes
122
infrastructure, private ownership
77

portals 123
restrictions and regulations,
China 60–2
streamlining of information 122–3
United States
mobilization of cyberweapons
58–9
security policy 48–52
see also cyberspace; World Wide
Web
Internet Access Providers (IAPs),
China 60
Internet Explorer 124
Internet protocol (IPv6) 16–17
Internet Service Providers (ISPs) 5,
49–50, 123, 130
interoperability 163–4, 201
Interpol 154–7
interrogations
filming of 227
use of harsh techniques 191
investigation *see* criminal
investigation; police investigation
investigators *see* detectives
invisible feature, of surveillance 212
IT *see* information technology

Joint Task Force-Computer Network
Defense (JTF-CND) 58
Joint Task Force-Computer Network
Operations (JTF-CNO) 58
jurisdictional boundaries, US
cybersecurity 83

Khawadja, Momin 2
knowledge
courtroom evidence 183–4
from intelligence policing 143
in investigation 182, 190
knowledge workers 143, 182, 187,
225, 226
Koval, Adam 22

late modernity
personal information

as currency 115–19
dissemination of 115
see also information exchange
technology as pointer to flaws
in 4
threat to privacy 113
tools and toys of 21–3
law enforcement
information technology 139–40,
142–4
US cybersecurity 73–6, 81–2, 83
Licklider, Joseph Carl Robnett 49
Linden dollars 127
Linden Lab 92–105, 106, 126, 127
location awareness 19
location factors, criminal
investigations 178, 179t
'looking into' 222–3
'looking out' 222, 223–4
Lord, William 59
loss prevention assistance 74
Loyalty Group 122
loyalty programmes 113, 122

Mafiaboy 46, 47
markets, personal information as
currency 118–19
mass surveillance 198
MATRIX 141
Meikar, Silver 47
messages, in criminal investigation
182
MI5 221
MI6 216, 221
Microsoft 20, 22, 123, 124
middle classes, visual surveillance
critique 224–5
military
convergence of policing and 52–3
cyberspace as potential theatre of
operations 50–1
cyberweapons 53
technologies 7, 23, 140, 216–17
Mitnick, Kevin 52
MMORPGs 88, 89

modernity *see* late modernity;
postmodernity
Montreal police, videosurveillance
project 29–44
MRTDs (machine readable travel
documents) 201
MSN 20, 123
music management packages 124
music piracy 131
MySpace 125–6

NASA 22, 49
National Criminal Data Bank
(NCDB) 149–50
National Criminal Intelligence
Service (NCIS) 145–6
national cyberspace 51–2
National Databank Branch
(Australia) 148
national general databank (Belgium)
148–9
national identification systems *see*
ID cards/systems
National Justice Institute (US) 140,
236
National Police Security Image
(IPNS) 159
national registries 197
National Registry (Belgium) 148–9
national security
cybercrime as threat to 52
technology
as a new threat to 2–3
as a new way to protect 3
US cybersecurity agencies
preoccupation with 48
National Security Presidential
Directive 16 (NSPD–16) 58
National Strategy to Secure Cyberspace
51
NATO 47
Nazis 196, 215
neoliberal governance 93, 94, 101,
104–5
netizens 125, 131, 135

network communication analogy,
   cybersecurity study 69–70, 71
Nineteen Eighty-four 15
NIPRNet 59
nodal clusters, cybersecurity
   analysis 70–80
nodal governance, cybersecurity
   study 67, 69–71

Office of Criminal Justice Programs
   (OCJP) 68
Office of Emergency Services (OES)
   68, 71, 72
online dating 20
online forms, concern over security
   146
open source code 94, 95
operational advantage, Europol 155
Operational Support Directorate
   (Australia) 148
operational (tactical) analyses 157–9,
   161–3
Orwell, George 15, 24

pain-induced technologies,
   application to terrorists 191
panoptic sort 198
panopticommodity 119
panopticon 119, 133–4
participatory democracy 24
participatory panopticon 119
passive looking out 224
Patriot Acts 25, 215
pattern-recognition systems 140–1
personal cybersecurity 130–1
personal information
   databases 19–20
   information revolution 197
   late modernity
      as currency 115–19
      dissemination of 115
      see also information exchange
   privacy defined as total of all
      forms of 114
   provision of, in cyberspace 119

surveillance 199
   unauthorized use of 132–3
personal responsibility, cyberspace
   protection 129
personal space, desire to protect 113,
   114
personal surveillance 198
personal websites 125
Pickton, Robert 185
piracy 79, 131
police
   data mining by 146
   investigators *see* detectives
   as knowledge workers 143, 182,
      225, 226
   lapses in professional behaviour
      17
   in urban environment 230
   use of crime mapping 6–7, 140,
      235
   use of technology discourse
      244–5
police cameras
   charged-couple device (CCD) 17
   see also police videosurveillance
police databases, flagging methods
   for suspicious activities 146
police departments, executive
   powers 156
police investigation, fiction 169–70
Police Reporting and Occurrence
   System (PROS) 150
police videosurveillance, local
   impact study 27–44
   crime and policing 32–5
   disorder and symbols of disorder
      35–7
   effect of proximity to cameras
      37–40
   literature 27–8
   discussion 40–2
   conclusion 43–4
policing
   accountable objects of 234
   control and surveillance 225–9

convergence of military and 52–3
ideology and practices 229–32
militarization 7, 140
Montreal 32–5
risk communication 225–6
strategies 232–8
technology 2, 142–4, 227–9, 244
see also intelligence-led
    policing; inter-jurisdictional
    cybersecurity study; self-
    policing; technopolicing
'policing at a distance' 201
political capital 70
politicians, use of technology
    discourse 244–5
population classification, ID systems
    203
portals 123
position emission tomography (PET)
    22
'positive power' 119
post-clearance work 186, 190
postmodernity
    Foucault's surveillance metaphor
        218
    social relationships 218–38
postwar surveillance 215–16
pragmatic approach, criminal
    investigation 185–9
pre-crime data mining analysis
    161–2
The President's Analysis 16
priority identification processes
    159–61
prison system, socialization 217–18
privacy 112–35
    cyberspace regulation, China 62
    data mining 144
    data protection 199
    debates over the right to 112
    defined as total of all personal
        information 114
    different conceptions of 113–14
    disposable 112
    flexible space 126–32

industrial information exchange
    119–26
information, surveillance and
    crime 132–5
need to redefine 25–6
reduction of, as social problem
    120
threat to 112–13
videosurveillance 27
private industry
    technopolicing 245
    US cybersecurity 76–8, 83
private islands, Second Life 103–4
private networks, cyberspace
    protection 130
private policing 118–19
proactive policing 142
problem-oriented policing (POP) 142
Proceeds of Crime Act (2002) 146
profiling 122, 170, 198, 223
Project Witness 17
property rights, virtual worlds 106
protection behaviours, cyberspace
    129–30
public security environment,
    cyberspace protection 130
public-private partnerships,
    countering cybercrime, US 57t

radio frequency identification (RFID)
    15–16, 195
A rape in cyberspace 91
Rapsheets.com 20
rationality, use of IT in law
    enforcement 142
real-time identification (RTI) 150
record linkage 198
Recording Industry Association of
    America (RIAA) 131
reflexive profiling 223
reflexive space 126–9
regional task forces, cybersecurity,
    California 71–3
registration, cyberspace applications
    124

responsibility, cyberspace protection 129–30
responsibilization 5, 80, 94
result-oriented investigations 187
RFID *see* radio frequency identification
risk analyses 159–61
risk communication 225–6
risk management 229
risk managers, general public as 80
risk society 117
risks
    cybercrime 131–2
    cyberspace 133
    personal information as currency 116–17
    of victimization, indifference to 80
robots, in policing 7
Royal Canadian Mounted Police (RCMP) 149–50, 160, 243–4
rules of conduct, Second Life 97–8
Russian hackers, Estonia 46–7

safety, trade-off between freedom and 25
Sarbanese-Oxley Act (US, 2002) 72
satellite images, spectographic analysis 244
scepticism, usefulness of IT 164–5
scientific expertise, in courts 187
scientific policing, criminal investigations 170, 178–81
search engines 123
searchable databases 194, 198–9
Second Life 92–105, 106, 126, 127
secrecy, of information 113–14
Secret Service (US) 74
secrets
    desire to confess 114
    right to keep 113, 114
secure space 129–32
securitization of habitat 103–5
security
    individual surveillance 135
    see also cybersecurity; data security; human security; insecurity; national security; technosecurity
security goals, internodal relations, cybersecurity 81
security monitors, dispersed ownership 17, 18
self-policing 105
Sensecam 22
Serious Crime Bill (2006–7) 146
Singapore, criminal intelligence service 151–2
Singapore Police Force 151
SLEIPNIR 160–1
smart technologies 16, 19, 199–200
Smith, Catherine 105
Smith, Charles 187
sniffers 23
social capital 70
social class
    distinction, videosurveillance 38
    spying 214
    visual surveillance 224–5
social control
    advocate of surveillance 225–9
    ID cards/systems 199
    spying 214
    through gangs 38
    through socialization 217–18
    visual surveillance 221–5
social function, surveillance as an evolving 214–17
social networking 126–7
social networking sites 125–6
social peace, gang protection 35
social relationships 218–38
socialization 217–18
software applications, data collection 124–5
software piracy 79, 131
sorting systems *see* ID cards/ systems
'sousveillance' movement 24
sovereignty-affirming strategies 130

spectographic analysis, satellite
  images 244
spending habits, analysis of 121
spies 211, 214
spying 211–12, 215
spyware 125
state
  decline of power in
    contemporary society 119
  power to access and use personal
    information 133
  see also governance; government
strategic analyses 157–9
structural supports, internodal
  relations, cybersecurity 82–3
subvocal speech systems 22
surveillance 209–38
  background 210–14
  behaviour modification 134
  citizen-owned security monitors
    17
  of civilian populations 196, 212,
    215
  complicity in 213
  constraints 214–17
  electronic 217–18
  focus and targets of 213–14
  globalized 119, 200–1
  ID cards/systems 194, 195, 199,
    206
  individual 135
  networks of seeing machines
    18–21
  'panopticon' metaphor 119, 133–4
  personal aspect 213
  radical diffusion of 134
  reduction of privacy 120
  reliance on technological and
    commercial expertise 199
  resistance to 135
  robotic 7
  social relationships 218–38
  sociological problem 212–13
  taxonomies 222
  web activity, China 59–60, 62

  see also counter-surveillance;
    dataveillance; police
    videosurveillance
surveillant assemblage 201, 228
Switzerland, operational analysts 161
Symantec 68
symbolic capital 70, 81
symbolic disorder 35–7

tactical (operational) analyses 157–9,
  161–3
Taser 7
TCP/IP protocol 49
technocrime 1
  constructive approaches 4
  government through 5–8
  as a pointer to flaws in late-
    modern society 4
  policing *see* policing
  responses to 1
technology
  evidentiary 187
  investigative 184
  late modernity
    as pointer to flaws in 4
    tools and toys 21–3
  limits to postwar surveillance
    215–16
  military 7, 23, 140, 216–17
  networks of seeing machines
    18–21
  policing 2, 142–4, 227–9, 244
  reduction of privacy 120
  smart 16, 19, 199–200
  terrorism and failure of 190–1
  trends in literature 2–3
  world of data 15–18
  see also information technology
technopolice brigade 6
technopolicing 1, 6–8, 243–6
technosecurity 1
telescreen 15, 24–5
terrorism
  application of pain-induced
    technologies 191

data mining to detect 141, 162
failure of technology 190–1
new forms of surveillance 200–1, 212–13
see also counter-terrorism; war on terror
Terrorism Information Awareness 141
third party loyalty programmes 122
Total Information Awareness 141
tracking 16, 223
trade-off, between safety and freedom 25
True.com 20

United Kingdom, criminal intelligence service 145–6
United States
   fight against cybercrime 52–3
      from defence to offensive operations 58–9
      key actors 54–7t
      legitimizing as warfare 53
      militarization 63
   growth of intelligence gathering organizations 216
   inter-jurisdictional cybersecurity study 66–85
   law enforcement technologies 139–40
   security environment 48–52
   surveillance of civilians 215
universal aspect, of surveillance 213
unmanned arterial vehicle (UAV) reconnaissance drones 23
urban anonymity 114
urban environment, police in 230
user-created content, SL platform 95

user-friendly cyberspace 122–5
USSTRATCOM (US Strategic Command) 58

videosurveillance
   threat to privacy 113
   see also police videosurveillance
violence, as a means of information extraction 191
virtual communities 50
Virtual Earth 224
virtual payment 121
virtual protection 224
virtual worlds 88–107
   deviant behaviours 90–1
      governing, case study 92–105
   game spaces as sites of criminological inquiry 88–92
   reasons for studying 89
visual surveillance 221–5

Wal-Mart 15
war on crime 243
war on drugs 52, 139
war on terror 205, 212
weapons technologies 7, 53, 216–17
'Web 2.0' 125, 127
web pages, individualization 128–9
Wikis 125
Windows Live ID 123
World of Warcraft 89
World Wide Web 49–50
   browsers 125
   surveillance, China 59–60, 62
wrongful convictions 189

YouTube 40, 129, 224